The Cruising Multihull

The Cruising Multihull

CHRIS WHITE

International Marine
Camden, Maine

Published by International Marine

Copyright © 1990 International Marine, an imprint of
TAB BOOKS, a division of McGraw-Hill, Inc.

Library of Congress Cataloging-in-Publication Data
White, Chris.
    The cruising multihull/Chris White.
        p.   cm.
    Includes index.
    ISBN 0-87742-264-8
    1. Multihull sailboats—Design and construction.
2. Sailing.
I. Title.
VM311.C3W47   1990
623.8′ 1223—dc20   90-4747
                                                      CIP

The name "International Marine" and the International
Marine Logo are trademarks of TAB BOOKS. Printed
in the United States of America.

Questions regarding the content of this book should
be addressed to:

International Marine Publishing
P.O. Box 220
Camden, ME 04843

Typeset by Douglas & Gayle Limited, Indianapolis, IN
Printed by Arcata Graphics, Fairfield, PA
Design by Patrice Rossi
Illustrations by the author unless otherwise noted
Production by Janet Robbins
Edited by J.R. Babb and Tom McCarthy

Dedication

To Kate:
sailor, friend, wife, and mother

Boats and books about them
would never get done
without your help

Contents

Acknowledgments
ix

Introduction
xi

CHAPTER 1/A Boat for Cruising
1

CHAPTER 2/The Specifics of Multihull Design
45

CHAPTER 3/The Trimaran
57

CHAPTER 4/The Catamaran
76

CHAPTER 5/Resisting Leeway
96

CHAPTER 6/Rudders and Steering
106

CHAPTER 7/Rigs
117

CHAPTER 8/Auxiliary Power
138

CHAPTER 9/The Specifics of Multihull Construction
149

CHAPTER 10/Safety and Seamanship
184

APPENDIX A/A Catalog of Production Multihulls
238

APPENDIX B/A Review of Multihull Designers
254

APPENDIX C/Two Designs from the Author
256

Index
263

Acknowledgments

In the development of the modern cruising multihull, I am a second generation participant. In the 1950s and 60s, the first generation of designers and builders produced an enormous variety of craft—some good and some bad, but all had to be tried. Few really new ideas have been introduced since then, although some bad ones have been discarded and the good ones further refined. Us "youngsters" now involved in multihulls owe a great deal to those who in good faith and at their own expense developed the art of designing and building sailboats with two and three hulls.

In more recent history, my editor at International Marine Publishing, Jim Babb, really deserves much of the credit, or blame, for this book. Without his urging I certainly never would have undertaken a project of this magnitude. Writing a book is a lot like building a boat: It takes much more time, money, and help than you can imagine when you begin.

To help get my bearings straight on a number of topics I solicited information from many sources, and I wish to thank the following for their considerate contributions:

Dan Blachley, Jim Brown, Steven Callahan, Charles Chiodi, Lock Crowther, Meade Gougeon, Walter Greene, Bruce Hays, Derek Kelsall, Brad Murray, Dick Newick, Michael Reppy, John Shuttleworth, Malcom Tennant, James Wharram, and Richard Woods.

Introduction

Cultural conditioning defines what is "normal." Because European civilization has no tradition of multihulled sailing craft, we of European descent tend to look askance at boats with more than one hull.

But tally up all the sailing craft ever built on this planet and you might be surprised to find that the *majority* had more than one hull. For thousands of years, multihulls were the vehicle of choice throughout much of India, Indonesia, Malaysia, southeast Asia, parts of China, the Philippines, Polynesia, Melanesia, and Micronesia. This is a huge chunk of the earth's surface—substantially larger than the areas frequented by single-hulled sailing vessels prior to the Renaissance and the age of European exploration.

All sailboats, single-hulled or multihulled, are subject to the same laws of physics. Everything floats by the same principle. All boats moving through the water meet resistance from the waves they create and the water that "sticks" to the hull surfaces. Sails know only the forces of wind flowing past, never the man-made theories that justify their shapes. Wind and waves are every bit as savage today as they were in antiquity. If the multihull worked so well for so many millions of people for so many thousands of years, why then isn't every boat a multihull?

Working on the assumption that, given time, people inevitably find the most efficient solution to the problem at hand, the reason seems obvious: European cultural history is based on trade, and not just trade, but trade on a grand scale. Throughout the evolution of naval architecture, the driving force has been to design vessels to transport large quantities of goods from one place to another as inexpensively as possible.

The culmination of this quest is the giant supertanker, effectively a lake of oil surrounded by a membrane of steel, which serves, at least most of the time, to keep the oil and seawater from mixing. Manned by only a few sailors, carrying more tonnage per pound of hull material than anything ever has, it is efficient and *profitable*.

Compared with a multihull, a monohull moves bulk cargo far more efficiently; it requires less power to push it through the water; its simple shape and greater enclosed volume compared with surface area makes it significantly easier and cheaper to build. If the task at hand is to move lots of stuff from here to there, a slow-moving, heavy-displacement, single-hulled vessel unquestionably is the best choice.

Trade carried out in these efficient, single-hulled vessels drove our society's development, making possible a standard of living that enables many of us to sail, not for profit, but for pleasure. Why turn our backs on these efficient monohulls that have served us so well?

Easy: As individual cruising sailors, we are no longer transporting bulk cargo. We have completely different reasons for voyaging.

Dr. David Lewis, in his excellent work on Polynesian seafaring, *We, The Navigators* (The University Press of Hawaii, 1972), lists in order of importance the reasons for oceanic voyaging among the islanders of the Pacific:

1. Adventure
2. Pride of the navigators
3. Raiding and conquest
4. Deep sea fishing
5. Trading voyages
6. Tribute and empire

The first two reasons (the modern equivalent of reason 3 might be "drinking and conquest") accurately describe what motivates modern man to abandon his TV and set off across the seas—*Adventure!* If this is why you go to sea, then you, like the islanders of the Pacific before you, will find a multihull ideal for your purpose.

Of course, exactly the same reasons led to the development of the supertanker, but in *exactly the reverse order*. If you go to sea to build empires and transport cargo, the single-hulled vessel is for you.

People sailing in quest of adventure are not bulk cargo. The stores and equipment a voyager carries are minute compared to a load of coal or grain. People are lightweight, high value, and time-sensitive goods who need a fast, comfortable, level-riding, seaworthy boat. For thousands of years the multihull has been the vessel of choice for that purpose—and it still is.

A Boat for Cruising

O f all man's inventions, few can compare with the sailboat—the nearly perfect vehicle with an inexhaustible supply of power; existing between two constantly moving mediums, drawing energy from each; able to sail around the world without refueling, not once or twice but hundreds of times. Our modern-day addiction to the massive combustion of fossil fuel to accomplish even the smallest task makes the elegance of the sailboat even more profound.

This book is about boats intended for cruising. To me, sailing a capable, responsive boat long distances to see new things and have new experiences is the ultimate joy. Opinions differ as to what sort of boat is best for cruising. The diversity of sailboat designs suggests that there really is no best type of boat. There are many good ones, each with its own characteristics that make it well-suited for cruising. This book deals with a specific type of sailboat: multihulled boats, catamarans and trimarans.

Multihulls differ from most monohulls in that they use no heavy ballast to augment their hullform stability. Instead, their ability to resist the heeling force of the sails comes from linking slender hulls to create a boat with great overall beam. In the same way that spreading your feet increases your ability to withstand a strong wind, a boat with widely separated hulls has great inherent stability to resist the overturning force of the sails.

Compared with a single-hulled boat, the multihull is much lighter for a given length, it has much greater overall beam, and usually draws less water. And it has *speed*. A good cruising multihull can sail up to twice as fast as a similarly sized monohull, although on the basis of daily averages the differences are smaller.

A multihull heels much less than a monohull, usually no more than 10 degrees. When sailing downwind it has no tendency to round up or broach, nor does it suffer from the monohull's unpleasant rolling motion, which can make steering difficult and life below uncomfortable.

A general feeling exists among cruising sailors with single-hull experience

that the multihull is intrinsically dangerous. They wonder about the multihull's inability to right itself if capsized, and about the integrity of such a seemingly elaborate structure. These are valid questions; after all, lives are at stake. But the answers are complex and many times the questions themselves are wrong.

In the pages that follow I will try to address these questions, and to outline the differences between single-hulled and multihulled boats. I'll try to illustrate the current state of the multihull art; help you decide whether a multihull is right for you, whether you want a catamaran or a trimaran, whether you should build it yourself, have one built, or buy a production boat. Once you see the whole multihull picture you should be able to decide whether they're your kind of cruising boat.

I also will draw upon lessons learned on the race course. Racing multihulls have been in the spotlight for the last few years, and this has had an enormous impact on the evolution of the multihull in general. The boats are faster, more stable, and better looking than ever before; the engineering has been refined, the materials better understood.

Yacht racing is a useful testing ground for new ideas and construction methods. Cruisers should not ignore the successes and failures of the race course. Where else can the outer limits be explored with some control, and with such thorough analysis? But like the actor who becomes typecast in unbecoming roles, the multihull often finds itself associated exclusively with "blood-and-guts racing." This is a sad oversight. The modern multihull has many attributes that make it well-suited—even ideal—for cruising.

I might as well say right now that, deep in my bones, all things considered, all risks weighed, a cruising sailor is at least as safe in a well-designed multihull as in a single-hulled, ballasted boat. I say this after having pulled one sinking boat off the rocks and having seen the onset of hypothermia and panic in the face of a woman who slipped overboard from the heeling deck of a monohull. Sailing involves risks on many fronts; if it is to provide an acceptable level of safety, *any* cruising boat must address all risks from all sources.

I do not mean to suggest that *all* multihulls are safe for offshore use. This is patently untrue, and there are a few multihulls in which I would be afraid to cross the bay. This holds true for monohulls as well, but the features that make a monohull safe or unsafe for a particular use are well understood and thoroughly documented. For multihulls, this same information is difficult if not impossible to find. That's the purpose of this book.

Compared with the century or more of development behind the ballasted monohull yacht, the multihull is the new kid on the block. Although they have a thousand-year history among the indigenous peoples of the Pacific Ocean, the first modern multihulls of any size to sail offshore were doing so in the 1950s—only thirty-odd years ago. The progress of design knowledge has been, or seems to have been, slow and at times painful. But looking back at the ground that has been covered, the theories tried, the materials and construction methods invented—usually on a shoestring budget—I have to say that great strides have been made.

And now it seems multihulls have arrived—or at least they have their boarding passes. Once the domain of the lunatic fringe, multihulls now are almost respectable. Indeed, recent issues of every magazine from *Cruising World* to *Forbes* have carried articles on multihulls. Their old image—low-rent boats built in backyards or "cost-effective" production designs—is on its way out. Now we should see some magnificent vessels.

Acquiring a Boat

In the labyrinth of decision-making that surrounds the purchase of a cruising boat, perhaps the first choice to consider is exactly how to go about acquiring a boat. Good cruising boats—monohull or multihull—cost money, usually lots of money. The materials used to build a boat are expensive and used in abundance. Labor, the largest expense, is measured in thousands of hours. Other than your house—perhaps even including it—a cruising boat may well be the most expensive thing you ever buy. And as with a house, you can acquire one in several ways: You might buy a used one, you might buy a factory-built prefab, you might commission a custom builder, or you just might build it yourself.

Build It Yourself?

Many sailors can't afford a production or custom boat or are unwilling to indenture themselves to the finance company for 15 years, so they elect to build their own boat. This can reduce upfront expenditures greatly because so much of the price of a production or custom-built boat is labor. Because you can buy materials as you need them, the costs can be spread over a long period.

But there are costs involved other than money when you build your own boat—such as gallons of sweat and often some blood. Several years of obsessive work at night and on weekends and holidays can have far-reaching effects. More than a few marriages have foundered on the rocks of boat construction. Is it worth it? Sure, if you're willing to stay the course—and retain your perspective. Despite what you may think at the time, a boat really isn't worth more than a marriage.

Figure 1-1. Although building your own boat requires a massive commitment of time, resources and energy, it can be one of life's most rewarding experiences.

There is much satisfaction in sailing a boat you put together with your own two hands. Few man-made objects come as close to actually being alive as a boat, and the personality of the owner-built boat usually is unique. Owner-built boats often are the best thought-out and the most durable and,

perhaps most importantly, if you build it yourself you can fix it yourself—anywhere, anytime.

Multihulls in particular have a long tradition of owner building. Literally thousands of Piver-, Brown-, and Cross-designed trimarans, as well as a similar number of Wharram-designed catamarans, among others, were launched from backyard boatyards around the world in the early years of multihull development. In the context of that early stage of design evolution, many of these were magnificent boats; many were anything but.

I will discuss owner building in depth in Chapter 9. For the right person, building your own multihull can be one of the high points of your life. For the wrong person, it may well be the lowest.

A Production Boat?

Very few people have the time or inclination to build their own boats, so the

Figure 1-2.
The needs of many cruising sailors can be filled by a good production boat. This is the Event 34 from Prout — the world's largest manufacturer of production multihulls. (Photo courtesy Prout)

standard way to acquire a boat is to take something off the end of a production line. By using expensive molds to form glass and resin into the various components, boats can be constructed quickly. Unfortunately, this highly capital-intensive form of boatbuilding is feasible only if large numbers of identical boats can be sold.

The demand for multihulls is growing rapidly, but by conventional monohull standards the market is still quite small, and this limits the selection of factory-built designs. Currently in the U.S. there are only four fiberglass boatbuilders producing stock cruising multihulls, and all of these builders are small by industry standards. The situation in Europe is better, with

JUDGING PRODUCTION-BOAT QUALITY

Faced with a gleaming, finished boat from a production builder, it often is difficult to see those portions of the boat that would allow one to determine how well (or how poorly) it was put together. For reasons I have yet to appreciate, most production builders choose to cover the interior of the boat with different forms of carpets, fabrics, and liners. "Monkey fur" is what one builder I know calls a particularly nondescript variety of this stuff. That this material is effective in trapping salt mist and as a result will forever mildew doesn't seem to bother the boat buyer.

Despite the barriers, the careful boat buyer should manage to find a few places to stick his head where the manufacturer thought no one would ever bother to look. These are the places to find telltale signs of construction care, or lack thereof. Is the laminate neat? It should be free of glass splinters and puddles of resin. The core, if there is one, should be visible through the inner skin. Are there white areas indicating bubbles between the skin and core? How are secondary bonds handled—hull to deck, crossbeams to hulls—the salesman should know. Push on the topsides. Do they deflect noticeably? In a cruising boat they shouldn't.

One key is a careful look at the exterior; kneel down and eyeball the topsides, deck, and cabin. Are they fair?

Moldmaking is an art similar to boatbuilding; slipshod boats often come from slipshod molds. Are there noticeable distortions in the hull topsides at the internal bulkheads? There shouldn't be. On deck, are the fittings and hardware bedded in sealant and properly reinforced with backing plates?

Often the best way to judge quality in any boat is to look at an old one, not a new one. In fiberglass boats, cracked or crazed gelcoat is not a good sign. At best, it indicates that the gelcoat was carelessly and thickly applied; at worst, it means that the underlying laminate is inadequate and flexing excessively, and may have been damaged. Check all highly stressed areas of the boat—mast step, chainplates, crossbeams, rudders and steering gear, center- or daggerboards—for signs of overload: deformations, cracks, delaminations.

All of these defects are design or construction failures worthy of correction. Big problems often start as little problems and grow over time. A boat that is well designed and built should show no indication of structural deterioration even after 10 years. If evidence of problems exist, and they are structural and not cosmetic in nature, be sure they have been corrected in the later sistership in which you are interested.

approximately two dozen multihull builders, some of whose designs are finding their way to the U.S. through various importers. (For a selection of some of the production multihulls now available, see Appendix A. Also, check the ads in *Multihulls* magazine, 421 Hancock Street, N. Quincy, MA, 02171. New boats on the market appear there first.)

The practical implication is that finding a stock boat that suits your needs can be difficult since the choice is so limited. For those accustomed to the wide range of high-quality, off-the-shelf monohulls, the narrow selection of production multis is bound to be a bit of a shock. But if the multihulled boat of your dreams currently is built on a regular basis and the price and quality are within reason, you are in luck—buy it. If not, don't despair.

Custom Built?

Custom or one-off boatbuilding will never be the cheapest way to build a boat but, when you consider that you can always get what you want, the extra expense will, to many, seem justifiable. The construction quality of a custom boat often is far superior to what rolls off an assembly line, and this can be especially important to a long-distance cruiser. One-off construction methods can produce boats that are stronger and lighter than typical production boats. Because multihulls need high strength at low weight they can benefit greatly from the highly efficient structure available in a one-off.

The big problem with custom building is that, for most people, it is a completely unfamiliar process. In this day of mass-produced goods you can

Figure 1-3.
A custom-built boat can be tailored to an owner's specific requirements. *Damiana*, a 42-foot trimaran designed by John Shuttleworth, not only has comfortable cruising accommodations, but is *fast*, placing third in the Open TransPac in 1987 and winning Class III in the 1988 C-STAR. (A. Fitzpatrick photo)

go your whole life without ever needing to have something made just for you. Like a custom-built house, the process of building a boat involves an owner, architect, and builder—all of whom have to find a common ground to produce a successful boat (or home).

One-off boats take a lot of time to build. It isn't unusual for a small shop to spend 8 to 12 months building a typical cruising boat. (It is also not unusual to wait that long for many production boats.) The cost for a one-off boat can vary considerably depending on the level of spit and polish required in the finished product and the number of mechanical systems (refrigeration, electronics, desalinators, etc.) installed in the boat.

A custom gold-plater with all the trimmings certainly is going to cost *lots*; yet a well-finished but simple boat often will cost no more than a production boat of equal quality. How could this be? The labor-saving efficiencies of the boatbuilding factory come at the expense of high overhead costs, advertising expenses, and various fees and commissions which add to the cost of an otherwise cheap boat. Unless the level of production is very high the economic benefits are meager.

But the primary reason to consider going the custom-built route is because you really can get just what you want. In a cruising boat, accommodations, equipment, deck layout, and sail-handling systems are all critical for easy operation—and every experienced sailor that I know wants things arranged his way to suit his own sailing needs. This can be done on a production boat to some extent, but all too often the original equipment must be moved or replaced. The owner of a custom-built boat can have it his own way right from the start.

What Kind of Cruiser Are You?

Cruising means different things to different people. To some, a big cruise is sailing across the bay for a weekend; for others, it is a trek across the ocean for a year. Not every cruiser need go foreign to live the life. The great inland waterways of the East and Gulf Coasts of the U.S. allow long-distance, protected travel. Like geese, thousands of cruisers migrate north and south annually in search of pleasant weather.

A boat designed to function perfectly for inshore use or coastal cruising may be completely inadequate offshore. Conversely, a vessel built for the rigors of long-distance bluewater sailing will be expensive overkill if it never leaves the Intracoastal Waterway.

For these reasons it is important to define arbitrarily the different kinds of "cruising." Starting with the safest style of cruising and proceeding to the most risky we have:

> • *Dock cruisers* (boats that seldom leave the dock)

- *Waterway cruisers* (boats that seldom leave the inland waterways)

- *Coastal cruisers* (short hops in the ocean)

- *Offshore cruisers* (anything can happen and you had better be prepared for it)

Although these are arbitrary classifications with considerable room for overlap among categories, they do allow prospective boat purchasers to begin to define realistically who they are, and consequently to find a boat that is neither more nor less than they need (although given my druthers, I'druther err on the side of a too-capable boat than an incapable one).

Another system for classifying multihulls has been proposed recently, but its categorical distinctions are mostly between racing and cruising, with no mention of the distance cruised or frequency of offshore travel. Although this may be useful as a yardstick for measuring a boat's performance, it does little to determine the boat's intended patterns of use.

Classifications borrowed from racing can, however, carry a great deal of information regarding the intended capabilities of boats. For example, the Ocean Racing Council (ORC) has developed a straightforward classification system for rating monohull races:

- *Category 0* races are long-distance, open-ocean races where the boats involved must be "capable of withstanding heavy storms and prepared to meet serious emergencies without expectation of outside assistance."

- *Category 1* is similar, but the races are shorter.

- *Category 2* races are "of extended duration, along or not far removed from shorelines or in large unprotected bays or lakes, where a high degree of self-sufficiency is required of the yachts but with the reasonable expectation that outside assistance could be called upon for aid in the event of serious emergencies."

- *Category 3* is a race across open water, most of which is protected or close to shorelines.

- *Category 4* is a short race in warm, protected waters.

While this classification system was developed for racing, it is useful for cruising boats because it takes into consideration the need for seaworthiness and the ability to cope with a variety of conditions. Coastal cruising, for example, generally would encompass the ORC Category 2. Offshore cruising would match ORC Category 0 or 1, depending on the distance between ports. Category 3 and 4 would be analogous to waterway cruising, depending upon the season and the locale.

An important facet of the ORC regulations is that, for a given type of race, the boats participating must conform to certain construction guidelines that help guarantee their structural seaworthiness for the anticipated conditions. The regulations also make skippers responsible for carrying safety equipment appropriate to the level of risk—an idea that many cruisers would be wise to adopt.

Boats participating in Category 0, 1, and 2 events must conform to the "Guide for Building and Classing Offshore Racing Yachts," developed by the American Bureau of Shipping. This guide specifies strength requirements for hull, deck, and rudder. Boats designed to conform to the ABS guidelines can be expected to hold up well in heavy going. Unfortunately, the formulas used in the ABS guide are not well suited to light-displacement boats, especially multihulls.

Most sailors and boats will alternate between the different types of sailing; each type has its appeal. For the purposes of further discussion, however, "cruising" means being equipped and prepared for an occasional offshore passage such as described by ORC Category 1 or 2, unless stated otherwise.

Why a Multihull?

Volumes have been written on (to borrow a phrase) the desirable and undesirable characteristics of cruising boats. Each author has his own opinions, which differ wildly one from the other. Often, the designer's criteria for judging the suitability of a cruising boat may differ markedly from an experienced cruiser's actual requirements. Although there is no broad consensus on *anything* concerning boats—with the possible exception of the colors of running lights—certain characteristics are mentioned more frequently by more cruisers than any others. They are:

- *Accommodation.* Comfortable interior spaces for long-term habitation, good galley facilities, excellent light and ventilation, adequate load capacity to carry cruising stores and equipment.

- *Performance.* The ability to go to windward, good average speeds, good light-air performance, reasonable speed under power.

- *Shoal draft.* The ability to cruise many regions inaccessible to boats drawing more than four feet.

- *Ease of handling and comfort under way.* Efficient hull forms that can be propelled with a sail plan designed for shorthanded sailing. Good self-steering properties.

- *Stability.* Minimal heeling, minimal rolling downwind and at anchor.

- *Safety.* High degree of survivability from severe weather and shipwreck, effective damage control in case of collision, security against man overboard, structural integrity, and some redundancy in essential systems and structures.

Accommodation

There is an enormous variety of accommodation schemes for multihulls, from the ultra-Spartan, one-cup, one-spoon, one-bucket approach favored by the high-performance raceboat set, to the refrigerator-freezer-microwave-equipped boat with multiple king-size beds and Jacuzzis that has not left the dock in three years—with 57 varieties floating between these two extremes. Practically everything has been tried, and I suppose that alone speaks volumes for the versatility of the multihull concept.

Broad diversity notwithstanding, a number of common traits make multis attractive for just "living aboard." The first is the lack of pronounced heeling and rolling. It is easier to walk around on a cat or tri both sailing and at anchor; you will not be thrown from your berth, things stay where you put them, the accommodation plan does not have to be designed to function at right angles to the earth's surface. Multihull designer/broker Bill Symons calls it "no bruisin' cruisin'." This is a near-perfect description of the multihull phenomenon, and something I tend to forget about until I go sailing on a "lead mine" and come back battered and bruised from bouncing all over the boat.

A second big comfort factor with multihulls is that for the most part their accommodations are well above the waterline, and they stay that way. This allows large ports to be placed at eye level, not at arm's reach above. What a relief for the cook or navigator to be able to see outside; it helps so much to avoid seasickness. And this also makes excellent ventilation possible: hatches and vents can be positioned at the sides of the decks and in the hull's topsides without the drenching consequences if this were done on a monohull.

Figure 1-4.
A) Spartan cruising interior of *Hopscotch,* a 34-foot fast cruising trimaran designed for economical construction by the author. B) Simple yet effective interior of the author's *Juniper,* a 52-foot cruising trimaran. (Jim Brown photo) C) Spacious, light, and airy bridgedeck saloon of *Peregrine,* a 46-foot cruising cat designed by Roger Simpson. (Purcell photo)

A

B

C

Interior layout becomes more flexible in a buoyant, non-heeling yacht. For instance, you can locate plumbing fixtures and their drains anywhere in the multihull that suits the accommodation plan without worrying about the back-siphoning that can occur when a heeling monohull dips its sink or toilet below the waterline.

Another appreciated feature of multihulls is that any bilge water and engine drippings stay in the bilge and do not periodically wash the inside of the cabin, as they can when a monohull heels, infecting all they touch with their characteristic lingering odor.

Figure 1-5.
No bruisin' cruisin' —
taking it easy in the
bow nets of a big
cruising cat under
spinnaker.

While the quality of the accommodation space is excellent on all multis, the quantity of space can vary radically from boat to boat. Compared with a monohull of equal length, a trimaran often will have less interior living area, a catamaran often more. Cats with large bridgedeck cabins can have up to twice the interior space of a monohull of similar length.

Too much of a good thing can be as bad or worse than too little, however. There's nothing wrong with space *per se*. Interior volume in and of itself weighs little, contributes greatly to the ambience and "feel" of the interior, and if the cabin is properly streamlined it should add little windage.

But sailors have a way of filling up *space* with *things*. This seems related to the "wasted space" syndrome: "I paid for it; why not fill it up?" This is not a healthy attitude for multihull sailors. If unchecked it leads to bloated, overweight designs that sail poorly and look worse. It is much better to realize that every boat has its limits; that for a certain length, beam, and sail area there is only so much you can put aboard without making the boat ungainly—provided of course you do want to cruise. If you intend to stay at the dock, anything goes.

Deck space on a multihull normally is huge compared to a monohull. This allows you to carry a dinghy aboard and out of the way. Better yet, it can be a real cruising dinghy, big enough to do the job safely. In fact, it is realistic to carry two dinghies on many multihulls; family cruising pretty much demands two avenues on and off the boat.

Most monohulls solve the dinghy-storage problem by going the inflatable route, which is fine until you have to row it. In addition, an outboard-equipped inflatable boat trailing astern provides an incredible temptation to thieves; there are few places you'll want to leave such a craft unattended, a concern hardly consistent with carefree cruising. On the other hand, boats with oars (and those stored on deck or in the netting between hulls) are seldom molested.

Many cruising boats carry sailboards these days. The monohulls lash them against the forward stanchions, where they obstruct visibility and the flow of water over the decks. How many hundreds of stanchions have been folded over this way? The multihull usually offers several out-of-the-way places to stow watersports equipment and other necessary cruising impedimentia, such as bicycles.

Performance

Throughout history, speed under sail has been of great military and commercial significance. Empires rose and fell by the military control of sea lanes. Naval superiority hinged on vessels that could out-sail their adversary. The best designs for sailing ships were as secret then as the designs for submarines are today.

Even after steam engines replaced sail aboard military vessels, speed under sail still was important commercially. The fastest sailing ships were first in port with their cargoes, and thus received the highest price. Understandably, passengers wanted to reach their destination in the shortest time and booked passage on the ships with the best record for speed. Fast boats made money.

If there has been a single force driving the development of recreational sailboats, it has been the quest for better performance. So many of the things that we take for granted in fast sailboat design today were regarded as heresy only a short time ago. Outside ballast was a novelty resisted for decades, as was the strong and simple Marconi rig and rudders separated from the keel—all features that now would never be exchanged for their predecessors.

Certainly there are other desirable attributes for a sailboat besides speed, but a pattern emerges over and over again: All else being equal, faster designs are better. The customers—military, commercial, pleasure—prefer them. For a cruising yachtsman who has no intention of dominating sea lanes or being the first boat in port with a cargo of silks and tea, speed has several advantages.

The one mentioned most often? Fast boats are more fun to sail, and they *talk* to you: Pull on the sheet and she accelerates; fall off to a reach and the whoosh of wind in the sails sounds like Neptune breathing. Cruising frustration often is related to poor performance. Working too hard trying to whip a reluctant barge upwind or uptide when you have too far to go and too little time to get there is not much fun for anyone.

Not all cruising multis are fast boats. When you consider their windward and light-air performance, some are quite slow indeed. The owners of the slow multis invariably claim that speed is not important, that they have all the comforts of home and are in no hurry at all. For them the multihull's advantages are nice accommodations, shoal draft, and level sailing (or more often motoring). I can understand this perspective but I do not subscribe to it. Sailing is the reason I go cruising in the first place and cruising in a boat that sails well is important to me. Still, I want to be comfortable. And this is precisely what multihulls have going for them. You *can* have it all. Comfort, safety, *and* performance. Having it all means careful design compromise, but a beautiful blend is possible. The blend is not always easy and not always cheap, but it is there for the taking.

Fast *is* fun, provided you can go fast comfortably, without white knuckles. A good cruising multihull will go fast without your knowing it, and that is the way it should be. Often, especially on big cats, the thrill seeker will be disappointed. There is little or no heel, little or no wake, no bow wave to speak of—just a mild hissing below. "Isn't this boat moving?" "Sure, look at the Loran. We're averaging 11.5 knots!" This is exactly the kind of speed you want in a cruising boat: effortless speed.

Contrast this with the typical fast monohull. You can get a big ultralight monohull (ULDB) up to this kind of speed by close reaching with a spinnaker, pushing it to the limit, creating enormous strains within the rig, battling a broach, ready at any moment to jump on the sheets. But who needs that kind of cruising? I don't. A multihull makes much more sense. Take a boat that can sail in control at 20 knots, take it easy and reef her down, and speeds up to 15 knots (steady speeds, none of this "I saw the needle touch . . ." guess-work) are easy—and relaxing.

Much cruising is done in unfamiliar territory. Indeed, that is almost the definition of cruising. And many times the serious cruiser finds himself without reliable charts or aids to navigation. From personal experience I can say that no lights (even major lighthouses) or buoys can be trusted in the Bahamas, Turks and Caicos, Haiti, Dominican Republic, and most of the West Indies. What does this mean to the cruising sailor? Simply that you sail at night at your peril. Almost always it is necessary to arrive at a destination before dark or else stand off until the next morning when you can see your way in.

Most cruising is done in short daysails, widely interspersed with longer passages. A boat that can sail comfortably 30 to 50 percent faster has a much greater daylight range, and this translates directly to a wider choice of harbors and less need to sail unfamiliar waters at night.

Even in New England, where the waters are exceptionally well charted and aids to navigation frequent and reliable, being able to make tracks is a real boon. The usual summer conditions create lots of thick fog, which is not a great deal of fun to sail in, and can be hazardous in crowded waters. The fog often burns off in midmorning and rolls back in by mid- to late afternoon. In between is a five- to six-hour window of clear sailing. If the wind is blowing you easily can knock out 50 miles or more in a multihull. A fast monohull would be lucky to do 40. Ten miles in a pea-soup fog is nice to avoid if possible.

Circumstance forces many sailors into a pattern of weekending, with perhaps an annual two-week cruise. The higher average speeds of multihulls can nearly double the cruising radius. This may allow the owners of a fast boat to include three or four cruising destinations for every one available to the owners of a slower boat. Cruising is fun, but cruising in the same small area each weekend quickly becomes mundane.

Another advantage of speed is the ability to deal with adverse currents. Whether caused by tidal flows or ocean winds, the water is often moving, and not always in the right direction. Tidal currents can run three knots or more. If you can only sail at seven knots and the current is against you at three knots, your speed made good is four knots. If you can sail at 10 knots, however, your speed made good is seven knots—an increase of 75 percent over the slower boat. If you are beating to windward against such a current the slow boat may make good only one and a quarter knots, while the faster boat can buck the stream at three knots—nearly two and a half times faster.

Evading storms is yet another reason in favor of speed. If something big is headed your way, your safest recourses are seeking good shelter or getting out of its way. In either case an extra hundred miles made good can mean a *big* difference. Nowadays, with the availability of inexpensive weather facsimile machines, you have a good chance of staying clear of the worst weather provided you can turn on the speed when required and get onto the "safe side" of the approaching storm.

Ian Johnston, skipper of the well-traveled trimaran *Balena* (also known by its sponsors' names: *Bullfrog Sunblock* and now *Verbatim*), states: "Our weatherfax is so useful, a tremendous safety feature, and we would be most reluctant to part with it. It has brought us into a new sailing era, where we no longer are making educated guesses about our environmental predicament, but simply plotting our position on the maps and watching the progress of the weather around us. It is a great morale booster *knowing* what's coming and going, rather than just supposing. With *Bullfrog's* speed we can alter course and position ourselves on the right side of a low or high pressure system and even make runs from extremely bad weather."

Exactly how fast is a cruising multihull? Many cats and tris can and do go very fast for short periods, but the average speed made good over distance is always much less than the highest speeds recorded. A reasonable comparison of the relative average speeds of a multihull to a well-sailed monohull over distance can be seen in this example.

In 1989, the 50th Marblehead to Halifax Race allowed multihulls to participate for the first time. This 360-mile race is one of the preeminent events on the East Coast, although regarded as more of a cruising or family race than a go-for-broke, crash-and-burn extravaganza. About 90 monohulls and 13 multihulls started the race. *Juniper,* my 10-year-old, 52-foot cruising trimaran, started in the last class (two hours after the first monohull classes), with a crew of three, including myself. No effort was made to strip the boat. We had cruising stores, water, and fuel aboard since we planned a leisurely cruise home after the race. The first 200 miles was in light winds, mostly reaching. *Juniper's* 20-year-old hand-me-down spinnaker and reacher were much better than nothing for these conditions, but far from ideal.

Near Cape Sable, Nova Scotia, the fog came in thick and the wind began to build to around 20 knots. We were moving well, averaging about 13 knots on a very close reach. Ahead, visible on the radar screen, was a smudge going the same direction. After a few minutes a large monohull came into view, a new Baltic 64 named *Sarah Kate*, which we passed about 75 yards to windward. I was surprised to see how fast she was going—charging along at hull speed, rail down, a plume of spray flying from her bow—although we passed her going about three knots faster.

We crossed the finish line about three to four hours ahead of the *Sarah Kate* (10 percent faster over the course), which was the third monohull to finish. A few days later I had a chance to go aboard her and was immediately impressed by the size and power of the boat—the available horsepower produced by the enormous rig was astounding. The headstay was 100 feet long (compared with *Juniper's* 40 feet). In common with other big modern racer/cruiser monohulls, the rigging was tensioned by a hydraulic ram under the mast step, which lifts the mast up with a force of 50,000 to 60,000 pounds. The roller furling units on the jib and staysail—essentials to handle such a rig—were first class, but the list price on one furling unit alone is more than the cost of *all* the materials that went into *Juniper*. Everything on deck was huge and very expensive; the smallest winches on the boom were two sizes larger than my largest sheet winches.

Down below the boat was magnificent: beautiful joinerwork, plenty of nice accommodation, even a built-in TV/ VCR. I hesitate to compare the two boats, they are so different, but on my return to *Juniper* she felt like a dinghy—light little masts, toy winches—and yet we smoked 'em. Were we as comfortable? Probably not (no movies). Were we as safe? I think so. Would we have done as well if the race had been a dead slog to windward in 35 knots of wind? I'm not sure. Could the three of us handle our boat well without ultra-expensive equipment? Absolutely. Could we afford a boat like *Sarah Kate*, even if we wanted one? No way.

This is one of the great problems trying to compare monohulls with multihulls. To have a valid basis for comparison, some aspect must be called equal. But what? Length? Performance? Cost? Accommodation?

Perhaps a more mundane example of multihull sailing will better illustrate the kind of speed to expect from a fast-sailing multihull. When daysailing along the New England coast, there usually are plenty of other sailboats in view. On *Juniper* in a breeze, it normally takes us about 20 to 30 minutes to overtake a garden-variety cruising sailboat when we spot it ahead on the horizon, and an equal amount of time to leave it hull down in our wake. Passing dozens of boats with ease may not be proper Puritan ethic, but it sure is fun.

Shoal Draft

Figure 1-6.
A shallow-draft boat that can be beached for repairs is a powerful advantage for self-sufficient cruisers. Searunner 31 *Shadowfax* being repaired on the beach in the Exumas after an encounter with a reef.

All boats need some water beneath the keel, but the more depth you need for safe operation the more restricted your available cruising areas become. I find it comical to see what the sellers of many performance-oriented monohulls advertise as "cruising" boats. Six, seven, even eight feet of draft is common! Haven't these people ever looked at a chart? There are many places you just cannot go with this kind of draft, and as anchorages and mooring spaces fill up, shallow areas become increasingly desirable.

In the U.S., money for dredging projects has been in short supply in recent years, and this situation is likely to get worse before it gets better. The practical implications are shoaling channels and harbors; many inlets are no longer maintained at all. Much of the Intracoastal Waterway is accessible only to shoal-draft boats. A cruising boat that can reduce its draft to three feet or less is able to get into many places safely where a deeper-draft boat can no longer go. A big cruising multihull with retractable fins and rudders will float in only 20 inches of water.

Because of their shoal draft, cats and tris are easy to put on the beach for maintenance. In many regions the tidal range is too small to dry out the hull of a fixed-keel monohull, but is sufficient to expose the bottom of a multihull completely. Beaching is a nice option when you need to get to the bottom for a minor repair or an emergency quick fix. Cruising means self-reliance. Needing only two feet of tide and a protected beach makes finding a quick "haul" pretty easy.

There must also be a safety gain associated with reduced draft. After all, the deeper a boat the more rocks there are to hit and shoals on which to strand. Much cruising relies on eyeball navigation; in poor light or murky water it is difficult enough to get around with a very shoal boat. I can't imagine how people manage with deep draft.

Ease of Handling and Comfort Under Way

For a given length, a multihull is much lighter than a ballasted monohull. This results in a boat that requires less energy to push through the water and thus needs less sail area to achieve adequate performance. It is astounding how fast a good multihull sails in strong winds with deeply reefed sails. The small sail area combined with the modest heeling—typically 10 degrees or less on a trimaran, half that on a cat—make those heavy-wind days much easier to tolerate. And of course those same small sails and level ride make sail handling easier in moderate conditions, too.

A monohull can give good sailing performance; certainly there is a trend in that direction: "Performance cruisers" have been the hot sellers for some time now. The designers make the monos go fast, however, by making them big, deep and tall. The restrictions of deep draft have been mentioned, but few people consider the problems of cruising with tall rigs. There are many fixed bridges on the East and Gulf Coasts of the U.S. with clearances of 65 feet. If your stick is taller, too bad. In practice, a 45- to 50-foot multihull will not be hindered by this sort of height restriction, but many performance monohulls will.

Most cruisers spend much of their time sailing in light winds. In many cruising monohulls this is the signal to break out the iron topsail. But it is so much more agreeable to sail than motor *if* you can make good progress—not an easy task with many cruising monohulls. One of the joys of sailing a fast cruising multi is to have a relaxing, enjoyable 30-mile sail while everyone else is having a dull 30-mile motor.

Good multihulls truly excel in light air. Their efficient hull forms enable them to accelerate in just small puffs of wind. When running and reaching, this quick burst of speed brings the apparent wind far enough forward to enable the boat to make exceptional progress under working sail alone, and avoids the need to hoist a spinnaker. And when spinnakers and reachers are flown, the multihull's wide beam makes the use of spinnaker and whisker poles, with their attendant complications and handling problems, unnecessary. Dousing these light sails on a multihull's wide, level deck is a snap.

Few multihulls are difficult to steer; those long, narrow hulls like to go in the direction they are pointed. There is little yawing, and strong rudder action seldom is required. Not only does this make the helmsperson's life easier, it also makes autopilots more effective.

Beating to windward against substantial waves will never be comfortable in any boat—and a multihull is no exception. If there is a bright side to windward bashing in multihulls, it is that at least the angle of heel remains modest, which does much to simplify the basic tasks that are so important to maintaining the crew's effectiveness and optimism: cooking, washing, and sleeping—all activities that are hard to perform tilted 35 degrees from vertical (see Figure 1-7 and the accompanying sidebar).

The motion of multis going to windward in waves is quite unlike the motion of a single-hulled boat. Some describe it as jerky, others call it quick; I call it different. Waves are made by wind; big waves are usually accompanied by big winds. Big winds make multis go fast, and going fast against big waves quickly becomes uncomfortable far out of proportion to the increased speed.

Although the boat may be physically capable of going 12 knots under these conditions, the motion below will be more or less intolerable. This has an easy remedy: *Slow it down*. Roll up some jib, put a reef in the main, keep the speed to 8 to 9 knots, and she will be a dream—the off watch can relax and the cook can cook. Sailed in this conservative fashion, the motion of a well-designed cruising multihull will be no worse than a monohull in the same conditions, and often better. And the multihull *still* will be going faster.

Running and reaching are the preferred modes of travel, and most long cruises are organized to take the prevailing winds from astern. The multihull is *ideal* for downwind sailing. There is no better boat for long, downwind passages. Where the single-hulled sailboat has a rolling, corkscrewing motion as it meanders through the waves, the multihull will charge along without a care.

Faster sailing means that waves overtake the boat more slowly and less frequently. Occasionally, beautiful surfing conditions develop that have to be experienced to be appreciated. Sheet leads can be moved outboard readily, allowing exceptional sail control without the complications of whisker poles. Steering control is sure, with a light helm and no tendency to broach before

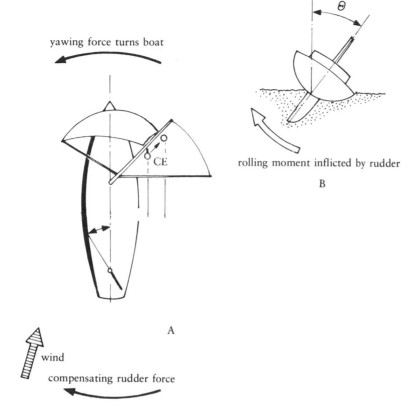

yawing force turns boat

θ

CE

rolling moment inflicted by rudder

B

A

wind

compensating rudder force

Figure 1-7
A) Substantial rolling causes the rig to be displaced to the side of the boat, introducing a yawing force which turns the boat. B) The heading can be corrected by a counteracting rudder force, but the rudder force tends to accentuate the rolling. (Adapted from *Seaworthiness the Forgotten Factor*, C. A. Marchaj. IMP and Adlard Coles, 1986)

waves. Even the harshest critics of multihulls readily concede their superiority downwind.

In fairness, big multis in tight places must be handled with caution. Under sail they can accelerate rapidly, leaving scant time to make decisions. Powerboaters in particular seldom realize that *this* sailboat *moves*, and often will not be ready to yield right-of-way. Monohull sailors blinded by heeled, overlapping jibs often don't realize that the sail seen well in the distance a few minutes ago may now be only a few boatlengths away. After a couple of near misses I *never* exert our starboard tack right-of-way unless it is readily apparent that the other skipper has seen us.

If you love short tacking through the yacht club's moorings, don't plan on making a lot of friends if you're doing this with a big multihull, which can be 16, 24, even 30 feet wide. I remember once sailing through a very crowded Edgartown, Massachusetts anchorage in a gusty summer wind in my old engineless 31-foot trimaran. Our too-rapid progress momentarily obstructed by swinging boats, I had no option but to sheet in, head up, and cut very close to the stern of a large Hinckley. Running out of room, the trimaran's high-flying windward float dripped saltwater into the Hinckley's dinghy as it flew over. The owner, who was sitting in the cockpit, spilled his martini and most definitely was not amused. These days we have a nice diesel and motor in to Edgartown.

Stability

Sailing downwind, single-hulled boats develop the peculiar and uncomfortable characteristic known as "rhythmic rolling." Because everyone is so familiar

---

FEELING SEASICK?

Those of us who have sailed multihulls for many years have become so accustomed to the comfort of our low-heeling, low-rolling cats or tris that we forget about the macho "heeled over and hanging on" attitude that permeates so much of sailing. In the same respect, those who sail single-hulled boats become so accustomed to the heeling and rolling that they often claim it poses no disadvantage, and in fact is half the fun.

In the world of yachting, very little basic research is ever done. With the exception of America's Cup-style keels, little money gets spent for scientific investigations of the practical aspects of sailing boats. This situation differs markedly from that of the military, where money abounds for studies of all kinds. Of particular interest is research funded by the U.S. Navy.

One significant problem the Navy has experienced is a reduction in crew performance due to the motion of ships, specifically the smaller ships. For example, destroyer escorts, which are about 420 feet long and displace over 4,000 tons, suffer frequently from wave-induced rolling.

Studies by J. B. Hadler and T. H. Sarchin of the Naval Ship Research and Development Center and the Naval Ship Engineering Center found that, " . . . about 50 percent of the time while in operation these ships experienced troublesome roll. The operators indicated

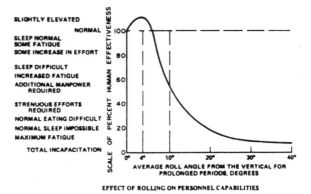

EFFECT OF ROLLING ON PERSONNEL CAPABILITIES

that continuous rolling with amplitude in the 10- to 15-degree range seriously degraded human performance, making it difficult to walk along passageways or even to sleep. . . . At more than 15 degrees, most activity, except basic ship operation, ceases."

Other studies, by Warthurst and Cerasini, also of the Naval Ship R&D Center, conducted aboard the *USS Glover*, " . . . showed three distinct regions of human performance for various amounts of roll. These are from 0 to 4 degrees, 4 to approximately 10 degrees, and more than 10 degrees. They correspond to ranges at which personnel can work at various rates of efficiency [see with this behavior, it is regarded not as a threat, but as an unfortunate fact of life. A great many factors contribute to rolling, and it is not easy to isolate the individual components of the complex whole that influences a particular boat's motion in a specific seaway.

One dominant factor is the pendulum effect of the ballast keel. Because a monohull has low hullform stability, an external force, such as a wind gust or wave, easily heels the boat until it reaches equilibrium. The keel then rolls the boat back upright and a little beyond, resulting in considerable residual motion.

This pendulum-effect rolling is only the tip of the proverbial iceberg,

Figure 1-7]. It should be noted that *a small amount of roll can be beneficial* [my italics]. The region from 4 to 10 degrees of average roll shows a marked deterioration in performance, progressing from some fatigue through the requirement for additional manpower to perform a motor task. At more than 10 degrees, normal functions such as eating, sleeping, and movement around the ship range from difficult to impossible." (From a paper entitled, *Seakeeping Criteria and Specifications,* by Hadler and Sarchin, Naval Ship Research and Development Center, 1973.)

So much for the advantages of sailing on your ear! As the graph illustrates, only 10 degrees roll angle cuts crew performance in half. At 20 degrees the crew's ability to eat, sleep, navigate, and generally stay alert decreases to one fifth their normal capacity. Perhaps the most interesting result is the approximate 10 percent increase in performance with an average 4 degree roll. Maybe this feature is akin to a rocking chair: It feels good, it's relaxing, therefore it's easier to concentrate on the task at hand.

Some will argue that studies of this nature do not apply to cruising sailboats. But why not? Isn't the small crew of a cruising sailboat, who must do everything themselves, subject to even greater demands than the crew of a naval ship, where there is a complete division of labor and each crewman is responsible for only one or two tasks?

The typical husband/wife cruising team must keep watch, steer, tend sails; navigate using piloting, Loran, possibly radar, SatNav, and celestial techniques; keep tabs on the weather, operate the radio, cook, clean up, eat, sleep, and command the boat. That is a long list of complex tasks for a crew who have been deprived of sleep and who must concentrate much of their energy on not being thrown across the cabin.

So many boating accidents are simple mental mistakes, or compounded minor errors, attributable to fatigue. Any reduction of crew performance due to the boat's rolling or other motions is cause for concern. If the boat's rolling motion can be reduced by just a few degrees the crew will realize a large benefit in performance. The cruising multihull rolls far less than its single-hulled counterpart, and thereby relieves the crew from an important but unnecessary burden.

What did the Navy conclude from its research? Among other things, they decided that applications requiring a very steady platform at sea were best suited to, of all things, a catamaran hull form. "A primary intent of this configuration is to attain high speeds in a seaway with small attendant motions."

however, because it can combine with other seemingly harmless forces to result in wild motions that can be exceedingly uncomfortable if not downright dangerous.

These "harmless forces" include: the slight variations in stability that occur when a boat sails in waves; the rolling force of small waves that closely match the boat's own period (time) of roll; rolling forces produced by the wind in the sails; rolling forces produced by the rudder as the helmsman tries to contain the heeling-induced yawing.

Most of these forces are small and easy to deal with in a multihull, but the single-hulled boat with ballast keel can rapidly develop a "child-on-a-swing" syndrome, where a small input of energy at the right time can induce a very large rolling motion that can build out of control. This can lead to a variety of difficulties, including broaching, knockdowns, or capsizing.

Here is a typical scenario for the onset of rhythmic rolling in a single-hulled boat: As the boat begins to heel significantly the sails are displaced from their position directly over the hull to a position some distance to either side. This tends to turn the boat to the opposite side, requiring a rudder correction. For instance, if the boat heels to starboard, the power of the sails pushing forward against the hull resistance—which is pulling backward—creates a force couple that turns the boat to port and can start the rolling process. The rudder action required to straighten the heading further adds to the rolling.

In addition, aerodynamic forces of the sails themselves further accentuate the rolling. The respected sailing theoretician C. A. Marchaj describes this feature well in *Seaworthiness, The Forgotten Factor* (International Marine Publishing, 1986): "A rig can extract energy from the wind in a self-excited manner by its own periodic motion in such a way that the sail can be regarded as a *rolling engine*, which operates even in steady (non-oscillating) winds. Consequently the boat [a monohull] *may be knocked down, even in a condition where the size of the waves is insignificant.*"

Figure 1-8.
How's the Jello doing, Marybelle? (Jo Hudson cartoon courtesy Jim Brown)

A classic example of this roll-out-of-control behavior is included in the "Final Report of the Joint Committee on Safety From Capsizing," by the U.S. Yacht Racing Union and The Society of Naval Architects & Marine Engineers, 1985. Referring to the need for high stability it states:

For those who cannot appreciate the need for this in big boats, a withdrawal report by a 60-footer [*monohull*] in the St. Pete-Fort Lauderdale Race of 1984 is instructive: "At approximately 1340 EST while running under spinnaker and full main, boat entered violent roll cycle. On deep roll to port boat buried end of boom and mainsail preventer held boom in water. Boom apparently collapsed as boat took deep roll to starboard (windward) and lay on beam ends (80-85 degree angle of heel). Boat remained in this position with a good portion of spinnaker and 10 feet or so of pole in water until force on pole caused spinnaker car control chain to break. Pole then shot up vertically with reference to water plane relieving pressure on spinnaker sufficiently to allow boat to right itself..." The "death roll" was so violent and deep that crew members on the starboard rail were completely submerged and "grinders" were hanging vertically from the pedestals. [And maintaining a death grip on the handles, no doubt!] The weather associated with this incident was reported as wind 20 gusting to 30.

Safety, like beauty, certainly must lie in the eye of the beholder! In my view this boat was extremely lucky that its mast was not broken by the spinnaker pole and that no crew were lost; a "death grip" indeed. Twenty gusting to 30 knots is not a lot of wind. If that is all it takes to knock a 60-foot boat flat when running, something is very wrong.

A cruising multihull sailing shorthanded, spinnaker up, and going 50 percent faster than the boat in the above example, *never* would have done this. Why? Because their great stability at low heeling angles nips rolling problems in the bud. If a boat fights off wind- and wave-produced rolling forces early—before they can get started—they don't build to dangerous levels. Add to this the elimination of the ballast keel and its bad-behavior-amplifying pendulum effect, the roll-dampening effect of the widely separated hulls, and the absence of pronounced heeling, which prevents the steering problems caused by the sail plan being physically displaced to the side of the yacht.

Much of monohull seamanship is devoted to dealing with the consequences of low stability. Designed, built, and sailed well, the cruising monohull seldom is threatened by its rolling behavior, but it certainly isn't comfortable for the crew and can hardly be viewed as a desirable trait. The multihull, on the other hand, is so docile in this respect that no attention need ever be given to this sort of ill-mannered behavior.

Safety

Over the last 20 years, so much has been written questioning the safety of multihulls that many sailors who are initially attracted to them abandon the idea. After all, these boats are uniformly condemned as unsafe by an elite cadre of experts. Who would be foolish enough to go against such respected opinions? Let's address this issue right up front, point by point.

Much of the criticism has been leveled by authors of yachting books with no firsthand multihull experience, which they admit readily. But rather than writing about the things they do know, they're somehow compelled to give multihulls a quick once-over. These authors have blasted as unsafe the whole breed of multihulled boats. They claim that multihulls are unable to go to windward, unseaworthy, prone to breaking up at sea, always on the verge of capsize, and most likely the result of someone's perverse death wish.

The arguments: Francis Kinney, in his revised version of *Skene's Elements of Yacht Design* (Dodd, Mead & Company, 1981), a well-regarded textbook, lays out the "conventional wisdom" pretty well on page 9 when he states that multihulls have, " . . . an inherent tendency to capsize. When knocked down by a squall, a catamaran will not lie on her side and right herself again, but will flip right over upside down with her mast pointing at the bottom. Granted, small ones do provide great sport speeding close to shore. Although I may be wrong, in my opinion you should never go to sea in one, because it might be a fatal mistake."

Not satisfied with such a broad condemnation Kinney goes on to state, " . . . but the inescapable fact is that all multihull craft tend to tear their hulls apart. They may sink from leaking badly at strained joints, or just fall apart and sink after capsizing." Subject closed.

Take no prisoners, Mr. Kinney! But could he be right? Sure, small beach cats can be turned over pretty easily if you catch a heavy gust and you don't ease the sheets in time. An open-cockpit ballasted monohull could capsize in the same conditions and, unlike the multihull, may well sink in the process. Does that make all monohulls a "fatal mistake" offshore? Of course not. Cruising-size multihulls are extremely difficult to overturn and present only minor risk of wind capsize (more on this later in this Chapter and in Chapter 10).

To complicate matters, knockdown and capsize mean different things to multihulls and monohulls. The post mortems after the 1979 Fastnet race established two categories of knockdown for monohulls: The less severe, or B1 knockdowns, laid the mast over to horizontal. The more severe B2 knockdown encompassed anything that went past the mast-horizontal position, including a complete 180-degree capsize and a 360-degree roll over.

The B1-type knockdown's angle of heel conforms roughly to the point at which the monohull reaches its maximum righting moment. In a single-hulled boat, the word *capsize* becomes a vague term. Has the boat capsized if the masthead is 20 feet underwater? Or is this still within the category of a knockdown? Certainly the boats that "stick" upside down have capsized, but most of the time another big wave helps them roll back upright, or else they sink. In either case the defining term *capsize* becomes superseded by another adjective.

With multihulls the situation is reversed. Knockdown is the nebulous term and capsize is very much a black-and-white issue. Either the boat is capsized or it isn't.

Applying the B1, B2 definitions to a multihull would lead one to call a knockdown any action that caused the multihull to reach the heel of its maximum righting moment. This squares pretty well with my definition of a multihull knockdown: a gust that lifts clear of the water the main hull of a trimaran or the windward hull of a cat. While there still is a good chance of avoiding capsize, your margin of safety is very thin once you start flying a hull.

Heeling angles for a multihull knockdown will vary depending on the design in question, but most trimarans will begin flying the main hull at 15 to 20 degrees of heel. Catamarans will be near lifting the windward hull at about 5 to 8 degrees. Capsize is easier to define from a multihull's standpoint: The boat is inverted 180 degrees.

Do all multihulls "tend to tear their hulls apart?" Admittedly, there are great strains that must be dealt with in the structure of a cat or tri; there also are great strains that must be dealt with in a monohull. Have you considered the strain that develops between the deep fin keel and the hull bottom of a single-hulled yacht? There is no place in the hull structure of a cruising multihull that is subjected to such highly concentrated loads. Does the fact that more than a few monohull keels have fallen off in recent years make *all* monohulls structurally unsound?

Figure 1-9 illustrates what can happen to a keel boat when the engineering or construction is not done properly. This boat sank in shallow water and was recovered. The bending load of the keel tore open the bottom and down it went. Similar incidents befell, among others, the ULDB *Charley* and the maxi-racer *Drum.* A particularly embarrassing episode occurred at the highly hyped launching in Maine of the *Nantucket Splinter,* whose deep keel fell off and whose mast went through her bottom shortly after launching. Oops!

These are just three examples of well-known incidents. A quick walk around most boatyards will reveal many other deep keels in various stages of "falling off."

In an effort to gain another small fraction of a knot, the current trend in performance-cruising monohull design is to employ bulb or wing keels. These keels have more volume down low, thus the ballast weight exerts a larger righting force. Unfortunately, this increases the strain at the keel-to-hull joint. Of course the better designers and builders know this and engineer the hull to accept the strain without damage. Nevertheless, it is an enormous strain, significantly greater than the strains in the crossbeams of a cruising multihull. Does the same logic, "They may sink from leaking badly at strained joints, or just fall apart and sink after capsizing," work here?

The American Bureau of Shipping publishes a *Guide for Building and Classing Offshore Racing Yachts* that details the structural requirements for hull, deck, and keel attachment for monohull sailboats. These data were derived largely from examining the extensive pool of information regarding boats that have failed in service. A monohull built to ABS standards will be strong enough for safe use offshore without being excessively heavy or overbuilt.

To perform as they should, safe cruising multihulls can and should be

Figure 1-9.
Multihulls are not the only boats subject to great strains that can "tear their hulls apart." The bending strain of this monohull's keel tore her bottom open and down she went.

constructed much more lightly than these standards require. Why can a cruising multihull, which according to the "sailing experts" suffers so terribly from "tearing its hull apart," be built successfully with much lighter hull and deck scantlings than a comparable monohull?

The multihull does not slam its hull bottom as it sails to windward over waves. Why? There *is* no hull bottom! Well, almost. As it reenters the water after being airborne, the narrow hull presents so little resistance to the surface that pounding seldom if ever happens (unless the multihull has very low underwing clearance). On the other hand, the monohull presents a huge area of underbelly to be slammed. If the boat is heeled substantially the pounding also will occur on the forward topsides, requiring very stout construction there as well.

And because the hulls are not being pulled constantly beneath the surface by a massive chunk of lead ballast, the multihull spends its time on top of the water rather than beneath it. Consequently, the hydrostatic forces (the pressure of the water outside the hull trying to get in) are lower.

A third reason that safe cruising multihulls are built more lightly than safe cruising monohulls is that the consequences of failure are so much less severe in a multihull. Think about it. If a big leak can mean uncontrolled flooding and sinking, it is of paramount importance that big leaks be prevented, even if this means adding a great deal of otherwise unnecessary weight to the structure of the boat. For a multihull, the "big leak" is not nearly so radical a problem. Certainly you want to avoid large leaks in *any* boat, but because a multihull is just that—multiple hulls, each of which is slender, for the most part above water, and *has an inherent tendency to float*—flooding is easily contained and controlled and presents little danger to a well-designed catamaran or trimaran.

Mr. Kinney's uninformed brand of criticism—well-meaning though it may be—has never been particularly productive. To successfully argue a point, it is not only necessary to understand both sides of the issue, but to understand the focus of the argument. I have yet to meet anyone who has given up driving a car because there was a crash at the Indianapolis 500. And I am sure that the pioneers of aviation had to deal constantly with the advice of well-meaning but inexperienced and uninformed kibitzers.

Mr. Kinney goes on to summarize very accurately why he feels the way he does, and this hits on the real meat of the issue: "The old feeling that a sailor acquires in childhood is basically right. That is, the single-hull sailboat with a lot of ballast as low on her keel as possible is the safest."

The real issue for Mr. Kinney, and others, is *habit*. Very few old dogs learn new tricks. I am no exception. As a boy I learned to sail unballasted centerboarders—Lightnings, Blue Jays, Sunfish, and the like. When it came time to build my first cruising boat it was natural for me to consider an unballasted, responsive boat—but one that I felt had sufficient stability for safe offshore sailing: a trimaran.

There is no question that there have been some horrendous multihulls built. I've seen more than a few cats and tris that made my flesh crawl. Anyone who has cruised has seen these boats. Many were built in the 1960s by nonsailors who were off chasing an elusive dream before having their noses very rudely rubbed in the reality of the open ocean. Abandoned or sold cheap, these boats now lie scattered about the world, often functioning as floating immobile homes.

Some early proponents of multihulls made voyages in their creations and wrote books about their misadventures. A few of these sea stories read like comic opera. They were unseaworthy, unable to make reasonable progress to windward, difficult to handle, and often unfinished inside or just plain poorly built. And worst of all, their owners still had nothing but praise for their craft! This did not go unnoticed by the yachtsmen of the day. It is easy to see why the good multihull boats were ignored; the bad ones made such an easy target for criticism.

But there were some very fine boats built even in the early days of the modern multihull. Beginning in the 1950s, Rudy Choy, Woody Brown, Warren Seaman, and Alfred Kumalai designed and built several dozen magnificent catamarans. These boats competed very successfully in long-distance races, winning such notable events as the TransPac. They also cruised thousands of miles and worked daily carrying passengers for hire. These boats stand in sharp contrast to the "accepted wisdom" regarding multihulls.

The arguments: In his book *The Ocean Sailing Yacht, Volume 2* (W. W. Norton & Company, 1973), Don Street levels a broadside against multihulls for being the epitome of unsafe watercraft. Certainly Mr. Street has a right to his opinion; unfortunately he presents much of it as fact. While he would be easy to ignore on the subject of multihulls because he knows so little about them, many people turn to his books to learn more about cruising boats in general and are convinced by these baseless attacks that *all* cruising multihulls are dangerous.

Mr. Street, a well-known, experienced sailor, pours forth his accumulated wisdom into a well-done, well-illustrated book—a definitive work on the subject of cruising boats. I know that if I were an inexperienced sailor and met an expert such as Don Street who said essentially that I would be a suicidal fool ever to set foot in a cat or tri, *I* would be influenced. Who wouldn't? Who would trust his life or the lives of his family to a boat so thoroughly damned by such an august source? There is just too much money, emotion, and peer pressure involved in the selection of a cruising boat to contradict the "experts."

For many years, antipathy has festered between some sailors of monohulls and multihulls. Just why this is so is a good question. In the early days of multis in this country, back in the 1870s, the often-abrasive Nathanael

Figure 1-10.
"Cheap" multihulls
such as this one gave
multis a black eye
from which they are
still recovering.

Herreshoff and others built a number of catamarans that did very well racing—*too* well:

> The general interest in catamarans of that time was caused by N. G. Herreshoff's *Amaryllis,* which competed with single-hulled craft in the Centennial Regatta held on June 22, 1876, off the New York Yacht Club's Staten Island station. *Amaryllis* raced in Class 3, which was open to all boats between twenty-five and forty feet in length. There were eleven starters in the race, including the best of the large-sized sandbaggers of the time. In the first part of the race, the wind was light and *Amaryllis* did rather poorly. This put her in a place where she would have to pass most of the fleet if she were to win, but when the race was about half over, a nice sailing breeze sprang up and *Amaryllis* sailed gaily through the fleet to win by twenty minutes and two seconds over the next competitor, the famous sandbagger *Pluck and Luck.* Some in the class were forty or more minutes behind. (From *An L. Francis Herreshoff Reader,* by L. Francis Herreshoff, International Marine Publishing, 1978.)

Consequently, multihulls were banned from racing in the prestigious events, a ban that largely continues. This certainly did not help the development of better multihull designs. Given the importance of yacht racing, few designers would continue to work in a field in which they could not see their creations perform. Try to imagine the history of multihull development if those early efforts had been embraced by the yachting community instead of disqualified as "unsporting."

The more recent thorn in the side of the yachting world was the way in which multihulls reemerged in the 1960s. You remember *The SIXTIES:* "Hey man, I'm splitting for the coast to get my head together."

Sparked by Arthur Piver, a "cultural movement" evolved around the trimaran. The core of this movement gained much promotional mileage from the "cheap-boats-for-ordinary-people" theme. It didn't matter that a good multihull, like any good boat, is not cheap to build. Why risk confusing someone with the facts? And this theme meshed nicely with other antiestablishment themes in vogue at the time such as the down-home, do-it-yourself movement. Let's face it, lots of multihulls were built by *hippies,* for want of a better word.

Take a weird-looking boat, often built and crewed by minimally skilled crazies who plainly took great glee in passing gold-plated monohulls like they were going backward; add to this potent mix the many flagrant violations of good boatbuilding practice done in the name of economy and embryonic multihull development, and you have a situation tailor-made to annoy the tradition-bound, crewcut yachtsmen of the day. This antiestablishment perception colors the views of many today. Although Mr. Street would probably deny it, I suspect that this is a large part of the reason he takes such a dim view of multis. But enough with emotion and historical perspective; let's examine the "facts."

Mr. Street presents a number of arguments that form the core of his "multihulls-are-no-good" sentiment. The first and by far the most important negative is that multis are not self-righting if capsized, and that this has caused tremendous loss of life. His second point is that "a catamaran or trimaran is completely unforgiving." He means that you are on the knife-edge of disaster at all times when sailing a multihull. His third point is that multihulls are inherently weak and prone to holing and other unspecified structural failures. His final argument is not so much against the boats but the people who own them: The people who sail multihulls just don't know what they are doing.

The counter-argument. If capsized, a cat or tri will not self-right—absolutely true. But this must be viewed in light of the fact that a seaworthy multihull is not an easy thing to overturn and can be capsized only by extreme conditions or gross negligence. And still, no matter what happens it will not sink.

It is often said (derisively of course) that a multihull has ultimate stability when upside down. Again, this is true, and I am glad of it. By comparison, a ballasted monohull has ultimate stability resting on the bottom. I'll leave you to decide which is a better situation: standing knee deep in the capsized cabin hanging up your belongings to dry? Or treading water looking for floating debris to clutch for your last hour on earth? Think about it.

Figure 1-11.
"Dear, are we sailing on the knife-edge of disaster?"

If a ballasted monohull were knocked down but did not self-right, it would be a total disaster. Thus it is only natural that the monohull sailor considers any boat that does not right itself immediately after capsize to be a death trap.

Why is self-righting ability considered so important? Self-righting has no value until you've capsized. The more likely a boat is to capsize the more important the self-righting feature becomes. Most ships are not self-righting; neither are the commercial fishing boats that work the North Atlantic all winter long. If the vessel has great dynamic stability to start with, capsize is unlikely and self-righting ability is not required. Capsize, as has been shown in *Seaworthiness, The Forgotten Factor,* by C.A. Marchaj, can happen to *any* boat, but is much more likely to happen to some than to others.

Two major factors contribute to a boat's ability to resist capsize. The first is the boat's stability, which is the ability of a vessel to resist the force of wind and wave trying to overturn it. There are different ways to measure stability, but unfortunately the feature we want to measure—a boat's dynamic stability when facing a combination of wind and waves—is the most difficult to quantify. It is not difficult to see, however, that from the perspective of resisting capsize, more stability is better than less stability.

An easy way to compare the energy required to capsize different boats is to compare their static stability curves. In the *Ocean Sailing Yacht, Volume 2*, Don Street presents a greatly distorted chart of stability curves that he would like you to take at face value because it bolsters his argument. Missing from Mr. Street's stability graph is the truthful representation of a multihull's huge

Figure 1-12. As everyone knows, the Achilles heel of a multihull is her inability to recover from capsize. Extending that logic, the Achilles heel of a monohull is her inability to recover from sinking. (Jo Hudson cartoon courtesy Jim Brown)

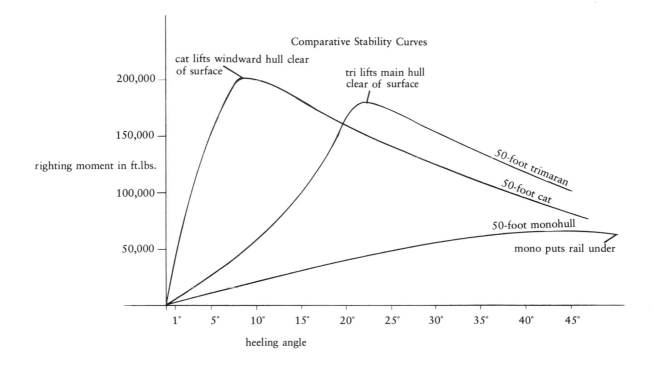

Comparative Stability Curves

cat lifts windward hull clear of surface

tri lifts main hull clear of surface

200,000

150,000

righting moment in ft.lbs.

100,000

50-foot trimaran

50-foot cat

50-foot monohull

50,000

mono puts rail under

1°   5°   10°   15°   20°   25°   30°   35°   40°   45°

heeling angle

Figure 1-13.
Comparative stability
curves plotted from
three actual boats of
comparable size.

stability at low angles of heel; unlike a monohull, they don't need to lay over on their sides to access their stability.

If his graph were an accurate representation of the way things really are, I would agree that a multihull would not be a good idea. With only monohull-like stability at low heeling angles and high stability inverted you would be saddled with the worst features of both kinds of boats.

Truly representative stability curves for monohull, cat, and tri are presented for comparison in Figure 1-13. These curves are drawn using actual values from three real boats of normal form, all of them the same length. Characteristic of a multihull is the very steep rise in the stability curve with the first few degrees of heel. As wind or waves try to tip the multihull it fights back—quickly and effectively. Where the single-hulled boat must lay over 30 or 40 degrees before developing an appreciable counterforce, a catamaran has it right away, the trimaran shortly thereafter. The practical implications are obvious: little heeling, no rolling tendency and the associated steering problems, and more sail-carrying power.

The gust that knocks the monohull on its ear, spilling crew across cabin and deck, will add only a few degrees of heel to the nearly level ride of a multihull. A monohull designer will point to the portion of the stability curve beyond 30 degrees. Since their boats spend so much time heeled to that level and beyond, they are forced by circumstance to rate with importance stability at great heeling angles; a multihull designer finds this part of the static stability curve meaningless.

Another major factor that contributes to a boat's capability to resist capsize is its ability to retain steering control at speed in large waves. A boat that broaches in heavy weather is very likely to be rolled over—if not by this wave, quite possibly by the next or the one after. The two features of multihulls that stand out so prominently are their tremendous stability and the ease and control with which they can be steered at high speed. Conditions under which many monohulls would broach out of control, at great risk of being rolled over, will not begin to trouble a well-designed multihull.

In 17 years of active multihull sailing I have yet to see a multihull broach. Their slender hulls and pronounced lack of heeling combine to resist broaching. This is not to claim that no multihull has ever broached; given extreme conditions, they can. And some designs behave better than others. I know of two examples:

During the 1972 TransPac Race, the 37-foot trimaran *Bacchanal* was well on the way to a record passage, surfing fast and hard under spinnaker. At a change of watch during the night the new helmsman, who had just come on deck from the bright lights below, became disoriented and lost control of the boat during a high-speed surf. The boat broached badly, momentarily shoving the outrigger (float) under water. The crew managed to release the spinnaker sheet, however, turn downwind, and resume racing, shaken but sound. The other incident I know of occurred when a 31-foot cruising trimaran sailed into a river entrance from the ocean. Large swells were breaking over the bar, but their severity was not obvious from seaward. The skipper was quite ill and needed medical attention, so the decision was made to go in. At the line of breakers the boat was hit very hard and broached; a wall of white water then carried it (sideways) at high speed for 100 yards or so until well inside the bar. No damage resulted.

Both cases involved older trimaran designs with relatively full-bodied main hulls—length-to-beam ratios of 6 to 1. Currently, designers prefer slimmer hulls, which subsequently steer and accelerate better. Despite the fact that both broaches were caused by varying degrees of "operator error," I feel that neither would have occurred with newer designs.

Put bluntly, because they can be difficult to control in heavy going and are thus much more likely to spin out or broach before a wave than a multihull, monohulls desperately need to be self-righting. Preparations for disaster should be in direct proportion to the likelihood of its occurrence.

Another reason that lack of self-righting ability is so feared is that a monohull capsized for any length of time often will lose its watertight integrity and fill with water. Many boats, in fact, lose their watertight integrity during the capsize itself. Ports or hatches may be stove in or even left open. In a ballasted boat this is disaster. With a crew less resourceful than, for instance, the Smeetons, during their well-documented pitchpoling incidents aboard *Tzu*

Hang, a capsized and severely damaged monohull most probably will sink. In the open ocean without a boat, your chances for survival are very, very slim.

Ninety-eight percent of the time, you could not capsize a good multihull designed for offshore cruising if you set out to do it on purpose; the energy required to turn the boat over is just not available.

Certainly multihulls *have* capsized. The majority of these have occurred during races, however, where the desire to win overcomes the better judgment of sensible seamanship. Other multihull capsizes can be attributed to faulty design or construction, or poor seamanship—of which far too many early multihull aficionados were guilty. But very, very few good boats of reasonable size sailed by experienced crews in a cruising context have capsized.

Even then, an offshore capsize, while an undeniable calamity, is far from a death sentence. With some preparation, reasonably comfortable survival within the boat is possible.

Designer/sailor/author "Trimaran Jim" Brown summed it up pretty well when he said to me, "The hard part, Chris, is convincing sailors that waiting for rescue is an acceptable consequence of capsize. It's almost as if they'd rather be dead than contemplate living in an upside-down boat. . . The SARSAT (Search and Rescue Satellite) system, Argus transponders, and hand-held VHF radios all offer appealing technological counters to the threat of waiting, but preparation for living through the aftermath is still the most important aspect, and the hardest to get people to think about and perform."

The only truly dangerous demon is the one you will not confront. Capsize is a fact of life. A multihull sailed offshore should be designed, constructed, and sailed to offer the greatest chance of avoiding capsize. But capsize preparation is still essential. Just as monohull sailors prepare for sinking, and everyone prepares for fire and medical emergencies and man overboard, the offshore multihull sailor must acknowledge the risk of capsize *and prepare for it* (see Chapter 10).

Mr. Street suggests that the death toll from multihull capsizes is so large that no one knows what it might be. This is an interesting point, and he has not been the only one to suggest this. As a member of the multihull fraternity, which is a fairly tight-knit group, I hear about most of the accidents that occur. To my knowledge the total number of deaths that are multihull related is actually quite low.

In an effort to arrive at a hard number I have asked many designers, builders, and multihull sailors worldwide for information on accidents that are not well known. Because of the difficulty of trying to obtain accurate information over too large an area, I limited my inquiry to fatalities that have occurred in the Atlantic Ocean, including all adjacent seas, i.e., Gulf of Mexico, Caribbean, North Sea, etc. The results are tabulated below:

Total multihull-related fatalities (Atlantic Ocean and peripheral seas) in boats 25 feet or longer from 1960 to August 1989: 28 Deaths in 19 accidents.

Of these, 13 deaths in 10 accidents were racing related (five boats were being singlehanded). These break down as follows:

- 3 men overboard

- 1 suicide

- 2 unknown causes

- 7 deaths in 3 capsizes

Fifteen deaths in nine accidents happened aboard cruising boats (two boats were being singlehanded). These were:

- 1 death from collision; 34-foot cat (American, 1988) run down at night by high-speed powerboat.

- 2 deaths from collision with rescue vessel; American trimaran improperly "modified" by owner experienced major structural failure causing crew to abandon ship, 1982.

- 1 death, cause unknown; American man singlehanding dugout canoe catamaran across the Atlantic reported missing (late 1960s).

There were eight deaths in four capsizes:

- 35-foot trimaran (American) capsized by hurricane Amy, 1975; skipper a diabetic, lost insulin and died from medical complications, crew saved.

- 30-foot cat (German) capsize, one fatality.

- 30-foot cat (English) capsize, one fatality, 1979.

- 30-foot cat (Bay of Biscay) capsize, one fatality.

Seven other deaths were not capsize related:

- 3 deaths, 30-foot cat (English), unknown cause; explosion or collision suspected.

- 4 deaths, 30-foot cat (Dutch); sank in gale.

Racing was arbitrarily defined as being in a particular location due to a race, whether or not the race had actually started. This would include delivery to the race start.

Some interesting points:

- Of 28 fatalities, 4 were due to man-overboard; 14 percent of the total.

- No deaths occurred in cruising multihulls over 37 feet in length.

- Three of the four cruising capsizes that resulted in fatalities were in production fiberglass boats with minimal flotation capacity.

- The worst cruising multihull accident in terms of life lost was due to the boat sinking, which is highly unusual for a multihull. A multihull that sinks is inexcusable.

In all probability this list is not complete; it would be next to impossible to find every accident that may have occurred during 30 years over millions of square miles of ocean. I do feel that it is very close to complete.

Considering the extreme nature of so many of the multihulls in use, i.e., the wretched home-builts, the ruthless racers, the experiments, and the designs "improved" by first-time boatbuilders, the number of fatal accidents is well within the bounds of the definition "safe."

From a statistical perspective this is a relatively small sample from which to draw conclusions, but it is the only sample we have. So, with some caution I present the following:

- No fatal accidents occurred in cruising multihulls over 37 feet in length. Whether this is indicative of the smaller number of large multihulls or a great safety gain in the larger sizes cannot be proved.

- Capsize has been the major cause of fatalities. Strangely, the cruising boats have suffered most in this regard, despite relatively few capsizes compared with racers. Most of the capsize fatalities involved fiberglass catamarans that had minimal flotation placed high enough in the boat to be effective when capsized. I believe that most of these cruising fatalities could have been avoided if these boats had floated higher.

• While there have been many more capsizes of racing multihulls (probably on the order of 10 to 1), they have resulted in far fewer fatalities per capsize. I attribute this to the fact that the racer's progress often is monitored, making help available earlier; the light, often foam- or balsa-core racing boats float very high if dumped; and the racers and their boats are prepared for capsize, while cruising sailors generally are not.

Comparing Apples to Apples

Meaningful safety statistics for cruising boats would be compiled in the same fashion as for accidents involving passenger aircraft: deaths per passenger mile. Unfortunately the information required to formulate such a statistic is not available from any source. No one has any idea of the number of single-hulled or multihulled boats actually cruising, the number of miles sailed, number of people aboard, or the number of fatal accidents that may occur beyond the immediate coastlines. Not a single person, organization, or government agency even will venture an educated guess.

The U.S. Coast Guard compiles statistics on all the reported boating accidents occurring on "the oceans, the Great Lakes, or bays and other tidal waters" of the U.S. These statistics can provide some insight into the level of safety for a given type of boat by correlating them with an estimate of the number of boats actually in use. But by its own admission, the Coast Guard believes that 90 percent of non-fatal accidents go unreported, although it feels that most accidents involving fatalities are.

According to the National Marine Manufacturer's Association, U.S. sales of auxiliary powered monohull sailboats averaged 3,800 units a year during the last decade (38,000 total). Assuming the same sales level for the previous 15 years and that all the boats wrecked, retired, or decommissioned in the last 25 years roughly equals the number of boats sailing that are more than 25 years old, you reasonably could assume that there are about 95,000 auxiliary powered monohull sailboats in use in the United States. The U.S. Coast Guard's boating statistics for the five-year period 1983 to 1987 inclusive lists 36 fatal accidents on auxiliary powered sailboats 25 feet or longer—an average of 7.2 fatalities per year, or about one death per 13,194 boats annually.

The best estimates (compiled from interviews with various multihull sailors, designers, and publishers) on the number of multihulls 25 feet or longer currently in use in the U.S. is about 3,250. This seems quite reasonable considering the volume of plans sold by Piver, Wharram, Brown, Cross,

Crowther, Newick, and many other designers, as well as the production boats built by Prout, Catalac, Performance Cruising, Stiletto, MacGregor, and others.

During the five-year period from 1983 to 1987 there were no reported cruising multihull fatalities in the U.S. or adjacent waters. Going back another five years, there were two reported fatalities in the 10-year period from 1978 to 1987 inclusive. This averages to 0.2 fatalities per year or, taking the number of boats into account, one fatality annually for every 16,250 multihull sailboats over 25 feet in length. This fatality rate is somewhat lower than the rate for monohull auxiliary powered sailboats 25 feet or longer, and better than the average fatality rate for boating in general, which the U.S. Coast Guard "Boating Statistics" show as being one death per 12,500 boats annually (average value for the period 1978-87).

Because of the extreme difficulty of gathering reliable information and the small size of the statistical sample, neither of these fatality rates can be regarded with much faith. I am not ready to assert that you are 23 percent safer on a multihull. But it does show that there is some factual basis for the assertion that you can be at least as safe in a multihull as in a monohull. The big talkers in the yacht club bars would have you believe otherwise, but let's see some proof.

All the Risks Weighed

Man overboard. Cruising is fraught with many very real risks and dangers—from being run down by a ship to stopping a jibing boom with your head to inadvertently consuming a fish full of nerve-damaging Ciguatera toxin. There seems to be a broad agreement, however, that the greatest danger facing all sailors is falling overboard.

Of the 36 fatalities reported by the U.S. Coast Guard for auxiliary powered sailboats 25 feet or longer for the years 1983 through 1987, 29 deaths were attributed to man overboard—80 percent of the total! Why is man overboard so deadly? Because it can happen any time and all the time. It is a risk to which the crew is constantly exposed. Are you less likely to fall off a multihull than a monohull? I think so.

Plain old common sense suggests that you are much more likely to fall off a boat that can easily heel 50 degrees or more than from the comparatively level deck of a multihull. The statistics, sketchy though they may be, appear to bear this out. Of the multihull-related fatalities in the above list of Atlantic accidents, four deaths were confirmed due to man overboard (one of which, unfortunately, was well-known multihull racer and author Robb James). This works out to 14 percent of the fatalities. Compare this with the statistics for monohulls, where 80 percent of the fatalities stemmed from man overboard. Now you tell me which boat offers better footing.

In addition, the inherently greater freeboard and lighter weight of multihulls cause them to rise quickly to oncoming waves, which are unlikely to wash forcefully across the deck, taking unsecured crew with them. In 20,000 miles of cruising I can remember only one occasion when we took any appreciable quantity of water on deck. This was while beating to windward in 35 knots of wind opposed by a considerable run of tide. Because we were near shore, the waves were only about eight feet high, but they were very steep and close together. Sailing to windward at 10 knots we would occasionally punch through the top of a wave, taking a sheet of water several inches deep all the way back to the cockpit. It didn't hurt the boat, and it was even fun for a while. If we were faced with those conditions for any length of time we would have slowed down and allowed *Juniper* to rise to the waves rather than punch through them at such speed. You can always slow down a fast boat. You can never speed up a slow one!

Collision. Anyone who has sailed offshore knows that in addition to commercial ships and fishing vessels there is an awful lot of junk as well as large, living, sometimes unfriendly creatures floating around. A quick scan of the sailing magazines reveals frequent stories of damaging collisions with known and unknown floating objects. Whales seem to pose a particular hazard. Having had to dodge very close whales on several occasions, I do worry about the day (or night) when we might meet with a crash. Large logs, lost shipping containers, and who knows what else are reported frequently by voyagers.

Every cruising boat should be built strong enough to survive collisions, but it is impossible to guarantee that a boat will not be holed if it strikes something big and hard. Monohull sinkings from collisions with floating objects are not exactly rare, even though most monos are substantially overbuilt just to resist holing.

I know of one fine *steel* cruising monohull that sailed into a navigational buoy on a sunny afternoon in Long Island Sound because no one was paying attention. The boat wound up with a considerable hole at the waterline, and was saved only by sailing back on the opposite tack, keeping the hole above the water.

Contrary to Don Street's opinion, all boats can be holed. Even the strongest have gone down from gaping wounds—remember the *Titanic*? A multihull can indeed be torn open by floating debris, but the boat won't go to the bottom because of it.

Due to the elimination of the ballast keel and use of lightweight construction, the multihull *can't* sink. In addition, a well-designed cruising or racing multi has numerous watertight partitions built into its *multiple hulls*. This results in a half dozen or more watertight segments; often there are three partitions along each narrow hull. Due to the small volume of the bilges, flooding of any hull portion leads only to very small losses of stability. The boat can be patched as conditions permit and the journey continued. In dire circumstances the boat actually can be sailed considerable distances half full of water—it's been done. Boats that float no matter what are inherently a sound idea and this feature alone gives them an outstanding safety advantage.

With this in mind I have a challenge for Mr. Street: You drill a hole in the bottom of your boat and I'll drill a hole in the bottom of mine and we'll go sailing—no patching allowed.

Shipwreck. A calamitous event far more likely to happen than either capsize or sinking offshore in deep water is being wrecked on the coast. Often the cause is simple carelessness: Someone sleeps on the job or makes a basic mistake in navigation and suddenly the breakers are around the boat beating her down onto the reef.

Sometimes it happens slowly while the crew watches and fights for their lives. Picture the air white with a mixture of salt spray and rain, 60 to 70 knots of wind, horrendous seas, and Cape Hatteras 15 miles to leeward! How many hundreds of well-found vessels have succumbed to such an ending?

A well-designed cruising boat will be able to fight her way off a deadly lee shore, at least up to a point. Luck does play a part; there could be an exceptionally violent storm for the season, a failure of critical hardware or sails, an injury to the crew. Any of these things could turn the tide of battle against the sailboat.

History has shown the multihull to be most survivable in such a deadly situation. Because of its buoyancy and shallow draft, the multihull will ride well through the breakers, bounce over sandbars, and grind its way over reefs to the beach, where the crew can step off the boat onto dry land. Multihulls driven ashore on a sandy beach stand a very good chance of sustaining only minor damage, and recovery of the boat is possible.

The ballasted boat, on the other hand, is unlikely to make it to the beach. Forced to drag its ballast along, it cannot rise fast enough in the surf and it will lay on its side between breakers, getting the daylights pounded out of it, often filling with water and further compounding its problems. Somewhere in this nightmare the crew has to decide when to swim for shore—a highly dangerous situation.

Still More Conventional Wisdom

But they don't point and they can't tack. Many of the other conventional prejudices against multihulls also seem to have little or no basis in fact. The 1988 America's Cup defense was the final nail in the coffin of the "multihulls-don't-point, multihulls-don't-tack argument." The challenger from New Zealand, a radical 120-footer, was widely conceded to be the fastest monohull ever built, yet she was firmly trounced by a catamaran half her size. This really came as no surprise to anyone except for the way the cat could both out-point and out-maneuver the big monohull on the wind.

In a peculiarly ironic twist, Michael Fay, the instigator of the New Zealand challenge, made a point of complaining to the television audience at every opportunity about the mismatch, his argument being " . . . pity us; we have to carry 30 tons of lead around." Pity you indeed!

They break up. Although the superlight offshore racing multihulls sustain structural damage with some regularity, this is considered acceptable (probably because the individuals and sponsors involved are not billed for the cost of rescue). Big-money racing encourages pushing the limits, whether done in cars, boats, or airplanes.

A properly designed and built cruising catamaran or trimaran stands no more chance of structural damage than a ballasted single-hulled boat. Obviously in the creation of a multihull there are engineering and construction aspects that need careful attention, but that's true with any boat that can sail or power at 20 knots in the open ocean. Because multihulls are intricate, engineered structures they should not be built by people who take a single-mindedly casual approach to construction details. Is that fact sufficient reason to condemn multihulls out of hand?

Boating can be a hazardous, risky pastime: equipment fails, storms come, people don't watch where they are going, the dark and fog settles in thick at the worst possible moment. Murphy's Law functions best on the water, and complete safety is just not possible. However, planning, preparation, and prudence can make a huge difference in your favor. A multihull is a different sort of boat and sailing one safely requires a different sort of planning, preparation, and prudence. But the assertion by some that they are all inherently dangerous is ridiculous and naive.

The Specifics
of Multihull
Design

CHAPTER 2

Terminology

*B*efore discussing the features that make up cats and tris, we should define the parts that make up multihulls in general. This will eliminate regional variations in terminology, and ensure that we'll always be talking about the same thing.

All multihulls are made from *hulls,* not pontoons. According to my dictionary a pontoon is "a flat-bottomed boat or other structure used to support a floating bridge." No one likes to hear his or her multihull described as a pontoon boat.

A catamaran has two hulls of equal size connected by *crossbeams.* If it has an enclosed structure between the hulls, this usually is called the *bridgedeck* or *wing deck.* The underside of the bridgedeck that hangs suspended over the water is the *underwing.*

Trimarans are composed of one big hull and two smaller hulls. The big hull is the *main hull.* The two smaller hulls are *floats* or *outriggers.* These hulls are attached to one another by *crossbeams.* If there is a single large crossbeam instead of two it often is called a *wing beam* or *wing deck.*

A few designers and multihull sailors use borrowed Polynesian terminology to describe the parts of a trimaran. These words mean nothing in English, and their similarity can and often does cause confusion, but they do provide an emotional link with the multihull's Polynesian ancestry. For what it's worth these terms are: *vaka* for the main hull, *aka* for the crossbeam, and *ama* for the float. I will avoid them in the interest of clarity.

Design Considerations

Payload: What Do You Really Need?

Cruising means living aboard and coping with a wide variety of circumstances. To do this successfully entails carrying along much more gear than would be required for a weekend sail. Because a multihull has slender hulls, every pound loaded aboard depresses the hulls more deeply into the water than would be the case with a monohull of similar size. In addition, the weight of crew, food, water, fuel, and gear represents a larger percentage of the total weight of a multihull than a monohull. This does not mean that a multihull cannot carry a sufficient payload. It can, provided a *realistic* assessment is made of the gear's weight so that enough volume can be designed into the hulls to support it.

The key word here is realistic. Realism, it turns out, is heavy. The total weight of all the minor bits and pieces comprising cruising essentials can add up to many hundreds, sometimes thousands, of pounds. Compared with an average daysailer or weekender, a cruising boat will carry heavier ground tackle, more spare parts, more fuel and water, a better dinghy, probably a sailboard, always snorkel gear, boom tents or awnings, maybe a bicycle, and on and on. Allowances must be made in the design stage for all this gear or the hull will float below its intended lines and not sail as it should.

Unfortunately for the prospective multihull buyer, there is no uniformity in the way designers separate the weight of the boat from all the things that are added to it later. Thus it can be difficult to discern what the actual payload capacity of a given design might be. Compounding this problem is the significant consumer bias, among multihullers anyway, toward boats that utilize lightweight, performance-oriented construction. Designers quite naturally like to promote their engineering talents by advertising the lowest weights possible.

I have found it frustrating to have one of my designs with, say, a cruising displacement of 10,000 pounds, compared with a very similar boat by another designer advertised as displacing 7,000 pounds. I know that, sans equipment, the weight of the two boats will be nearly identical. The issues are (1) how much displacement a design actually allows for payload and (2) exactly what constitutes payload as distinguished from the boat's normal equipment?

Short of putting a bare boat on a scale and comparing that weight to its stated cruising displacement, the only way to determine how much was allowed for the required cruising equipment is to examine the detailed weight estimate that was part of the early design process. In future years perhaps some standard will be adopted that will allow reasonable comparison among boats from different designers. For now this type of comparison must be viewed with skepticism. In addition to the truism that all boats cost more than advertised, it must be added that they all are sailed heavier.

For a rough rule of thumb, a very weight-conscious couple going off for a spell of extended cruising will need to allow about 1,500 pounds for personal gear, food, and water. Sailors who don't pay close attention to the weight they

Figure 2-1A.
Modern cruising trimaran. Design by Dick Newick. (Bruce Alderson illustration)

aft crossbeam

port float

Upstart

forward crossbeam

main hull

starboard float

Figure 2-1B.
Modern cruising catamaran. Design by the author. (Bruce Alderson illustration)

bridgedeck cabin

seagull striker

bridgedeck or wing deck

underwing

forward crossbeam

port hull

starboard hull

bring aboard often end up with considerably more. Monohull circumnavigator Gary Underwood, of the yacht *Alice Alakwe* of New Zealand, reports that, "We have weighed all our possessions aboard *Alice*, and it comes to 3,335 pounds, not including water but including food for 40 days—our norm."

I feel that a payload of 2,500 to 3,000 pounds is a realistic, comfortable range for most cruising couples. Most medium to large multihulls can carry that kind of payload without significant loss of performance. It should be noted, though, that this weight often will represent 30 percent of the all-up displacement. If the designer allows for less payload in his calculations, you will have to be very careful about what you bring aboard the boat or you will risk sailing overloaded. This can cause the underwing or underside of the crossbeams to be slammed by waves. At best this is uncomfortable; extreme cases of overloading have caused structural damage.

The Wide Performance Envelope

Designing a good multihull is complicated by the wide performance envelope inherent in these craft. Even the slower cruising multis can be surfed up to 12 knots on occasion—50 percent faster than the slowest monohull of comparable size. A performance-oriented cruising multihull can sail steadily in the high teens and surf large waves faster than that. I'm quite sure that I've surfed *Juniper* up toward 30 knots a few times!

Because the energy contained in moving water or air increases as the square of the velocity, when a boat's speed doubles, four times the kinetic energy becomes available to create lift and drag over hulls, fins, and rudders. If the speed triples, eight times the energy is available. This not only places very high loads on rudders, rigs, and sails, but also changes the way water flows around the hull and such appendages as rudders and fins.

It does not always follow that what works well at high speed works equally well at low speed; nevertheless a boat must be as functional when sailing at 3 knots as at 20. Thus multihull designs are by nature a compromise that must satisfy a broader range of conditions than would be required for a single-hulled yacht.

Picture your car with a state-mandated governor limiting its speed to 20 m.p.h. The steering and suspension could be rudimentary, the brakes would lead a simpler existence, the specific rubber compound and tread design for the tires would be unimportant, there would be no need for streamlining to reduce resistance at speed. In other words, a Model T Ford will do just fine. But remove the governor, put in a hot cam, fuel injection, and a turbocharger, and the design and construction of all these formerly unimportant components suddenly becomes critical. The faster the car—or boat—the more important the harmonious blending of these essential components becomes.

Sailboats That Don't Heel

The concept of linking together multiple hulls produces sailboats with highly desirable characteristics for cruising because high transverse stability can be obtained in conjunction with low overall drag. More stability means more sail-carrying power and better speeds; low overall drag means higher efficiency under sail and power: better fuel economy from smaller engines, and less sail to muscle around in heavy going. A boat with substantial stability is safer for offshore cruising as well. The risk of wind and wave capsize declines significantly as the stability of the boat increases.

There are two ways to increase the stability of a multihull: increase its overall dimensions—length, beam, or both; or increase its weight. For a variety of reasons, usually a combination of emotions and economics, the length of a boat often is fixed to some degree; thus the primary variables become overall beam and weight.

Beam and stability. Adding weight to a boat considerably increases its drag. A cruising multi is by definition already a "heavy" multihull because of its robust construction and its supply of water, fuel, food, stores, and equipment. Adding even more weight just to increase stability generally will not pay dividends. Adding beam, however, often has substantial benefits: At only slight increases in weight and windage, a boat's stability increases with little increase in drag.

In the early days of cruising multihulls, the designers drew boats that were quite narrow overall, at least by today's standards. To some degree this was a function of the materials and construction methods used at the time. It was just not possible to make the boats as wide as desirable without running into structural limitations. Since then, materials technology has improved enormously and the structural barrier is far less of an issue.

What is so good about increasing the overall beam of a multihull? Aside from the obvious benefit of larger accommodations, more beam increases transverse stability, which counteracts the heeling force of the sails. This permits the horsepower of the sail plan to be utilized more effectively and gives a greater margin for error in extremely gusty winds. More beam significantly increases the boat's resistance to capsize by large storm waves, and reduces the heeling and rolling motion as the boat conforms to the uneven surface of the sea.

Balanced against these desirable traits of increased beam are some practical limitations: Wider boats are more difficult to haul out and store, the extra width means there is more boat to build, and at some point structural limits once again come into play.

So how much beam is right for a cruising multihull? Why not make it ever wider? Until recently this question had no good answer, but now the experience of the out-and-out racing multihulls shows that there are limits to the effectiveness of increasing overall beam alone. If the separation of the hulls were increased without constraint, the transverse stability could become enormous but the fore-and-aft stability would remain unchanged.

The easiest way to envision the complex nature of stability is to imagine there is a model boat floating in front of you, and you can reach out and grab the top of the mast. Pulling the masthead sideways heels the boat. Pulling forward moves the boat ahead but also pitches the bows downward. If the boat is prevented from moving forward, the downward pitching will be even more pronounced. Moving the masthead diagonally results in other motions that are a combination of heel and pitch. In short, the value for stability can

Figure 2-2.
Longitudinal stability is
obtained the same
way as transverse
stability (see Figure
2-3). This holds true for
cat, tri, or monohull.

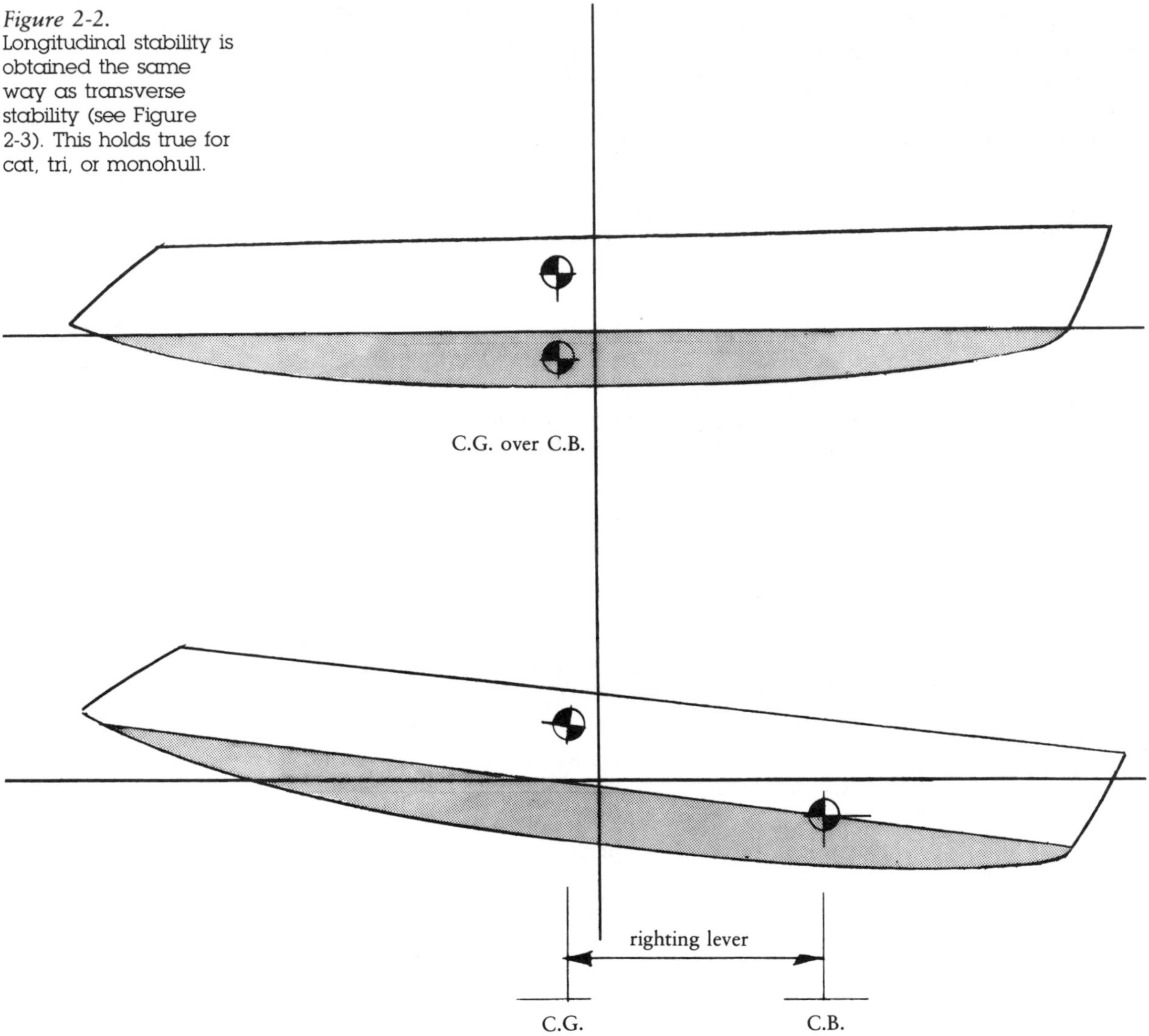

C.G. over C.B.

righting lever

C.G.   C.B.

be expressed through a range of angles that start from head-on, proceed
through the beam, and go to the stern. A cruising boat is in trouble if it has
great transverse stability but lacks longitudinal or diagonal stability. A boat
can be capsized from any side: forward, aft, or diagonally. Stability to resist
capsize must be provided for all directions.

The term used most often to describe a boat's stability is its *transverse
static righting moment*—a measure of the force needed to heel a boat on its
side around its fore-and-aft axis, expressed in foot pounds of work energy

plotted against the heeling angle. Originally developed for single-hulled vessels, this presentation has been carried over unchanged into multihulls. There is a problem in doing this, however: A monohull has very low transverse stability in relation to its longitudinal stability. Because of this, the designer is concerned primarily with increasing the low transverse stability and pretty much ignores

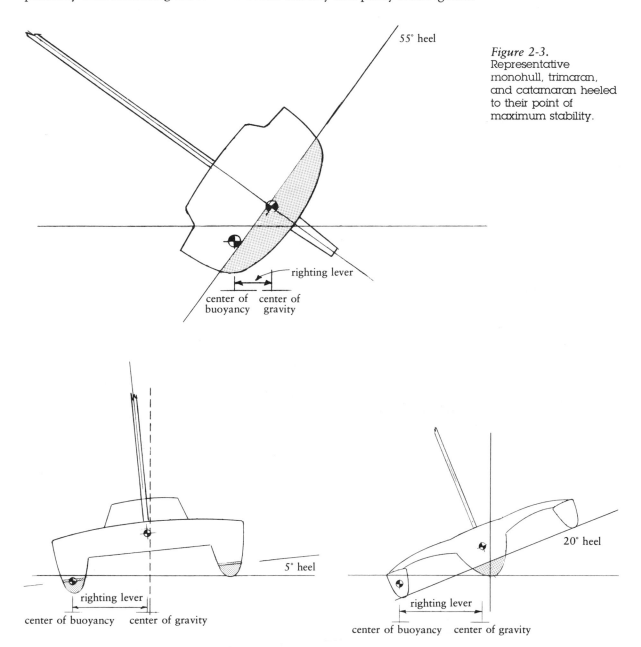

Figure 2-3.
Representative monohull, trimaran, and catamaran heeled to their point of maximum stability.

the comparatively much greater longitudinal stability. In his quest to make the boat stand up against the force of the wind, he may increase the midsection beam, harden the turn of the bilge, or lower the ballast weight.

In an extreme case, a multihull can present just the opposite set of conditions, with transverse stability exceeding the boat's longitudinal stability. Take, for example, a racing trimaran. For sail-carrying power, the boat is wide overall; for speed, the hulls are very narrow. The transverse righting moment is large because of the wide overall beam, but the longitudinal stability is fairly low in comparison because of the narrowness of the hulls. (The more water plane area forward and aft, the higher the longitudinal stability.)

Let's say the owner of this hypothetical boat is cleaning up on the race course. Not to be outdone, the guy who is losing races builds a similar boat, the same length but much wider, and installs a larger rig. This boat has enormous transverse stability but no more longitudinal stability than the first boat. As long as the rig heels the boat transversely everything is fine, but when this big rig starts to pull in another direction, watch out! All of a sudden the dramatic imbalance of righting moments becomes inadequate to prevent end-over-end capsize.

This places a practical upper limit on a multihull's overall beam. Increasing the beam does tend to resist capsize transversely, but has no effect longitudinally. A boat with a huge sail plan and the commensurately huge overall beam (in relation to its length) to carry it is far more likely to encounter a nasty surprise should something go wrong.

For a cruising multihull it seems good practice to maintain at least as much longitudinal stability as transverse stability. In a practical sense this means that the maximum desirable width of a multihull, measured from hull centerline to hull centerline, often can be related to its waterline length. A cruising cat with balanced longitudinal and transverse stability typically would have a hull centerline-to-centerline beam of about 40 percent of the waterline length. Substantially more hull separation than this has diminishing value; less separation fails to utilize the advantages that great overall beam can provide.

Trimarans are somewhat more complex to evaluate since the main hull and the floats are different sizes and shapes. Generally speaking, for a cruising tri, optimum separation of the two floats, centerline to centerline, seems to be in the neighborhood of 60 percent of the waterline length. These are approximate figures. Smaller boats often need proportionately more beam; large boats often can safely use less.

Coefficients for Comparison

Many of a boat's characteristics can be expressed in the form of mathematical coefficients. These numbers make it easier to compare one boat with another even though they may be of different size or design.

Displacement-to-Length Ratio

One of the most useful numbers is the displacement-to-length (D/L) ratio.

$$\text{Ratio} = \frac{D}{(.01L)^3}$$

Where: D = Displacement in long tons (2,240 lbs.)

L = Waterline length

This number is used widely in monohull design and thus is familiar to most sailors. The lower the number the lighter the boat is in relation to its length and the easier it is to push through the water.

Using the D/L ratio to compare the projected relative performance of a cat with a tri, a catamaran will appear slower because the formula treats the two hulls as one. Thus a different benchmark figure must be used to separate fast from slow. A performance-oriented cruising tri typically will have a D/L ratio between 40 and 60; a heavier, slower boat will be in the range of 80 to 100. If the D/L ratio is above that you'd better have a big engine! For a cat, the equivalent figures would be about 50 to 70 for a fast cruiser; about 100 to 120 for a slow cruiser.

Length-to-Beam Ratio

Another widely used coefficient of comparison for multihulls, the hull's *length-to-beam (L/B) ratio,*

$$\frac{\text{Max. Waterline Length}}{\text{Max. Waterline Beam}}$$

sometimes referred to as the fineness coefficient, is the length of the hull waterline divided by the waterline beam. Multihull aficionados love to think in terms of long, fine hulls so there often is a strong prejudice in favor of high L/B ratios. If the L/B ratio is too low (the hulls too fat), excessive wave-making will result and the boat will not be able to accelerate to the speeds that make multis so attractive.

Overemphasizing this number can be a mistake, however: The waterline beam is a result of the shape of the midships hull section and does not necessarily reflect the displacement of the hull. A wide, shallow hull may have less drag than a narrow, deep hull, for example, although the L/B ratio would suggest otherwise (see Figure 2-4). But a narrow, deep hull will slice through the waves better, and this is one reason that a high L/B ratio can be desirable.

A trimaran with a main hull length-to-beam ratio below 6/1 normally will make lots of waves. While this sort of hull can be coaxed to surf and almost plane if enough power is applied, it is not the best hull form for sailing. Eight

Figure 2-4.
Variations in hull L/B
ratio. Despite
appearances, each
hull has the same
underwater volume.

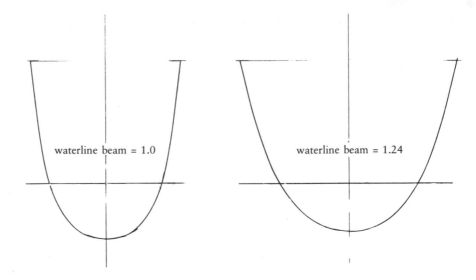

waterline beam = 1.0   waterline beam = 1.24

to one is a good compromise where adequate load-carrying capacity and reasonable speed can coexist. A hull of 10/1 fineness is pretty slippery, slicing through the chop cleanly and making few waves.

Cruising catamarans have *two* big hulls in the water all of the time; each catamaran hull should be somewhat finer than the one main hull of a trimaran. I feel that a hull waterline length-to-beam ratio of 8/1 is about the minimum acceptable value; 12/1 produces a very efficient hull; and 16/1 or more denotes a high-performance hull seldom consistent with the accommodation requirements of a cruising boat unless the cat is quite large.

Bruce Number

The *Bruce number,* another comparison coefficient frequently applied to multihulls,

$$\text{Bruce number} = \frac{\sqrt{SA}}{\sqrt[3]{D}}$$

Where: SA = Working sail area (no overlap) in sq. ft.

D = Displacement in pounds

compares a boat's sail area with its displacement, and is most useful as an indicator of light-air performance. All-out racing designs often have B-numbers in the range of 2 or more. The most conservatively rigged cruisers come in at about 1.0 to 1.1. In my experience, a boat with a B-number of less than 1.3 will feel very sluggish in light air. If the B-number is above 1.6 or thereabouts the offshore cruiser will find himself reefed down nearly all the time and regretting the unused mast length.

Pounds Per Inch Immersion

Consider a boat at rest in smooth water. If you were to load weights on it until it were depressed one inch past its load waterline, the amount of weight added would be equal to the hull's *pounds per inch immersion number*. This is a handy way to get a feel for a given design's sensitivity to overloading. The PPI is related directly to the area of the waterplane —the cross-sectional area of the hull at the waterline. The larger the waterplane the more weight it takes to immerse the boat an inch deeper.

Cruising cats, because they have two relatively large hulls in the water, generally have higher PPI numbers than tris. A 46-foot cat I designed has a PPI figure of 1,200 pounds/inch. If this design were to sail with an additional 500 pounds of fuel aboard, the boat would rest less than $1/2$ inch lower.

A trimaran of similar size likely would have a PPI of about 800 pounds; an equal quantity of extra fuel would depress the hull about $3/4$ inch.

Stability Number

Catamaran designer James Wharram and his assistants have devised a "stability" number that seeks to indicate the ease with which a boat may be capsized due to wind.

$$\text{Windspeed (in mph)} = \left(0.682 \sqrt{\frac{W \times (\frac{1}{2}BOA)}{0.001785 \times SA \times H}}\right) \times .555$$

Where: W = Weight of boat in pounds

SA = Working sail area

H = Height of center of sail area

from load waterline

BOA = Beam overall

This number purports to tell approximately how much wind, taking gust loads into consideration, will be required to capsize a boat with all sail up and sheeted flat amidships, wind directly on the beam, in flat water.

Obviously wide overall beam and a short rig will make any boat more difficult for wind to overturn. It is important to have great stability in a multihull, not only to resist wind capsize, but wave capsize as well. However, this formula tells us that a boat of low righting moment (narrow beam) and small sail plan is as stable as a much beamier boat with a larger rig. There is ample reason to think that this is not the case. As the Final Report of the Joint Committee on Safety From Capsizing found, the boat with more beam is less sensitive to loss of stability due to heeling and certainly more stable in waves due to the effects of inertia.

How useful is this "stability" number? It can find boats that are overrigged in relation to their hull stability, but I really don't think it is a broad measure of a boat's safety. Like all rules of thumb it oversimplifies real life. James Wharram asserts that boats with stability numbers below 24 knots have inadequate stability for safe cruising. I agree more or less, but safe sailing of any kind means knowing when to shorten sail. An enjoyable cruising boat should have enough sail area so that the reefs can be shaken out when the wind gets light and the boat brought back to life.

Applied Mathematics

Why do we care about all of these numbers with funny names? Because they provide some insight into a specific boat's potential performance in different conditions. A very low Bruce number means a boat will require a gale of wind to get going; you know without even sailing the boat that it had better have a decent engine. If what you want most of all is to go rocketing down tradewind swells, a long slender hull as evidenced by a low displacement-to-length ratio is something to look for. If you plan on a cruise down the Intracoastal Waterway with all of your possessions close at hand, the pounds per inch immersion number should be of interest.

Designers and some manufacturers often publish the vital statistics, and this gives the prospective boat buyer some means to compare various features that otherwise would be hard to measure.

The
Trimaran

*A*lthough the single-hulled boat can incorporate lots of beam into its hull without hurting performance, the trimaran has great *overall* beam but must keep the *hull* waterline beam to a minimum to realize the benefits of the multihull. Herein lies a problem: Where do you put the accommodation if the hull must be so narrow?

Every designer has his own solutions to this most troublesome issue; the following will help to define the three basic approaches.

Accommodations

Full Wing Deck

To obtain maximum accommodation in a trimaran, extend the main hull cabin structure all the way across the boat, from one float to the other. This results in a boat with three almost separate accommodation spaces. A short wander inside this type of boat will leave one awestruck by the available volume.

This bled-to-the-edge accommodation style was the avenue of choice for many of the experimenters in the early days of multihulls. Some boats of this concept were really hideous; others weren't quite as bad, although they seldom were pleasing to the eye.

Because the floats and connecting structure must contain sufficient volume for them to become worthwhile accommodation, this concept is truly effective only on large boats—over about 45 feet LOA.

Despite the houseboat-style accommodations, there are some compelling reasons *not* to extend a trimaran's cabin from rail to rail. At the very least it adds lots of weight and windage. This can make a boat awkward to control in close quarters and possibly difficult to steer in heavy going offshore. This type of craft often is considered an ideal retirement home because of its palatial accommodations, but it is likely to be the most strenuous type of boat for a

Figure 3-1A.
Full wing deck
trimaran.

Figure 3-1B,C.
Going for broke.
Accommodations on
this trimaran are
spread into all three
hulls, producing
maximum interior
volume and a deck
surface to rival a small
tennis court.

small crew to handle. If sailing is what you enjoy, you will enjoy it much more in a boat that sails well.

Accommodation in the wings is often cramped. Accommodation in the floats is even less attractive, at least when sailing. The occupant of the leeward float berth will be kept awake by the water washing rapidly by a half-inch of plywood away; the inhabitant of the windward float will be at the end of a pendulum, tracing an amplified version of the boat's progress along the ocean's uneven surface. Here a strong stomach is required.

Another important consideration is the amount of work involved in constructing a boat this way. It is just like building three boats, and labor hours will disappear into the black hole at an unbelievable rate. The final result will be an expensive, slow boat with large accommodations, only some of which are genuinely usable under way. This is precisely what a Virgin Islands charter company needs, but few cruisers will find trading speed, handling, and economy for 15 berths much of a bargain.

Partial Wing Deck

An improvement on the going-for-broke technique, and one used in most cruising trimarans, is scaling back on the cabin so that it extends only part way to the float. Typically this space becomes bunks and storage, and it is a method that can be used in practically any size trimaran. It does add some weight and windage, but if done well this is not excessive.

One significant point to consider is the clearance from the underside of the extended cabin, which is suspended over the water, to the waterline. Often this distance is minimal because the designer tries to maximize headroom in the berth above. But the lower this surface the more collisions it will have with moving water. Trying to sleep on top of a roaring volcano has its drawbacks. This problem can be alleviated to some extent by careful shaping of the hull-to-cabin extension.

Open Wing

The final method for incorporating accommodation is keeping everything big and simple, with all accommodation contained within the main hull. The evolution of racing trimarans over the years has shown that there are substantial advantages to reducing the exposed area of the connecting structure. (If it is not there it cannot pound or break.) For a cruising design it would seem that the loss of accommodation would be so serious as to offset the potential advantages, but this is not necessarily the case.

Because of the simplicity of construction, the hull may be increased in length without adding to the labor hours. The longer hull can provide much of the accommodation volume lost through elimination of the wing *and* substantially increase load-carrying capacity and longitudinal stability—two of the things that many cruising trimarans lack—at substantially the same cost.

I chose this technique when it came time for me to build my second offshore cruising trimaran (my first was a smaller boat with wing extensions), and I have never once regretted having a longer hull without wing decks hanging out over the water being slammed repeatedly by short, steep seas. Certainly a longer boat will cost more to put on the dock, but it pays big dividends when cruising offshore.

Figure 3-2A.
Partial wing-deck
trimaran.

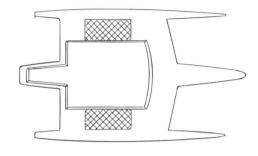

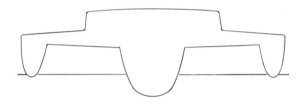

Figure 3-2B,C,D,E.
B) A more moderate approach. Extra
accommodation space is provided by extending the
cabin partway to the floats. (Michael Reppy photo)
C) Cabin extensions are shaped carefully to reduce
windage and smooth contact with wave tops. D)
Interior of the 42-foot Shuttleworth tri, *Damiana*, a
gull's-eye view of which is seen in Figure 3-2A,
shows the expansive accommodations modest hull
extensions can provide. E) *Charis II*, a 35-foot
Constant Camber trimaran designed by John
Marples.

C

D

E

B

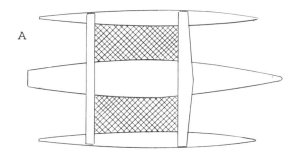

A

B

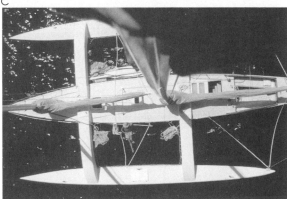

C

Figure 3-3.
A) Open-wing trimaran. B) Big and simple. *Juniper,*
the author's 52-foot trimaran. C) Compare this
gull's-eye view of *Juniper's* long-and-lean style with
the moderate hull extension approach of *Damiana,*
in Figure 3-2C. D) *Juniper's* interior shows that
accommodations need not be cramped in an
open-wing trimaran. E) Innovative storage
techniques are important to reduce weight and
provide sufficient space for essentials aboard long
and light multihulls. These two full-length drawers
contain much of *Juniper's* galley paraphernalia.

D

E

Figure 3-4.
Open-wing trimarans can work well in smaller sizes as well. *Hopscotch*, an Explorer 34 designed for economical construction by the author, packs Spartan but adequate cruising accommodations into a lean, fast hull.

Figure 3-5.
Smaller tris can stretch their accommodations by using a cockpit enclosure, such as this one aboard one of Ian Farrier's popular F-27s.

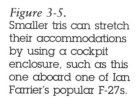

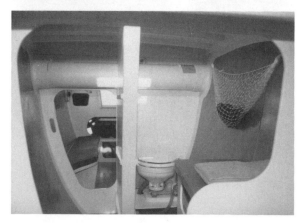

Main Hulls

The trimaran has two distinctly different hull types within the same boat. Essentially, the floats have a single purpose, which makes their shape relatively easy to optimize. The main hull, on the other hand, has many functions which complicate its design: it contains most if not all of the accommodations; it is always in the water carrying the weight of the boat; it supports the mast and most of the rigging loads; and it provides attachment and essential torsional support for the crossbeams.

A 40-foot trimaran designed only for sailing, with no consideration given to interior accommodations, would have a very narrow main hull with freeboard so low that standing inside would be impossible. But accommodations are the essence of a cruising boat, and a cruising trimaran's main hull must be enlarged to house the bunks, galley, and head. This points up the major conundrum in trimaran design: Everything you do to increase accommodation space moves the hull farther from its optimum slender shape.

The best cruising boats evolve by first designing the boat's interior and then figuring out the most desirable way to wrap a hull around it, while allowing for the crossbeams, mast support, and perhaps a daggerboard or centerboard. This is a classic design spiral: continuously adjusting the interior

Figure 3-6A.
Very slender main hull of a racing trimaran. Nice, but no room for accommodations.

Figure 3-6B.
Cruising trimaran main hull. More volume and freeboard provides comfort below. The hull's flare just above the waterline adds additional volume.

Figure 3-6C.
Juniper's main hull, with a 10:1 fineness ratio, is fast but roomy due to her 52-foot length.

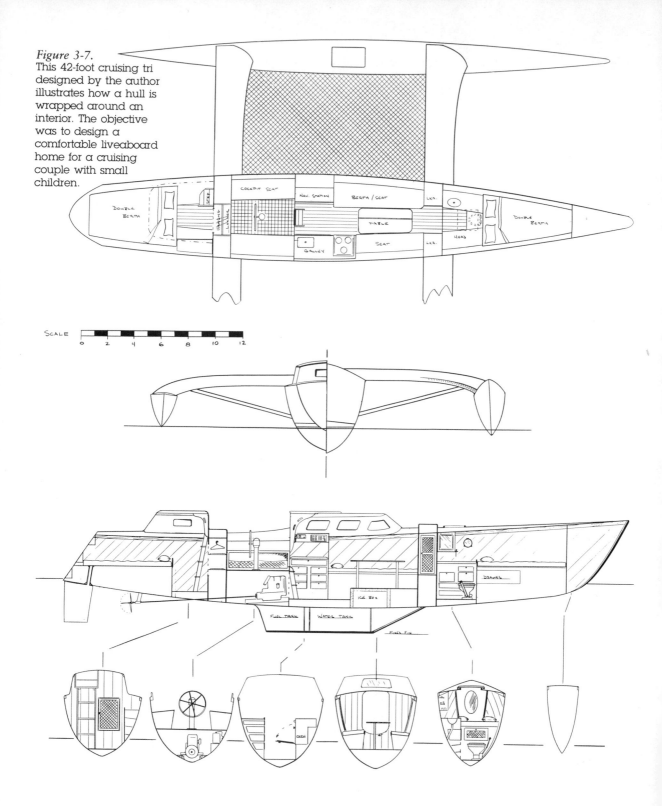

Figure 3-7.
This 42-foot cruising tri designed by the author illustrates how a hull is wrapped around an interior. The objective was to design a comfortable liveaboard home for a cruising couple with small children.

SCALE

0 2 4 6 8 10 12

so that it fits the envelope and vice versa. The only "truths" controlling the underwater shape may be expressed very crudely like this: "The pointy end goes forward; the blunt end aft!"

Beyond this, not much is sacred and every designer has his own idea of what is best, with wide variations in the overall slenderness of the main hull, its underwater profile, bow overhang, hull cross section, stern shape, etc. Nothing *has* to be a particular way, but each approach has associated benefits and drawbacks. Some familiarity with them will enable you to assess a given design's probable performance.

Faster designs get that way by keeping the hulls reasonably slender, but this also means that the hull will be driven through waves with real velocity and must not have protrusions in the topsides that unnecessarily obstruct water flow.

Boats with powerful sail plans benefit from a long waterline length with minimal bow and stern overhangs. This counteracts the pitching forces of the large sail plan.

Looking at the underbody in profile, some designs may have a very deep and narrow forefoot; others may be shallow and broad. The former is nice beating to windward in a chop but can make steering less sure when surfing downwind at speed. The shallow, wider forebody hull is great when surfing but tends to hobbyhorse when sailing to windward in sloppy waves.

Broad, shallow, U-section sterns dampen pitching motions but must be designed carefully or they can create lots of drag-producing turbulence. Double-ended sterns release water flow very cleanly but the hull needs to be longer to achieve the same displacement and pitch-damping qualities as a U-section stern.

A hull with a deep midsection and shallow ends will turn smartly but may not have enough volume (displacement) in the ends to allow efficient high-speed sailing. Conversely a hull deep in the ends has a high prismatic coefficient, which means that it is better at higher speeds, but it turns more slowly, making close quarters handling more difficult.

To some degree a deficiency in one place can be overcome by adding something elsewhere. For instance, if the best hull for the task looks as if it will be difficult to maneuver, the design of the rudder can be altered to compensate.

Floats

The trimaran's ability to carry sail is directly related to the size and shape of its floats. The distance from the float to the centerline of the main hull also has a profound effect on the boat's ability to stand up to hard wind, but as previously discussed, extreme overall beam can create other problems and should be avoided.

Big Float, Little Float

A tri with very small floats will be tender, heeling and spilling wind when pressed. In protected waters this can contribute to safety to some extent because it will not be possible to drive the boat hard enough to lift the main hull, which is often the start of capsize. If the boat is overpowered, the float will be pushed completely underwater and the boat will heel way over, at least by multihull standards, slowing down and spilling wind from the sails. Normally, a complete recovery is made from this type of knockdown in sheltered water. In heavy breaking seas this may not be the case, and the low-buoyancy float has fallen into disfavor during the last decade.

At the other end of the float-buoyancy spectrum is the current (1989) crop of racing trimarans. Their floats are designed to provide as much transverse stability (read *stiffness*) as possible, and thus are extremely full bodied—nearly a sideways oval in midship section—and typically as long as the main hull. Float displacement often is two or more times the overall weight of the entire boat. The high buoyancy and full section shape means that the main hull can be flown clear of the water for long periods. This reduces wetted surface, which is crucial to winning races—provided of course that rudders have been installed on the floats in order to steer!

It all sounds good on paper, but the result of such highly buoyant floats is an extremely uncomfortable boat. In a beam sea the windward float

Figure 3-8A.
As overall beam increases floats must be positioned higher to keep the weather float out of the water.

Figure 3-8B.
A similar, but substantially less exotic float on a cruising design.

occasionally will come down with a thunderous slam, shuddering the boat to its foundations. Oh, what price speed!

A cruising trimaran should have floats that contain enough volume to support the entire weight of the boat and then some. While the cruising sailor will never fly the main hull of his boat, a highly buoyant float will keep the crossbeams from dragging in the water, and will minimize the possibility of his boat tripping sideways over the float if the boat is caught by a huge, breaking sea on the beam. A good range for float volume in a cruising tri is 110 to 150 percent of the all-up displacement.

Float length can contribute to fore-and-aft stability; consequently most designers have gradually lengthened their floats over the years. And long, slender floats offer the same advantage as long, slender hulls: low drag.

Float Sections

Because the float spends so much time going up and down as waves pass beneath the hull, the sectional shape of the float can have a dramatic effect on the boat's overall motion. Very full or flat-bottom floats can pound viciously—not something you'd like for cruising. When beam reaching, the windward float often will hit the surface with some velocity. If the bottom of the float is too blunt this collision can send considerable spray into the cockpit where it *always* finds its way down the neck of your foul-weather gear. Give me a float that keeps me dry and I'll happily trade away a tenth of a knot of boat speed.

Everyone involved with trimarans has his own idea on the right shape for floats, but in a nutshell it boils down to several basic points: There must be sufficient buoyancy, especially forward, to resist heeling and capsize. The shape of the hull must be easy to drive through waves, which usually means slender hulls with fine entries and streamlined crossbeams. There must be sufficient length and volume aft to provide stability in heavy weather.

Hydrodynamic lifting floats have been tried on occasion. By carefully shaping the float's bow it is possible to create forces that resist heeling. At high speeds almost any shape will create some hydrodynamic lift, but large increases can be obtained by using special planing or lifting shapes. Dick

Figure 3-9.
Trimaran float sections.

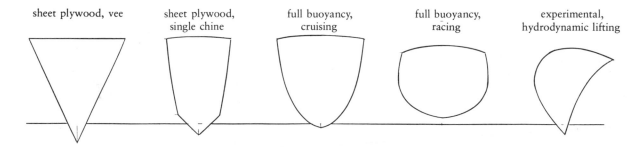

| sheet plywood, vee | sheet plywood, single chine | full buoyancy, cruising | full buoyancy, racing | experimental, hydrodynamic lifting |

Newick has experimented with what he calls a half-moon section. The concave outboard surface of this section can produce much lift at speed but it comes at the expense of hull volume (displacement). This can be detrimental at low to medium speeds because it increases wetted surface. The experiments continue.

There is one other minor detail of a cruising trimaran's float that bears mention—one that only a dedicated cruiser would consider worthwhile. Long overhanging float sterns are popular because they look fast and racy. Whether they are fast or not I'll let others debate, but they do have the extremely annoying habit of crunching dinghies. When anchored in harbor slop or roadstead swell, the float will move up and down considerably even though the main hull moves relatively little. Eventually, dinghies tied to the stern will find their way underneath the overhanging float stern and bam, bam, bam! Although this seldom causes real damage to the dinghy, it's noisy enough to get you up on deck quickly to see what the commotion is about. Of course

Figure 3-10.
(Below) A clean float exit makes little fuss at high speed.

Figure 3-11.
(Right) Wide beam and high-buoyancy floats are the necessary components of a fast and safe cruising trimaran.

this happens only on boisterous nights, about an hour after you've gotten to sleep.

Tying It All Together

One of the most critical elements in a trimaran are its crossbeams. Just as an airplane's wings must never fall off, a multihull's crossbeams must never break. To people unfamiliar with multihulls, a trimaran's float flying to windward looks as if it might break off under its own weight! Nothing could be farther from the truth. A multihull's crossbeams must be strong enough to withstand a force equal to *20 times* the weight of the float. The crossbeams can support the whole boat stood up on its side without damage.

Crossbeams must deal with a complex interrelationship of loads. A weakness in any area can lead to failure. The most basic load is the upward buoyancy of the float, which is being pressed underwater as the boat heels. Totally immersed, the float of a 40-foot cruising tri exerts an upward force of about 10,000 pounds. The boat's speed, force of the sails, and wave action exert a strong twisting force, sometimes referred to as the "knuckle-under" effect. If shrouds are led outboard, the crossbeams must deal with rigging loads. And then there's the weight of the float, which by itself is almost negligible—until it starts moving around with velocity, as it will when going fast in heavy seas.

There is no one "correct" design for crossbeams; many different methods have been used successfully. While some notable failures have occurred in the past, usually they resulted from a weak component or poor construction rather than from a bad design concept. Crossbeams are not a place to cut corners.

To Fold or Not to Fold

Before selecting a crossbeam type it is necessary to decide whether it is essential to reduce the boat's beam by making the crossbeams and floats foldable or detachable. If a boat will be constructed a long distance from the water, or if it must be transported periodically over the road, something other than permanently installed crossbeams must be considered. For a small daysailer or smallish lightweight coastal cruiser this presents no overwhelming problems. For example, Ian Farrier's well-known Trailer Tri and production F-27 Trimaran incorporate a unique folding mechanism that can make the trailering process much easier.

When the boat gets much larger, however, regular disassembly becomes a difficult and lengthy process, and thus it is done rarely. It is usually more difficult to construct a boat with removable or folding crossbeams, and strength often suffers.

In my experience, a large demountable cruising multihull is seldom if ever taken apart after the initial launching. If you are looking for a large, bluewater cruising boat, avoid the temptation of demountability.

Figure 3-12A,B.
Ian Farrier's F-27 uses a unique folding mechanism that makes launching this trailerable tri almost as easy as launching a monohull. In addition, the floats can be folded while afloat, allowing the F-27 to use narrow slips designed for monohulls. (Courtesy Corsair Marine)

Solid Wing Decks vs. Open Wings

Once the demountability issue is decided, the next major question in crossbeam design is whether to have solid wing decks or open areas covered with net. In the early days almost all trimarans had solid wing decks. As designs widen, however, the solid side decks have been replaced gradually by open areas spanned with net.

Solid decks provide better surfaces for walking and, because the decking blocks spray, they make for a drier boat. On the downside, they weigh more, they're prone to pounding, and the extra windage on the undersides possibly adds to the risk of capsize in ultimate conditions. On the other hand, nets are light, offer little windage, cannot possibly pound, and make great places to throw muddy anchors—not to mention provide first-class accommodations for stargazing.

Demountable Crossbeams

Aluminum tube. A simple demountable crossbeam that works well for small- to medium-size tris is illustrated in Figure-3-15A. In this configuration the crossbeam itself spans the boat in one section, functioning as a pure cantilever beam. To take the boat apart the floats are unbolted from the ends of the crossbeam, shear pins at the main hull sleeves are removed, and the beams slid out.

Figure 3-13.
This photo sequence of a trimaran float blasting through waves at high speed shows that streamlined crossbeams are not just cosmetic affectations.

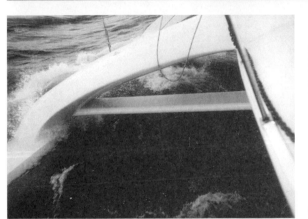

Figure 3-14.
To the truly dedicated lounger, few places on a boat can compare with the nets of a multihull.

In aluminum crossbeams, the welds (if present) are usually the weak spots and can lead to failure. Typically, welded aluminum (type 6061) has only about half the strength of unwelded aluminum—less if the welds are done improperly. In this type of crossbeam it often is possible to obtain the extrusion in lengths long enough to eliminate the need for welding.

Welded aluminum truss. Figure 3-17 illustrates an aluminum crossbeam fabricated from hollow rectangular tubing and aluminum plate; all the connections are welded. This beam was used on my 31-foot trimaran *Shadowfax,* and is a good example of how welding can be detrimental to aluminum. The crossbeam itself was not strong enough and probably would have broken eventually, but the initial failure occurred at the weld. As is usually the case with a built-up part such as this, once one portion of the beam failed

Figure 3-15A.
Simple demountable crossbeam made from aluminum tubing. Large diameter means no wire stays are required.

Figure 3-15B.
Smaller section aluminum tube crossbeam requires wire stays for support.

the integrity of the remainder of the beam was violated and it proceeded to break down. Of course this all happened while I was single-handing 200 miles offshore.

I got back home by sailing on the other tack. During the 30 hours this took I had a long "sit down" with the concept of weight-saving in multihulls.

Figure 3-16.
Failed chainplate attachment under crossbeam. Very high loads are present in crossbeam components and the load path must be fully considered.

Figure 3-17.
Failed welded aluminum truss. Welding aluminum reduces its strength by about 50 percent.

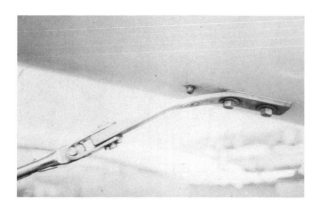
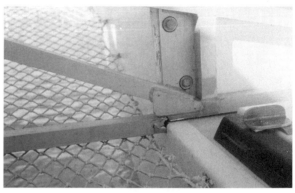

I decided that there are appropriate places to try to save weight and places, like crossbeams, where it is just too risky. Make the crossbeams strong and save weight by carrying less beer.

Permanently Mounted Crossbeams

Trimarans that are joined together permanently usually use wood/epoxy or fiberglass composite crossbeams. There are as many crossbeam shapes as there are multihull designers, but generally speaking, all are designed to provide maximum strength and stiffness at minimum weight and windage.

It is important to attach the hulls to the beams without weakening either. This usually is done by spreading out the loads by using high-strength, unidirectional fibers, integral bulkheads, or by using a wide bonding area, which minimizes the concentration of stress.

Arthur Piver used laminated lumber and plywood "box" section crossbeams in his trimaran designs of the 1960s. Borrowed from aircraft construction techniques, the box beam is a structurally efficient solution and is used in one form or another in the majority of tris that are tied together by permanently fixed crossbeams. Although these days most "box" beams bear little visual resemblance to boxes, technically they still are "box" beams. In many cases other materials have replaced plywood and lumber, although these are still excellent materials for crossbeams.

Figure 3-18.
Common box beam
with wire stay.

Figure 3-19.
Molded wing.
Attractive and strong,
but complex to build.

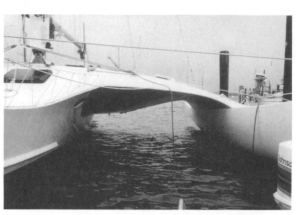

Newick-style wing. Dick Newick popularized a box crossbeam design he calls the "wing aka." Only one crossbeam is used, but typically it is quite large, often allowing space for double berths within the wing. Its large dimension makes the crossbeam very strong and resistant to flexing. Newick's designs are often stunningly beautiful; the complex curves of both top and bottom

Figure 3-20.
Molded composite
crossbeam. Beautiful,
streamlined, and light,
but it requires
expensive materials.

Figure 3-21.
Wood/epoxy box
beam with strut. Very
rugged, simple, and
effective.

wing surfaces add much to the boat's visual and functional appeal. The downside is that complex curves are complex to construct. Boatbuilders groan enough at the thought of building three hulls. Adding a fourth, in the form of a complex crossbeam, really hurts.

Juniper-style box beam and strut. This is a very strong, simple, easy-to-fabricate crossbeam that does not require exotic materials. It is sufficiently rigid so that shrouds attached to the floats hold the mast firmly, preventing it from "pumping," or moving slightly due to crossbeam flexibility.

CHAPTER 4

The Catamaran

Like trimarans, cats can incorporate living space in several basic ways. Because you cannot scale the human frame up or down to suit the boat, each method works better to a degree in different sizes of craft. The results range from sumptuous to Spartan.

Accommodations

Open-Wing Cats

The simplest form of cruising multihull is a cat without a solid bridgedeck: an open-wing cat. Like a Hobie Cat, the two hulls are connected by crossbeams or aluminum tubes and the gaping hole between them covered by a fabric trampoline or other lightweight, porous material. With just two slender hulls and simple crossbeams to construct, this style of multihull often is the least expensive to build. The famous Wharram catamarans have used this basic approach for many years.

Eliminating a cat's bridgedeck structure has the same advantages as eliminating the wing decks on the open-wing style of trimaran: there is less boat to build, and a lighter, often faster, boat can result. Because the designer has not had to provide enclosed standing headroom in a bridgedeck cabin, an open-wing cat usually will have good clearance to the underside of the crossbeams and trampoline, which reduces the chance of pounding. Provided the hulls are large—35 feet or longer—there should be sufficient accommodation for comfortable cruising.

Racing cats usually are open-wing designs. The increased weight and windage of rigid decks between the hulls would subtract from their already frightening speed. A few of the big offshore boats have been notable exceptions, however, and have included sufficient bridgedeck accommodations to provide a secure cockpit and central living space.

From a cruiser's perspective, the major disadvantage of an open-wing

Figure 4-1.
The cruising catamaran reduced to its simplest form.
The ubiquitous Wharram Cats trade palatial,
sheltered accommodations for low windage and
ease of construction. Larger cats of this type have
good accommodations in the hulls; smaller ones
expand minimal hull accommodations with
bridgedeck tents. (Martin Schöön photo)

Figure 4-2.
The high wind speeds
across the deck of a
fast cat have
prompted even the
pull-out-the-stops
racers, like the 70-foot
Jet Services, shown
here, to add
bridgedeck shelters.

catamaran is the lack of a secure, central cockpit and the inability to get from one hull cabin to the other without going outside. When the spray flies or the rain falls this becomes a most aggravating feature for long-term habitation.

A good illustration of this point can be found in the comments by German catamaran circumnavigator Wolfgang Wappl, whose suggestions were published in an interesting newsletter devoted to Wharram-style catamarans: "Why not have more shelter on deck, possibly some means of commuting from one hull to the other without getting soaked by that lashing monsoon rain, without getting waterblasted by the continuous heavy spray as the boat hurtles down the long tradewind rollers at 16 knots toward the Marquesas" (from *The Sea People/Sailorman,* January, 1989. Foss Quay, Millbrook, Torpoint, PL10 1EN, U.K.).

Full Bridgedeck Cats

At the other end of the spectrum from the super-simple open-wing catamaran is the palatial cat with a full-length bridgedeck cabin. A catamaran designed for large accommodations above all else can be positively cavernous inside. The two relatively large hulls provide space for completely private heads and sleeping quarters, and a vast connecting bridgedeck cabin provides a central living core.

The bridgedeck cabin is more nearly rectangular—room-like—than is customarily seen on any other type of sailboat, and this can give the interior a most welcome "open" feel. In big cats this cabin can contain all the comforts of home and then some: a large, well-equipped galley, a comfortable "living room," a navigation station that would do justice to a small ship, and more.

If the cat is large enough to carry the weight of these luxuries and if the design is balanced with an eye toward sailing, the results can be spectacular. Sadly, this is not always the case. The quest for ever more comfort and luxury often overburdens the vessel, causing it to lose its sparkle. For a boat meant to sail, compromise is the key to success.

To get from one hull to the other without crawling on hands and knees, the bridgedeck cabin must have reasonable headroom, with its sides extending outboard slightly past the inboard edge of the hull. As long as the boat is large and these features are done in moderation, the sailing and aesthetic properties of the boat are not greatly diminished. Of course one man's moderation is another's excess, and this is where problems develop.

Full standing headroom is almost a prerequisite for boat interiors these days—even on trailerable minicruisers. And unfortunately for boat designers, people are taller than they used to be. This means that the ceiling of a bridgedeck cabin will have to be 6 ½ feet from the floor, which is already a substantial

Figure 4-3. Three approaches to catamaran accommodation.

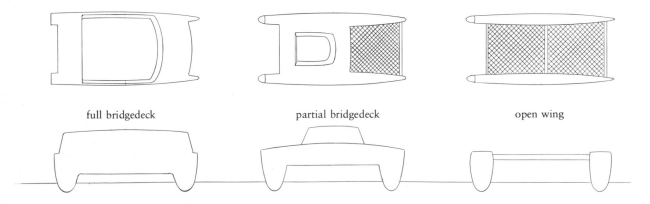

full bridgedeck   partial bridgedeck   open wing

Figure 4-4.
This Prout Q50 is a good example of a large bridgedeck cat designed to maximize accommodation. Because of the boat's size (49 feet LOA), it doesn't suffer from the ills of smaller cats that try to fit a quart into a pint pot. (Photo courtesy Prout)

Figure 4-5.
The bridgedeck cabin of Lock Crowther's *Deguello* displays the kind of light, airy accommodations only available in a catamaran.

distance above the waterline to avoid pounding on the wave tops. The profile height of the boat then becomes the sum of these two dimensions—normally 8 to 10 feet above the waterline in a cruising cat. No matter if the boat is 28 feet long or 68 feet long, the profile height is roughly the same.

This great freeboard makes smaller cats look awkward, and to some eyes just plain ugly. By using every design trick in the book—dropping the underwing clearance, streamlining the cabin, using attractive lines and clever paint schemes—the looks can be improved, but that does little to reduce the problems of excess weight and windage.

In larger cats, the bridgedeck cabin with standing headroom begins to melt into the rest of the boat and is no longer an eyesore. In fact, a very large cat probably would look worse without it. The weight and windage of large bridgedeck cabins comprise a much smaller portion of a big cat's total drag, and thus is relatively easy to live with.

A smaller going-for-broke style catamaran typically has a bridgedeck cabin that spans the boat's entire beam, extending forward and aft nearly the full length of the hulls, with the cabin floor dropped quite low to the waterline. There most definitely will be lots of "room" aboard this boat, and for dockside living and cruising protected water, this may be ideal. Long-distance open-water

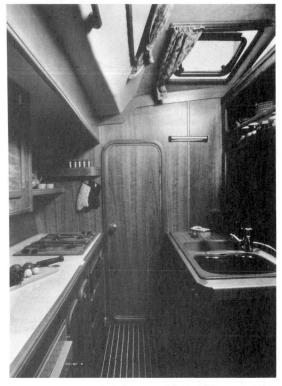

Figure 4-6.
The Privilege 48 shown here offers opulent accommodations while retaining good bridgedeck clearance and comparatively low windage. (Photos courtesy Privilege Yachting)

Figure 4-7A,B.
These older production cats display some of the features used in smaller catamarans to maximize accommodation and allow the boat to fit into a standard slip: bridgedeck extended forward to bow, narrow beam, and low underwing clearance. These features work, but only at the expense of sailing performance. Note the lack of underwing streamlining in Figure 4-7B.

A

B

sailing will show up the disadvantages of this approach, however, and the owner of this type of craft must expect excessive pitching due to the weight of the cabin in the ends of the boat, pounding of the low underwing surface, and a general loss of sailing performance. For a more detailed description of the problems surrounding this type of cat, see "Caveat Emptor," later in this chapter.

Partial Bridgedeck Cats

By limiting the bridgedeck accommodation to the maximum desirable instead of the maximum possible, a cat can offer exceptional living space and still provide exceptional sailing performance. In practical terms, this means scaling back the dimensions of the bridgedeck cabin and shifting some of the living functions into the hulls.

Everyone has his or her own feeling as to what combination of features best suits the needs. What is right for me would in all probability be wrong for you. For smaller cats—say under 40 feet—I prefer to confine standing headroom to the hulls, which then become the obvious locations for the galley and head, the only places that really need standing headroom.

A bridgedeck with approximately 3 feet of interior vertical clearance can

A

Figure 4-8A,B,C,D.
The author's Atlantic
50 cat design is a
good example of a
compromise boat. Most
of the accommodation
is within the hulls. The
low bridgedeck houses
berths and a
pilothouse, which also
has space for a chart
table and a small
dining area. (Figure
4-8B, Jim Brown photo)

B

C

D

Figure 4-9.
Jim Brown's Searunner 44 keeps a low profile by eliminating a bridgedeck cabin altogether. The bridgedeck houses large double berths with full sitting headroom. The balance of the accommodations are within the hulls. (Jim Brown photo)

Figure 4-10.
The Edel Cat 35 houses the galley and dining area in a comparatively small, low-profile bridgedeck cabin, and shifts the balance of the accommodation into the hulls.

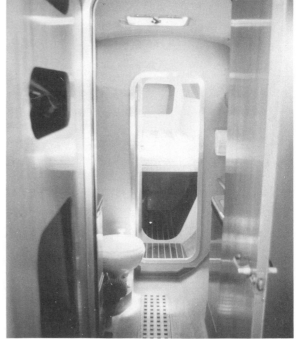

join the two hulls. This provides full sitting headroom for several large, comfortable berths. Aft of this is room for a secure central cockpit. Hull-to-hull commuting during wet weather can be resolved by incorporating a small "blister" in the deck and perhaps the underwing that provides sufficient headroom.

Depending on the size of the boat a smallish bridgedeck cabin with a comfortable eating/lounging area—or even a pilothouse—often can be worked in without spoiling the appearance if the headroom is kept modest. Cats over

Figure 4-11.
The Peter Spronk-designed *Skyjack*, a 45-footer, has many cruising miles as well as several Atlantic crossings behind her. Note her efficient deck plan and low, unobtrusive deck house.

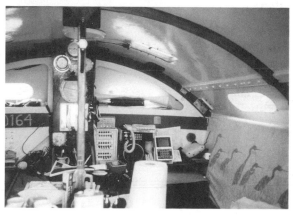

40 feet can have moderate amounts of standing headroom within the bridgedeck cabin; cats 45 to 50 feet in length can offer substantial areas of full standing headroom.

For boats that will sail offshore it seems best to move the bridgedeck back from the bows of the boat, normally a quarter to a third the length of the hull. Clearance from the waterline to the underwing should be maximized to prevent pounding, and the load of accommodations and gear should be consistent with the limits posed by the size of the hulls.

Even though the bridgedeck cabin has been scaled back in size, the total accommodation area remains substantial. Best of all, it is divided so that real privacy is available. Nice interiors, pleasing appearance, excellent performance: What more can you ask for in a boat?

Hull Shapes

By definition a cat has two hulls, each a mirror image of the other. This simplifies the design compared with a trimaran, which has two distinctly different types of hulls that must interact.

In the early days of cruising cats, most hull shapes were heavily influenced by the successful designs of Rudy Choy and partners. These incorporated very narrow hull beam, substantial hull freeboard, double-ended sterns, and often no daggerboards, fins, or keels. This is an easily built, fast, and very seakindly hull shape, but for cruising it has limited load-carrying ability, little accommodation volume within the hulls, and less than optimum windward performance.

More recently, cruising cat hulls have become fuller bodied in section to enlarge accommodations and payload capacity. Typically, modern cats have ample freeboard forward to keep the forward crossbeam and netted areas or decks above the waves, knife-like bows to better drive through waves at speed, and efficient, nearly semicircular hull sections amidships that minimize wetted surface. The hull then flattens to a U-shaped section in the stern, which tends to dampen hull pitching and enhances maneuverability. To improve windward ability, modern cats increase lateral resistance with daggerboards or fixed fins.

Bulbous Bows

About the only radical development in cat hull shapes in the last decade has been the use of bulbous bows. Primarily, Australia's Lock Crowther is responsible for this innovation, which looks more or less like a miniature version of the bulbous bow now standard on merchant ships.

The bulbous bow of a loaded ship is deeply immersed, and acts as a streamlining device to reduce hull drag. Because a ship operates more or less at a steady speed, the design of the hull form and bulb can be optimized for

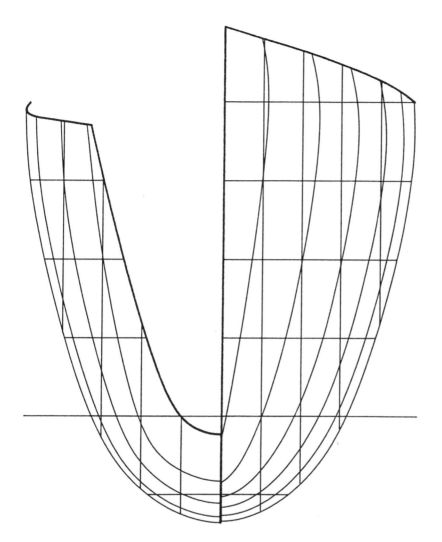

Figure 4-12.
Typical hull section of
a modern cruising
catamaran. This is the
40-footer shown in
Figure 4-13.

a particular speed-to-length ratio, producing a more efficient, easily driven hull.

This same logic doesn't apply to cruising yachts, however: Because the bulbous bow cannot be immersed deeply enough to free it from the effects of surface waves, and because cruising yachts seldom sail at steady speeds for long periods, the bulbous bow does little to reduce drag. It can, however, reduce a boat's pitching motion by increasing buoyancy forward, effectively lengthening the hull, and producing a shape that naturally resists plunging up and down better than the standard, narrow, vee-sectioned bow. Certainly anything that can reduce pitching can increase sailing speed.

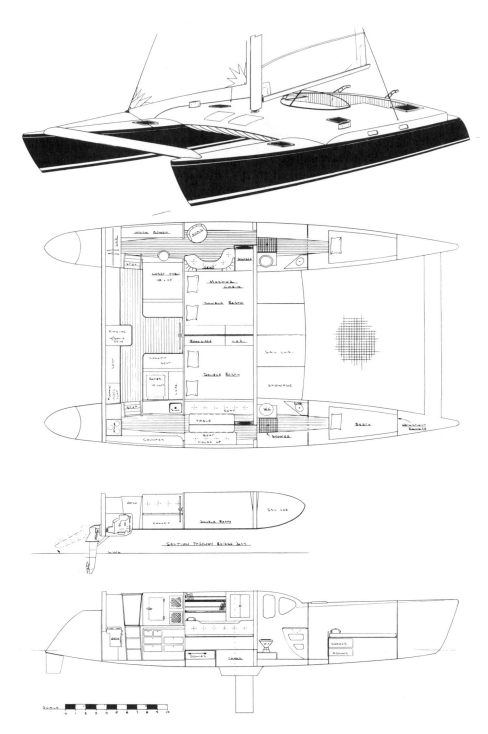

Figure 4-13.
This 40-foot cat by the author has the narrow bows, extensive use of netting, and low-profile bridgedeck with lots of clearance that typifies current thinking in performance cruising catamaran design.

The verdict is not yet in on bulbous bows, despite the myriad advantages claimed by the owners of cats retrofitted with them. But aside from being difficult to build, traditional bulbous bows tend to snag kelp, lobster pot warps, and flotsam—significant drawbacks in some cruising areas. And not only are bulbous bows conspicuously absent in the work of most designers, but Lock Crowther's own recent designs utilize a much more subdued version that is quite different from his original ship-like bulb, which stimulated so much interest in the concept.

Caveat Emptor

In a way, monohullers are lucky: They have many sources of information that offer reasonable advice on how to select a cruising boat suited to their needs. But for multihull enthusiasts, the situation is completely different. Multihulls have so little in common with monohulls that their literature is of little value in the decision-making process. Reliable information on multihulls is so scarce that many people have no way to evaluate what they see except to take the word of the salesperson. And as national opinion polls have shown, these people are deemed only slightly more trustworthy than politicians. Few of us believe that either of those groups has our best interest at heart.

Recently, a letter appeared in my mailbox from a cruising couple who wanted additional information about a design of mine in which they were interested. They had just sailed transatlantic in a 34-foot cat from one of the well-known European production builders, and had found the boat didn't live up to its advertising claims—a dose of reality that is all too common. It reads in part:

> We have become aware of certain shortcomings of our present cat over the past 6,000-plus miles, and would be interested to know how your design addresses them:
>
> 1. Bridgedeck slams to windward. We have literally been bounced off the bunks. I would not purchase another boat with this problem.
> 2. Indifferent windward ability. 100-110 degrees between tacks.
> 3. Non-protected steering station.
> 4. Limited load capacity due to excessively heavy construction; slow speeds.

Because this kind of disillusionment is so common, it may prove useful to examine these problems in detail.

1. Bridgedeck slams to windward. This problem results directly from piling too much accommodation into the boat. The underside of the bridgedeck cabin is pushed lower and lower to gain full standing headroom on a boat too short to tolerate it safely. To obtain even more living room, the bridgedeck is extended way forward, aggravating pitching and creating more low underwing area to pound. Pounding is dangerous; it can do very real damage to the boat and, perhaps most dangerous of all, it fatigues the crew. It is unrealistic to expect first-class seamanship from a crew unable to sleep.

   Ample underwing clearance—the distance from the water to the suspended underside of the bridgedeck—is most critical for a cruising boat that will spend time at sea. The underwing surface is big and often flat or nearly flat. If it is low to the water it can be pounded *hard* by waves.

   There are several important factors to take into account when designing the underwing to reduce pounding. The first and most obvious is to locate this surface as high above the waterline as possible. The second consideration is to minimize its area, especially the area forward, which contributes most to pitching and is most likely to be slammed by waves as the boat beats to windward. A third consideration, which is more difficult to evaluate without a lines plan, is how the shape of the hulls helps or hinders the pounding problem.

   A deep, narrow hull section generally is a soft-riding shape because it tends to slice through waves rather than ride up and over them. Conversely, full-bodied and beamy hulls have a quicker motion because they sail over the waves rather than through them.

   When a narrow-hull cat is heeled, the leeward hull will be depressed more deeply due to its smaller waterplane area, decreasing the available clearance of the underwing on the leeward side. And because the narrow hull will slice through the waves, their tops will reach higher up the hull and farther aft. The result is more collisions between wave tops and the underwing.

   In contrast, a cat with more volume in the hulls will depress the leeward hull and underwing less when heeled because the hull is more buoyant. Sailing into waves, the extra buoyancy in the hulls will force them to rise faster, lifting the underwing up and out of the way of the waves.

   None of these factors should be overworked. A fine line separates combinations of hull forms and bridgedecks that work well and those that do not. Multihull yacht design, like all yacht design, is a careful compromise between many conflicting requirements.

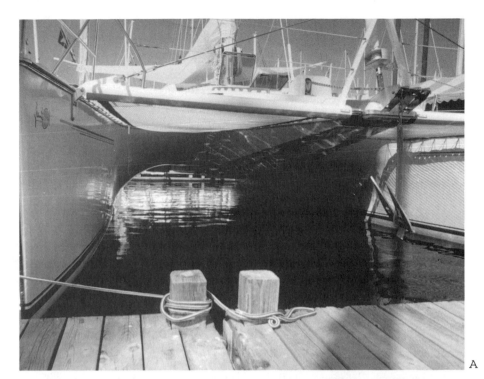

Figure 4-14A,B.
Good contrast of
underwing clearance.
The boat in Figure
4-14A exhibits good
clearance and will not
pound when sailing in
waves. The cat in
Figure 4-14B essentially
has no clearance and
drags a deep center
nacelle in the water.

A

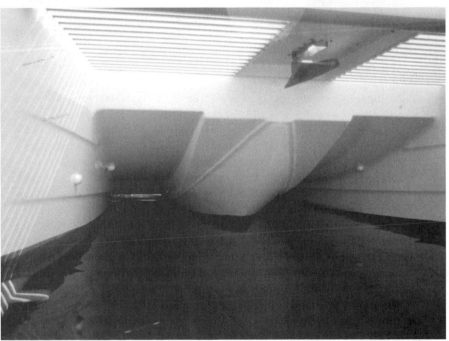

B

Shaping the flat surface of the underwing into a deep vee or a series of smaller vees often is used to drop the underwing surface closer to the water and increase the accommodations above it. Some builders refer to this structure as a *nacelle*. The idea is that the force of the wave collisions will be dampened by the cushioning effect of the vee section. I am sure this works up to a point, but often it seems to be grossly overdone. Dropping the underwing in the water adds a great deal of drag, and it can pound badly no matter what its shape if it is too low.

Remember that hulls, even slender ones, displace water. The water that *was* where the hull *is* had to go somewhere. Much of it gets pushed sideways as a wave; the two converging bow waves made by a heavy cat can be large enough to add appreciably to the ruckus of normal wave action that the two hulls must straddle. All of this turbulent water is moving aft with some velocity, and any barrier in its way will only slow the boat and create lots of noise in the cabin, disturbing the crew.

2. *Indifferent windward ability.* A boat of this type's windward ability suffers from the weight and windage of all the accommodations and gear aboard—there's just too much stuff on too short a hull and it can't get going. I know this design and I'd be surprised if they can make good 110 degrees between tacks. Without boards or deep fins, the saggy headstay and short rig cannot develop the power to climb to windward the way a cruising boat should. But to read the sales propaganda you would think it is a true ocean greyhound.

3. *Non-protected steering station.* While a protected steering station on a yacht is more a matter of personal taste than anything else, it is a big advantage to have a place to sit out of the wind and spray. In the world of commercial vessels, where people are expected to work and stay at sea for long periods, *all* boats have protected steering stations.

Few monohulls offer permanent shelter, although most serious cruising boats fit canvas spray dodgers of some sort. But a performance cruising multihull will sail much faster than a monohull, and thus will create more apparent wind. When beating to windward it is not unusual to have 25 knots of apparent wind across the decks when the real wind velocity is still under 15 knots. This constant gale in the cockpit can be very tiring to the crew, and some means of getting out of the wind is most welcome.

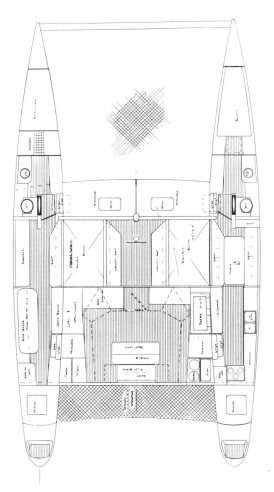

Figure 4-15.
The author's Atlantic 46, shown here, addresses most of the problems common to older style catamarans: High-clearance bridgedeck starts well back from the bow; deep daggerboards enhance windward ability; aft pilothouse provides a sheltered steering station and central dining/lounging area without adding excessive windage; long, slim, wood/epoxy or foam sandwich hulls produce a lightweight boat that can carry normal cruising stores without unduly hampering performance.

If I ever build another boat for myself it will have an enclosed pilothouse, or at the very least a place out of the weather with full visibility where I can sit on watch. Having sailed on one of my own designs with this feature some years ago I can report that it puts a whole new complexion on cold and wet weather. It is so much easier to stay alert and rested when your body heat is not being sucked away by the wind.

4. *Limited load capacity; slow speeds.* Both problems are rooted partly in the single-skin fiberglass construction used in this boat and several other production multihulls. A coreless laminate must be thick (read *heavy*) to obtain the required stiffness in the hulls. Heavyweight construction aside, load-carrying capacity is largely a function of hull length. If the overall performance is to exceed a monohull of the same length, a 34-foot multihull, cat or tri, will have somewhat restricted load carrying capacity to start with. If a cat or tri this size is loaded with lots of cabin space and interior appointments, heavily constructed, and then piled with gear for a long cruise, don't expect much in the way of speed. Payload capacity is important for a cruising design; it best can be improved by using strong but lightweight construction and having hulls of adequate length.

There is nothing wrong with having a lot of space on a multihull, as long as that space remains *space* and doesn't become filled with *things*. And as long as that space is high enough above the water, far enough back from the bows, and low enough in profile not to seriously hamper the performance of boats that are meant to *sail*.

Attaching the Headstay

One problem peculiar to catamarans is what to do with the headstay. There is no hull on the boat's centerline to attach it to!

Some cats with enormous bridgedecks that extend well forward install the chainplate right on the leading edge of the bridgedeck. While the wisdom of extending the bridgedeck forward to the bows of the boat is questionable from the standpoint of pitching and underwing pounding, it does provide a convenient solution to the headstay attachment problem. The bridgedeck must be built very strongly to resist the upward pull of the headstay, which in a large boat could easily reach 5,000 pounds.

Cats without decking forward commonly attach the headstay to the center of a tubular aluminum crossbeam run from bow to bow. Obviously the tremendous upward pull of the headstay is quite capable of breaking or severely bending the long and hopefully lightweight aluminum beam.

To solve this problem, a stout wire running from the ends of the crossbeam at the hull over a spreader at the crossbeam's center absorbs the headstay's upward pull, relieving the crossbeam itself of the intense bending load on its center.

Because of its functional similarity to the downward-pointing spreader and wire used beneath the bowsprit of a traditional boat—the "dolphin striker"—the upward-pointing catamaran version has been dubbed a "seagull striker." Who says multi-mariners have no sense of tradition?

Figure 4-16A,B.
The "seagull striker" counteracts the pull of the headstay at the weak point of the forward tubular aluminum crossbeam.

Figure 4-16C.
An alternative to a seagull striker is a headstay bridle attached to hulls. Bridle wire must be stout.

CHAPTER 5

Resisting
Leeway

*A*ll sailboats extract energy from both the wind and from the water flowing past the hull. While the sails are the engines that draw energy from the wind, there is another element less obvious but just as important: the hydrofoil formed by the hull and its appendages—the rudder and keel or fin—which derive their energy from the flow of water past the hull.

With nothing to oppose the force of the wind in the sails, a boat can only drift downwind like a balloon. But add an effective, immersed hydrofoil, and a boat can harness the power in the wind and sail across and against it. The more efficient the hydrofoil, the better the boat's performance.

Normally, the hulls of a cat or tri are narrow and deep relative to their width. This naturally efficient shape has an inherent tendency to resist leeway, and some multihulls will sail tolerably well to windward without additional fins or keels—the deep and narrow-hulled catamarans of Rudy Choy, for instance. By and large, all multihulls benefit from the addition of some sort of "keel" to improve hydrodynamic efficiency.

Because multihull stability derives from the wide separation of the hulls, there is no need to hang ballast off the bottom of the yacht, as is the case with monohulls. The only function of a multihull's "keel" is to resist the side force of the sails; it is relieved from the task of providing stability, too.

This simplification of the keel's function has significant advantages: First and foremost, it means that, since it contains no ballast, the keel can be very light. Thus it is easy to retract when not needed, allowing less drag in light air or when sailing downwind, and less draft in shoal water.

In their effort to reduce leeway, all multihulls fall into one of four categories: specially shaped hulls that use no fins, boats with fixed (non-retractable) fins, vertically retracting daggerboards, and pivot-up centerboards.

Leeway-Resisting Hulls

Asymmetric vs. Symmetric Hulls

The Micronesians, early builders of sophisticated multihulled sailing craft, often employed highly asymmetrical hull sections that developed leeway-reducing forces in the same way that an airplane wing develops lift. In ancient days this method was confined to the main hulls of Proas—single-outrigger sailboats that always keep the outrigger to windward. This means that the asymmetric hull would always have its low-pressure side to windward, and thus would be able to benefit from the asymmetry.

When the modern multihull era began to gain momentum in the 1950s and '60s, several designers applied this concept to their boats. For many years the champion of this idea was Rudy Choy of Hawaii, who, together with Warren Seaman and Alfred Kumalai, designed and built some of the finest catamarans that have ever sailed.

Choy's designs at that time relied on the asymmetric hull section to combat leeway. It soon became apparent on the race course, however, that the addition of a fin was essential in order to gain the best windward performance.

For an asymmetric hull to function properly it should be the only hull in the water. If a cat with asymmetric hulls is sailing level, the lift from each hull fights the other and no net benefit is realized. Except for the ever-popular Hobie 16, cats with asymmetry are seldom seen. That being said, however, there remain two reasons to consider asymmetry: The first is an interesting observation made by Rudy Choy that asymmetry made a boat much easier to steer down big waves at high speed. This seems due to the lack of a pronounced pressure wave on the forward outboard side of the leeward hull (which is flatter in an asymmetrical hull).

The other place to consider asymmetry is in special situations where the overall beam is restricted. By using an asymmetric hull shape, the center of buoyancy can be shifted outboard slightly and a gain in stability realized without increasing the overall beam.

Hull Section

The cross section of a symmetrical hull can be tailored to prevent leeway; this was the method used most often in the early days of cruising multihulls. A deep, narrow, vee-shaped hull section will develop significant resistance to the side force of the sails. This is fairly obvious by comparing the shapes in Figure 5-1. Section A would be much more difficult to push sideways through the water than section B.

At first glance this looks like an attractive way to go: The construction is simple and there is no centerboard trunk protruding into the cabin. But there are some problems with this solution to the leeway problem. The two big drawbacks are the additional wetted surface, which will hurt light air performance, and, of greater significance, the fact that a very narrow and deep

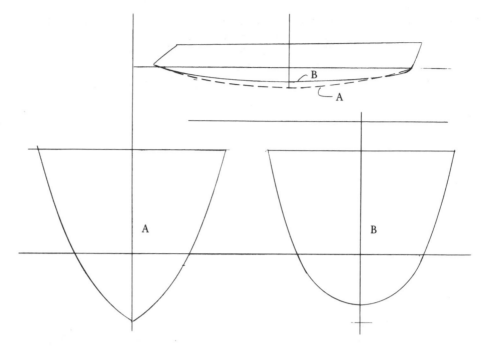

Figure 5-1.
Leeway-resisting hulls.
The hull section A
resists leeway better
than section B, but
section A has more
wetted surface drag,
and can be more
difficult to turn than B.

hull makes it difficult to turn. If enough "keel rocker" is used to allow good maneuverability, the hull normally has insufficient displacement in the ends and thus will hobbyhorse excessively. Over the years this technique has fallen out of favor, and most designers have moved on to other hull shapes.

Fins

Fixed Fins

A fixed, non-retractable fin is sometimes used to improve windward performance. If the hull is shaped to work with the fin, i.e., a section more veed than rounded over its length, the area of the fin itself can be fairly modest, preserving a reasonably shoal draft. The fixed fin is shunned by the racing crowd because it is a bit slower than a retractable board, but for cruising I think it has some advantages that are not widely appreciated.

I think the fixed fin is better suited to a trimaran than a catamaran. Cruising catamarans have two hulls in the water at all times, which is not terribly efficient from the standpoint of wetted surface. Compared with trimarans and monohulls, cats pay a drag penalty in very light winds when wetted hull surface comprises most of the hull drag. This tends to make cruising cats sluggish in light air even without fixed fins. The addition of two fins big enough to do the job will add more wetted surface and magnify this problem.

In addition, very long fixed fins will tend to make a cat slower to come about. A cat with lots of windage can be slow to tack as it is; long, shallow fins only exacerbate the problem. In my opinion a successful fixed-fin catamaran should have fins that are modest in length combined with an efficient hull shape and a reasonably powerful sail plan.

A trimaran, on the other hand, has very low wetted surface in light air, and a fixed fin does not place it at a serious disadvantage. Because tris pivot around the main hull during a tack, a fin (provided it is not too long) will not slow tacking excessively.

Fixed fins do have the major advantage of simplicity. The construction is straightforward, with no moving parts, thus maintenance is carefree. Centerboard or daggerboard trunks do not intrude on precious living space within the hull. Fixed fins also protect the rudder, a feature of special significance to cruisers. Normally the fin is deeper than the rudder and will take the full impact of grounding or striking flotsam. With the rudder thus protected it can safely be made non-retractable, further simplifying construction and maintenance.

As of this writing most production catamarans utilize fixed fins, the primary reason being that it is the lowest cost solution. The fin itself is quicker to build than centerboards or daggerboards and their associated paraphernalia, and the extra complication of a kick-up rudder can be avoided.

Because the typical multihull's fixed fin is hollow (it carries no lead), it can easily be made into tanks for the large quantities of fuel or water carried by cruising boats. This works out well because the weight of the tankage is located in the most desirable place (down low, amidships), and the space gained in the hull by the removal of the tanks can be put to better use.

Figure 5-2.
A fixed fin adds lateral plane without the complication of a centerboard or daggerboard, protects the bottom in groundings, and can be used for fuel and water tankage. Fixed fins do increase wetted surface, however, and can hamper light-air performance, particularly with catamarans.

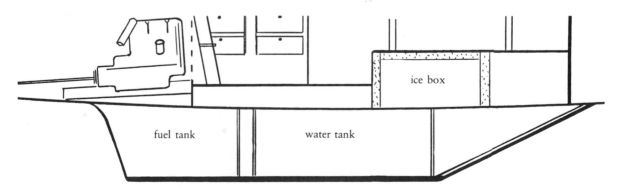

fuel tank

water tank

ice box

You will have deeper draft with a fixed fin; there is no getting around that. But by monohull standards a fixed-fin multihull is still quite shoal. My own boat, a 52-foot trimaran with a fixed fin, draws 4 ½ feet. Over many years of cruising I have wanted less draft a few times, but seldom has 4 ½ feet prevented us from having a good time. It also tends to keep me honest. While sailing centerboard boats I tend to think, "Oh, what the hell! Why not cut the buoy and save ourselves the distance —CRASH!" You just can't jump over the side of a large cruising boat and hope to push it off, so in the long run I've been very content with *Juniper's* draft.

Daggerboards

The vertically retracting daggerboard is the only leeway-resisting device now used in racing multihulls. The reason is clear: It has the best lift-to-drag ratio and therefore is more efficient than the other techniques for resisting leeway. And as the performance level of cruising multihulls has risen over the years, more and more daggers have found their way onto cruising boats.

A centerboard pivots on a shaft and can swing back into its trunk without damage if it strikes an obstacle. The daggerboard, as its name implies, resembles a knife blade that plunges vertically into the water from the trunk and is retracted the same way. It cannot swing back and up; if it strikes hard, something will have to give. This would seem an insurmountably bad feature for a cruising boat, but in practice a cruising daggerboard can work well if certain precautions are taken.

The most basic of these precautions is constructing the daggerboard trunk sturdily, so the trunk will not open up no matter what you might hit. If the board can cut into the back of the trunk and cause a major leak you have a serious problem.

From a construction perspective this is not a big deal; it is only a matter of putting enough meat around the base of the trunk to absorb the impact. On a hard grounding, one of two things will happen: either the boat will stop dead in her tracks without damage or the daggerboard itself will be damaged. In this case the board normally can be extracted through the top of the trunk and repaired.

Recently there has been a design carryover from the race course into cruising boats that I think is unwise and has been responsible for more than a few problems. In an effort to save weight, the daggerboard is shortened so that the top of the board is below the top of the trunk when in the down position. Because the board has less "bury" in the trunk, the load is greater where the board bears against the trunk walls. And of critical importance, if the board strikes something it is possible for the trunk to rupture because the top of the board bears on the trunk walls in an unsupported area rather than at the deck.

Several designers have developed daggerboard designs that are intended either to absorb impact or retract on impact and thus minimize damage. Dick

Figure 5-3A.
Typical daggerboard,
fully retracted.

Figure 5-3B.
Up-and-down control
lines are led to cockpit.

Figure 5-3D.
Racing-style
daggerboard. When
lowered, top of board
is near bottom of
trunk, and has little or
no support if it hits
something.

Figure 5-3C.
Daggers often are
positioned off-center to
give added space
below decks.

Figure 5-4.
The addition of a
"bumper fin" in the
way of the
daggerboard can
absorb part of the
shock of grounding.

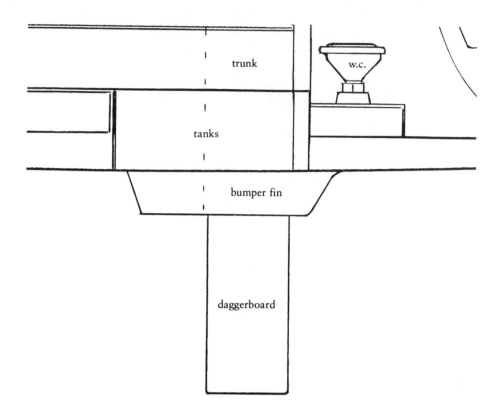

Newick has for many years employed a "crush box," which is a sacrificial lumber box contained within an extension of the lower end of the daggerboard box. The idea is to cushion the force of impact by smashing a sacrificial part that can be replaced cheaply.

Another interesting scheme was related to me by English multihull designer John Shuttleworth. In this method the daggerboard has a simple catch built into it at the top of the trunk that prevents it from coming up. The uphaul line that normally retracts the board is replaced by a smaller diameter nylon line winched very tight and placed in a sheet stopper. If the board strikes bottom, the top of the dagger will disengage from the catch, and the nylon line, stretched like a rubber band, will quickly retract the board. The report is that the system works, although if you strike a rock at high speed nothing short of a very stout trunk will save the day. Happily most groundings are softer.

A few years ago, while I was working on the daggerboards for a sharpie monohull design, I had an idea for an automatically retracting daggerboard. I have since incorporated this concept into a large cruising trimaran design, now under construction. Its simplicity makes it an attractive design. The daggerboard is wider than normal and its trunk is angled forward. By carefully

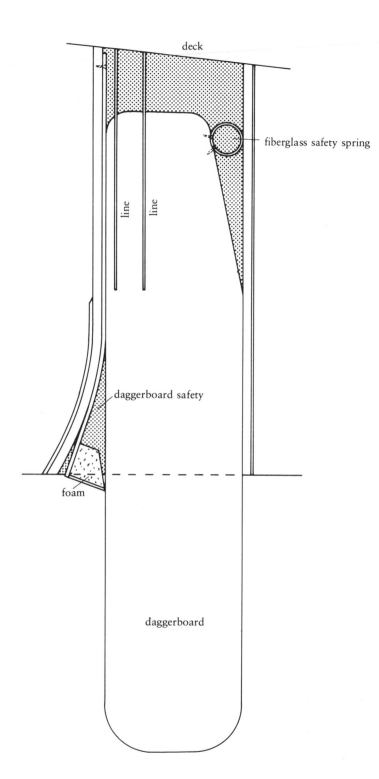

deck

fiberglass safety spring

line

line

daggerboard safety

foam

daggerboard

Figure 5-5.
The Newick "crush box." In this case, an easily replaced glassed-foam block attached to a flexible ash batten runs down the daggerboard trunk abaft the board to take the shock of grounding.

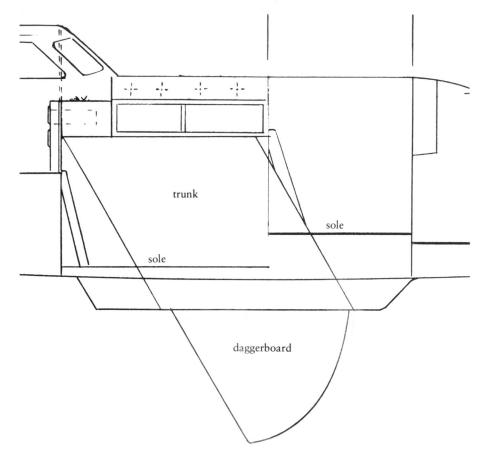

Figure 5-6.
Because this daggerboard is angled forward, it will be forced up into the trunk in the event of grounding.

trunk

sole

sole

daggerboard

shaping the board's leading edge and matching it to the sweep angle of the trunk, the daggerboard will, upon grounding, be forced up into the trunk.

This design combines the most desirable features of both the center- and daggerboards: Like the centerboard, it retracts on impact, but like the daggerboard, there is no open, turbulence-producing slot when the board is down. Nor is there a pivot pin to fail or leak.

As is the case with most daggerboards, its performance will be enhanced by the addition of low-friction materials where the board bears upon the trunk wall. Teflon, Delrin, or high-density polyethylene have all been used successfully for this purpose.

Centerboards

In theory, the pivot-up centerboard makes a lot of sense. The board, as used in a multihull, normally is unballasted and buoyant. A hold-down line pulls the board into the down position and is cleated in such a way that it pulls

Figure 5-7.
Older catamaran with
dual centerboards.
Note the long,
turbulence-producing
slot for the board.

free on impact, allowing the board to pivot up. In practice, however, there are some nagging problems with centerboards.

The trunk is by nature large and intrusive. A big trunk in a narrow hull often defines the accommodation plan, although this is more objectionable in some boats than in others. The bottom of a centerboard-equipped boat must have a long, open slot. Because this creates a great deal of turbulence it can really hurt the performance of a fast boat, and the faster you go the worse it gets. This turbulence also can create quite a lot of noise in the trunk, which can be most aggravating and disruptive to the off watch. The pivot pin and its attendant hardware cause a lot of problems. The construction details always seem more complicated on pivoting boards, and it is more difficult to extract the board for routine maintenance and painting.

The pivoting centerboard does shine in one area: Aside from seeing one or two centerboards that were damaged by forces applied sideways to the board, serious damage is uncommon.

CHAPTER 6

Rudders and Steering

Rudders

A multihull's rudder presents some unique design problems. Single-hull yachts almost always have a fixed keel of greater depth than the rudder, which protects it from damage should the boat strike the bottom. A multihull, on the other hand, normally has a very shallow hull and retractable "keels." With the board up, the rudder hangs much deeper than the hull and is vulnerable to damage. For protection, multihulls often employ retracting rudders, which are more complicated to design and construct.

Designing a multihull's rudder is influenced also by the boat's wide performance envelope. A multihull's rudder must be able to function properly from 0 to 25 knots. At low speed there must be enough rudder area to control the boat. At high speeds there usually is plenty of rudder area, but it may be prone to ventilation. This happens when air is sucked down from the surface along the low-pressure side of the rudder blade, and can cause a sudden and drastic loss of rudder lift. While this normally is not dangerous, it can make steering difficult. Because the pressure differential developed over a hydrofoil such as a rudder blade varies with the square of the water velocity, the faster a boat goes the more likely it is to experience ventilation.

On the positive side, compared with a monohull a multihull is generally quite easy to steer. Its long, narrow hulls like to track straight ahead, and the lack of significant heeling eliminates the helm required to correct the imbalance that ensues when a monohull's center of effort shifts bodily to leeward as the hull heels. These factors mean that the multihull rudder can be modest in depth, and this significantly reduces the bending loads on the rudder stock.

Surface-Piercing Foils

Transom-hung outboard rudders are used often on multihulls. This type of rudder works well with many types of self-steering gear and is easy to make retractable. There is one drawback: At high speed this type of rudder is much more likely to ventilate than a rudder located under the hull.

Any hydrofoil that pierces the surface of the water at some angle of attack will tend to pull surface air down along the low-pressure side. Some multihulls with outboard rudders have problems with the loss of lift due to ventilation and others do not. It seems that a well-balanced hull form that requires a minimum of helm to control the boat can better accommodate an outboard rudder than can a boat that requires constant and large rudder correction.

In problem cases, the ventilation of an outboard rudder sometimes can be controlled by the addition of ventilation fences, which are horizontal plates attached perpendicular to the rudder surface. These fences will prevent or at least discourage the surface air from being drawn down the entire length of the rudder blade.

By placing the rudder under the hull the direct link to surface air is broken, and the problem of rudder ventilation at high speed is lessened to a great degree.

Kick-Up Rudders

The rudder is one of a boat's most crucial elements. Lose it and you have *big* problems. Therefore one of the design essentials in a cruising boat is making the rudder damage resistant. If the boat has a fixed fin or keel that makes the draft of the hull deeper than the draft of the rudder, there is little risk of the

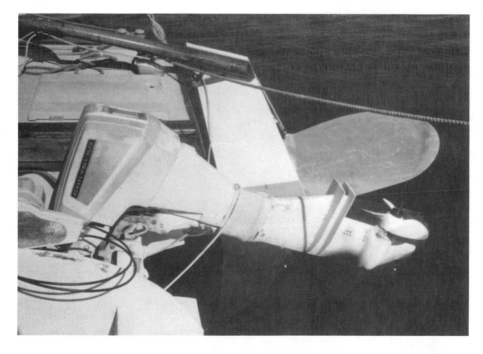

Figure 6-1.
The simplest form of kick-up rudder.

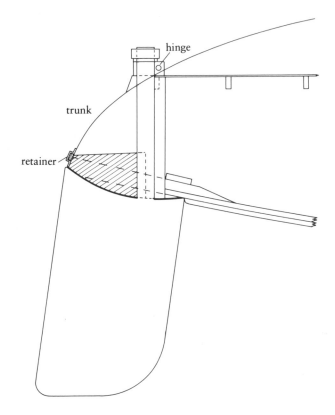

Figure 6-2.
Newick-style kick-up rudder. The rudder pivots up and aft through a hollow trunk.

hinge

trunk

retainer

rudder sustaining a life-threatening blow. But in a multihull with retractable daggerboards or centerboards, the rudder very likely will hang a foot or more below the lowest point of the hull when the boards are retracted, as they would be when sailing in shoal water. This means that upon grounding, the rudder will be the first object to strike the bottom. Few ordinary rudders can survive this kind of abuse.

The solution employed for many years has been to make the rudder retractable on impact. A good bump to the rudder will release it from its hold-down catch and it will swing up out of harm's way. Sounds simple, doesn't it? Usually it is not. A good kick-up rudder must retract when it should, and must not retract when it shouldn't. It is inherently more complex than a fixed rudder and thus more prone to maintenance problems. And last but not least it complicates the linkage that ties the rudder to the steering wheel or tiller.

Hobie-style rudder. Small beach cats such as the Hobie use pivot-up spade rudders that are linked by a tiller bar. Many larger cruising cats employ this basic system, too. If the construction details are thought out properly this is

Figure 6-3.
A seemingly radical
solution to the kick-up
rudder problem is
having a section of the
hull pivot upward.

a very straightforward and reliable way to go. The disadvantage is that you have surface-piercing foils that are prone to ventilation. In addition, unless remote steering systems are used, the cockpit must be placed where you can reach the tiller bar.

Newick-style rudder. An improvement on the Hobie-style rudder for larger craft can be made by installing the kick-up rudder under the hull. There are several construction techniques for doing this.

One popular method is illustrated in Figure 6-2. Here, the rudder is built into a trunk open at the aft end. If the rudder strikes the bottom it can pivot aft and up through the transom. Making this style work requires some careful thinking. Will the rudder retract properly if it is turned? Will the rudder shaft bearings be supported properly as the rudder retracts? How will the steering linkage be affected, and how quickly can it be brought back to a functioning position? These problems have been solved with varying degrees of success.

C-Class type rudders. Another type of kick-up rudder that has been used successfully on smaller cats, such as the 25-foot C-Class boats, is just starting

Figure 6-4
A vertically retracting rudder doesn't kick up on impact, but it does allow the boat to be steered in shallow water with a partially retracted rudder.

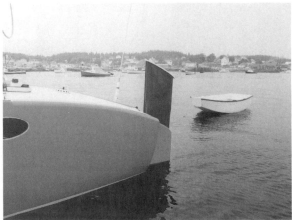

to show up on larger boats. At the outset it seems a radical solution to the problems inherent with the other types of kick-up rudders, but in reality it has many advantages. Basically, the rudder itself is built into the hull, just the way a fixed spade rudder would be, with rudder shaft bearings fixed in place. To make the rudder retractable the last few feet of the *hull* is hinged so that hull and rudder pivot up together.

There are several advantages to doing this. First, the highly stressed shaft bearings can be fixed into the hull, eliminating the problems associated with making the bearings movable. Second, the rudder and stern of the hull can be designed to practically any shape, since one does not have to retract within the other. And third, the separation of the hinges is very wide, which allows better triangulation so the rudder is well supported at all stages of retraction.

Vertically retracting rudder. By housing a transom-hung rudder in a form-fitting fiberglass sleeve a rudder can be made to retract vertically, similar to a daggerboard. This is a simple rudder to construct, and it offers the advantage of being usable in the partially retracted position. Uphaul and downhaul lines position the rudder at any depth. When sneaking around in thin water the rudder may only be one-third down, but it still will function well enough to maintain steerage. A hard accidental grounding could damage the rudder if it were lowered to full depth, so it is good practice to retract the rudder to less than hull draft any time the daggerboard is up.

Fixed Rudders

A fixed rudder can take many forms: inboard, outboard, with skeg, without skeg, balanced, or unbalanced. A transom-hung, fixed outboard rudder can suffer from the same ventilation problems as a transom-hung kick-up rudder, so it is desirable to get it under the boat if possible.

A *skeg* is a portion of the rudder's leading edge attached to the boat so that it cannot turn. A skeg can make the rudder less likely to stall (water flow becoming detached from the low-pressure side of the rudder surface) when turned hard.

I have come to believe that skegs are less effective than theory says they should be and it seems other designers have come to the same conclusions: Skeg rudders are seen much less nowadays than they were 10 years ago.

A skegless, or *spade*, rudder, hung beneath the hull is an efficient, simple rudder that is easy to construct and for these reasons used frequently. Often a small portion of the rudder surface extends forward of the rudder's turning axis. This area "balances" the rudder so that much less force is required to

Figure 6-5.
Spade rudder on a cat; non-retractable, but protected by the hull's draft.

steer the boat. Very little forward area is required. An excess will "over balance" the rudder, which will develop a mind of its own, making steering nearly impossible.

It should be obvious from the discussion on kick-up rudders that building a good, workable, low-maintenance, retractable or kick-up rudder will be neither easy nor cheap. But if a cruising boat has a deeply immersed rudder unprotected by the hull, clearly it is essential that *something* must be done to reduce the risk of serious rudder damage.

Figure 6-6.
Linking a catamaran's twin rudders requires extra thought, particularly if kick-up rudders are involved. For remote steering, cable systems, such as those illustrated here, work well, retaining good "feel" and being easily adjustable. They also can be readily adapted to some types of kick-up rudders.

An alternative is to use a fixed rudder and protect it by increasing the draft of the hull with the addition of a fixed fin. If the increase in draft is acceptable this is a simple and effective way of dealing with the problem. Even a design that has a centerboard or daggerboard can install a small deadwood "bumper fin" on the bottom of the hull around the exit slot of the board. This bumper fin can greatly reinforce the hull/trunk, and will confine any damage from grounding to the board itself. It also provides a rugged base for the boat to sit on when hauled or beached.

There is one aspect to cruising with the fixed fin/rudder combination that few multihullers appreciate. All cruisers go aground from time to time. A boat with a central fin at the deepest part of the vessel will ground at that one place, near the middle of the hull. In this position the boat can pivot, and it is often possible to turn the boat and sail off.

We have surprised ourselves many times by our ability to become unstuck in our ketch-rigged trimaran *Juniper*. We use the sails to turn the boat in the direction we want, sheet in, walk out onto the float to lift the main hull slightly, and off we go.

In the same situation with a kick-up rudder-equipped boat, the rudder will retract on grounding (assuming the centerboard is already up), the boat will lose steerage, and often will be blown into even shallower water, stopping only when the hull grounds. With the water too shallow to deploy the rudder and the hull grounded on a large part of its bottom, it will be difficult to sail off.

Regardless of the rudder type, the rudder's surface must be carefully shaped into an efficient, smooth, and symmetrical streamlined shape. Designers often use airfoil sections from the NACA (National Advisory Committee for Aeronautics) series to guide the shape of rudders and keels. If the construction is faithful to the designed shape everything should be fine. If there are unfair areas of the rudder it usually will begin to vibrate or "sing" at speeds exceeding 10 knots. Flat-plate rudders and other shortcuts common to monohulls or the early days of multihulls are entirely inadequate for a fast boat and may prove dangerous as well as frustrating.

Self-Steering

Wind Vanes

Wind vane self-steering systems have fallen from favor in recent years due to the wide availability and increased reliability of electric autopilots. There also is some sentiment in multihull circles that a wind vane does not work for a multihull. The theory is that the rapid acceleration of a fast boat and the large shift of the apparent wind prohibits the wind vane from holding a steady course. In my experience this is true to a point. Certainly there are some conditions in which an electric, compass-controlled autopilot performs better

Figure 6-7.
Wind vane connected
to a servo-tab on an
outboard skeg rudder.
A simple, reliable
system that works well
on most points of
sailing.

than a wind vane. But the wind vane has its advantages provided it is designed and installed correctly.

Having relied on the wind vane that Jim Brown designed for his Searunner trimaran series for many thousands of miles, I can state without reservation that a wind vane connected directly to a servo-tab on the main rudder is a very powerful and reliable system. It does not depend on electricity, which as all cruising sailors know can be fickle, and if it breaks you need not be a computer scientist to fix it. The harder the wind blows the more energy there is available to keep the boat on course. Beam reaching in tradewind conditions is somewhat like riding a rail; there is no course variation.

The wind vane hits its nadir in light winds, however. (Of course under power in a calm it is of no use at all.) For example, a fast boat broad reaching with 5 knots of breeze on the quarter will sail at about 5 knots, and the apparent wind will come around to slightly forward of the beam. With the sails trimmed and the boat sailing well, the crew decides to engage the wind vane. For a few minutes everything is fine, but eventually the boat starts to veer away from the wind slightly. As it does so the apparent wind quickly decreases in velocity, losing its power to turn the vane and thus correct the course. The boat continues to bear off unhindered until it loses its speed and the wind overtakes the wind vane. At this point the boat is headed off on a dead run, but the sails and vane are trimmed for wind slightly ahead. Now the wind catches up from astern, forcing a radical correction, and the boat heads up higher than the desired course. As boat speed builds she again falls off gradually, and the whole sequence repeats itself—a frustrating experience to say the least! In most ocean conditions, however, a good wind vane should deliver satisfactory performance.

Servo-tab coupled wind vane self-steerers are the only type commonly used on multihulls. The popular Aries self-steering gear, used extensively on monohulls, is a different type of system that uses a separate servo-rudder to generate power, transmitting it to the boat's main rudder through the steering system. I know of no one who has applied this type of steering to a multihull. My feeling is that the standard unit would be too powerful at the speeds at which a multihull often sails. If at all possible it would be better to use a servo-tab on the main rudder.

A servo-tab mounted on the main rudder has an additional desirable feature: Whether the tab is intended to be controlled by a wind vane or by an electric autopilot, it requires very little power to operate and easily can be done manually. In the event of a breakdown in the main steering linkage the boat can be steered by hand via the tab.

Electronic Autopilots

The electronic autopilot has come of age during the 1980s. Provided the unit selected is not too small for the job, the reliability has been good and is getting better. It should be noted, however, that the OSTAR racers often carry two or more backup units.

Because multihulls normally are easy to steer, most of the time a relatively small autopilot can do the job. At the upper ranges of the performance envelope, however, the steering loads can become excessive and may overload the system. This means that a larger, more expensive, juice-guzzling autopilot will be needed if you are asking it to steer the main rudder the way a helmsman would.

But wait! Remember the servo-tab? A small, inexpensive, power-sipping autopilot can steer a very large boat if it is linked to a servo-tab. The autopilot need turn only the tab; the tab muscles the rudder around by harnessing the energy provided by the water flowing past. You really must see it to believe it. Just a finger poking the bellcrank of the servo-tab will make the rudder jump.

If a servo-tab cannot be linked to the rudder, then a balanced spade rudder can keep the steering loads within the range of most small autopilots.

Figure 6-8A.
Outboard skeg rudder
with servo-tab for
autopilot.

Figure 6-8B.
Linkage from autopilot
controls trim tab.

Figure 6-8C.
Autopilot controls small
bell crank, which is
connected to rudder's
trim tab via push-pull
cable.

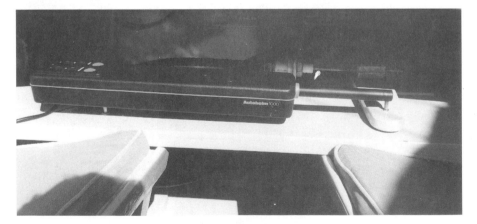

Rigs

W riters have devoted reams to sails, rigging, blocks, winches, and the associated paraphernalia of sailing in monohull-oriented books, and I see little need to rehash the subjects here just to consume paper. But there are some substantial differences and more than a few misunderstandings between rigs for monos and rigs for multis; I will try to clear up these gray areas.

A multitude of rigs and types of masts have been tried in multihulled craft over the last 30 years, with varying degrees of success. The rigs of cats and tris present some unique problems and on the whole are more difficult to engineer than those of a monohull.

The major consideration a multihull designer faces must be a recognition of the tremendous loads that a stable, almost non-heeling boat places on mast, rigging, and sails. Multihulls stand up to the wind; they don't roll over and play dead when a gust hits. The rig of an offshore cruising multihull must be adequate to the task.

The other significant difference from a monohull is the much greater staying base for the shrouds, made possible by the multihull's wider beam. This in itself is good because it permits a more efficient shroud angle. But some multihulls have flexible crossbeams that make the staying base slightly unstable (flexible), and this must be considered in designing a proper rigging plan and mast.

Masts

Most multihull rigs fall into one of three basic types:

- Conventional mast with inboard shrouds over spreaders.

- Conventional mast with shrouds led out-board, no spreaders.

- Rotating mast.

Conventionally Stayed Mast with Spreaders

This rig is more or less the same familiar, single, double, or triple-spreader plan that is so common on monohulls (see Figure 7-1A). The shroud chainplates are a short distance outboard from and abeam of the mast; spreaders compensate for the narrow separation of the shrouds. Aside from the need to increase the strength of the mast and staying wire to deal with the increased loads that a multihull can generate, there is no real difference from its monohull counterpart. This rig often is used on multihulls where overlapping headsails are desired or where crossbeam flexibility makes it impossible to attach the shrouds further outboard.

Conventional Mast With Shrouds Led Outboard, No Spreaders

These rigs are supported by shrouds led outboard as far as possible, which eliminates the need for spreaders to increase the effectiveness of the shrouds and reduces the compression loads on the mast (see Figures 7-1B and 7-2). This can be a very effective rigging plan on boats with wide beam and great structural stiffness. Catamarans with rigid bridgedeck structures can use this rig most successfully. If large headsails are used, they can be sheeted inside the upper shrouds.

If the boat has an exceptionally wide beam or is lightly built, problems can arise in keeping a mast of this type in column. Generally, it is impractical to eliminate the flexibility of the connecting crossbeams or deck structure. A successful way of dealing with this is to use only one cap shroud, led from the masthead as far outboard as possible, and hold the mast in column with a series of short spreaders and diamond shrouds (see Figures 7-1C and 7-3). With this arrangement the whole mast is free to move slightly without affecting the support of the diamonds, which are essential to keeping the spar straight.

The Rotating Mast

Another rig growing in popularity among multihullers is the rotating mast. This sounds like a radical solution unworthy of a cruising boat, but a complete examination of its features will show that the idea has merit for several reasons.

In theory, the rigging wire is always under tension and the mast always under compression. Picture the mast as a drinking straw. Stand one end on a table and lay your finger on the other end. Now push down lightly. The straw will resist your finger's pressure up to a point and then it will start to bend outward. Once it bends beyond a small amount its ability to resist compression falls dramatically and it will buckle and fail—just as a mast would. Thus the primary objective in mast design is to make a mast that best resists bending under axial compression.

The easy and light way to strengthen a mast is by increasing its diameter, or cross section. The problem with doing this is that the mast is also the leading edge of the mainsail, and a big lump of mast is the last thing you want on the leading edge of an airfoil such as a sail. And so the dilemma arises: Do we use a small-section mast held in column by many rigging wires, or do we use a larger, less aerodynamically efficient section that is stronger and requires less rigging wire to keep it straight?

The designers of monohull racing boats—and an increasing number of performance-oriented cruising boats—usually opt for the small mast with lots of wire approach. The result is a complex maze of rod rigging and a pencil-thin mast that often is on the verge of going for a swim; only one of these many interrelated components need fail and over she goes.

Why do yacht designers use these seemingly unseamanlike rigs? Because if they're intent on performance, they usually have no choice. A large-section mast is only efficient if it is given a streamlined section and permitted to rotate from side to side so that it fairs itself into the leading edge of the sail, reducing speed-robbing turbulence. But the monohull racing rules *prohibit* rotating masts.

Fortunately, we who design multihulls are free to do whatever works, and a rotating mast really works. This is not to say that a fixed mast is a bad idea in a multihull; it works well and can be extremely fast. But the rotating mast provides a structurally efficient solution to a variety of problems and can be beneficial to cruising boats as well as to racing designs.

Before going any further in this discussion, I should clear up some confusion

Figure 7-1.
The most common schemes for staying a multihull's mast. A) Conventional double-spreader rig. B) No-spreader rig; shrouds led outboard. C) Modification of B; diamond shrouds hold mast in column, cap shroud led outboard. D) Rotating mast.

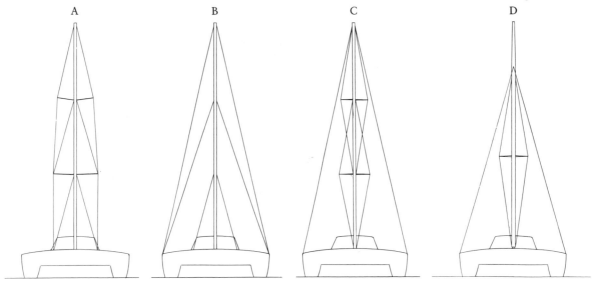

A   B   C   D

Figure 7-2.
Non-rotating mast, spreaderless rig. All shrouds lead outboard at an angle that eliminates the need for spreaders. This only works on wide boats with stiff, non-flexible crossbeams. Genoa sheets inside of upper shrouds.

Figure 7-3.
Small section, non-rotating aluminum mast held with one set of upper shrouds. Mast kept in column with multiple sets of spreaders. This works well for wide boats with flexible crossbeams.

in the terminology currently used to categorize rotating masts. At the extreme end there is the rigid *wing sail,* as used in the C-Class catamarans and the 1988 America's Cup defender *Stars and Stripes.* Because it can't be reefed, this is not a rig that I would advocate for cruising!

Scaling back the size of the rigid wing, there are a number of racing multihulls that have very large chord-length (the fore-and-aft dimension) masts equipped with soft sails that can be reefed. These are *wing masts.* The larger editions of these masts have been blamed for several capsizes in storm conditions, during which the boat became unmanageable under the large, efficient, and unreefable wing—a terrifying prospect!

A solution that works nicely for a cruising or cruising/racing multihull is sticking with the concept of an airfoil-section rotating mast, but scaling back its dimensions so that the unreefable sail area of the mast is not objectionable. For want of a better term we will call this a *rotating mast.*

Deciding what presents an objectionable amount of unreefable (or axe-reefable) sail will depend on the other characteristics and intended uses of the boat. As a general rule a mast area of less than 10 percent of total sail area seems to present no difficulties for offshore use. The smaller rotating mast sections are not that much larger than a conventional mast and, because they require far less rigging wire, the total windage of the rig in storm conditions often is less.

A rotating mast has some significant advantages for a cruising boat:

- Its larger section requires less rigging to hold it up (and thus fewer pieces to break), and often this rigging is not at all sensitive to tuning.

- Due to its efficiency, the total sail plan can be reduced in size. You will get the same power from less rig.

- At anchor, the mast presents very little windage, and there is less wire-rigging windage. Since multihulls generally have lots of wind drag at anchor anything that can be done to reduce it is welcome.

- A rotating mast can be built effectively by an amateur, since most are designed to be constructed in wood/epoxy. This means that out-of-pocket cost can be lower than for the store-bought aluminum variety, and that practically anything can be repaired with supplies carried aboard. Have you ever tried to find an inert gas welding setup in the boondocks?

A streamlined rotating mast of modest proportions also can be a very nice storm sail. I found this out firsthand during a 60-knot squall. We could sail 4 to 5 knots to windward under the tiniest scrap of jib and a trimmed mast. When the mast was "over sheeted" to the centerline and stalled, the boat

Figure 7-4.
Rotating aluminum
mast. Shrouds and
headstay attach at one
point. Small diameter
means mast must be
held in column with
multiple sets of
diamond shrouds.

Figure 7-5.
Rotating wood/epoxy
mast. Large section
reduces need for
additional wire support.

stopped. So long as the mast area is not excessive a rotating mast's ability to serve as storm sails seems to be a highly desirable trait—they can't flog themselves to pieces the way a sail can, and they are always rigged and at the ready.

The rotating mast is still evolving, and there are few standard construction details. Figure 7-8 illustrates a number of details that work well.

One nuisance that plagues all boats with rotating masts is what to do

Figure 7-6.
Full wing masts, like
this one aboard *Elf
Aquitaine*, have too
much unreefable area
and have no place on
a cruising boat.

about the invaluable masthead tricolor running light. Anyone who has lived with the tricolor knows that it has no equal for making the boat visible at night, and most would be loath to give it up. I know of two solutions to this problem.

One is prescribed by the International Regulations for the Avoidance of Collisions at Sea (COLREGS), which says that, in lieu of a tricolor, an all-round red light can be carried at least one meter above an all-round green light. Several boats have done this but I suspect the one-meter separation has not been observed.

The other solution, which after much head scratching I devised for myself, is to mount two tricolor lights one above the other, each turned 45 degrees to the boat's centerline. On starboard tack, one light is correct and turned on. On port tack the other light is switched on and the first light cut off.

Freestanding Masts

Freestanding or unstayed masts have been used on single-hulled boats for centuries. Recently they have gained popularity on a number of production monohull designs, such as Gary Hoyt's Freedom 40, and have been used in a few multihulls as well.

The first multihull that I know of to use this sort of mast was *SIB*—an

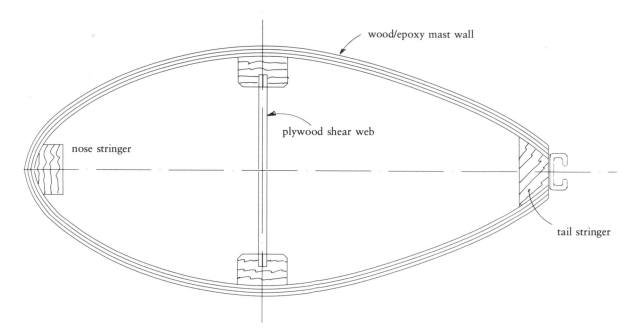

Figure 7-7A.
Rotating mast
construction.

experimental boat designed by Jim Brown and Dick Newick in 1978. I had the pleasure of building and sailing SIB (an acronym for **S**mall **I**s **B**eautiful) and was able to incorporate some of its rig's more successful features into my own *Juniper,* which I began building the following year. I was attracted to the freestanding rig by its low cost, simplicity, durability, and maneuverability under sail in close quarters. Although I have since changed *Juniper's* rig, after sailing the original unstayed rig for six years and 14,000 miles I feel that there are some applications for which it is particularly suited.

I should say first that this type of rig puts unusual loads into the hull and deck and for the most part cannot be retrofitted successfully into an existing multihull. From the bilge up, the hull and deck must be arranged to take the concentrated loads imposed by this type of spar.

The monohull presents few problems when incorporating a freestanding mast because the boat has a low righting moment (stability). Consequently, the mast will be stressed much less than the mast of a boat with dramatically higher stability such as a multihull. Consider for a moment a freestanding mast and sail embedded in a concrete slab ashore. The harder the wind blows the more energy the mast must absorb. Ultimately the mast will break at some point due to high wind velocity.

Compare this with the life of a mast in a tender monohull. As the wind velocity increases, the boat will heel, eventually laying over on her side. This presents less sail to the wind and relieves the mast from strain—quite an easy

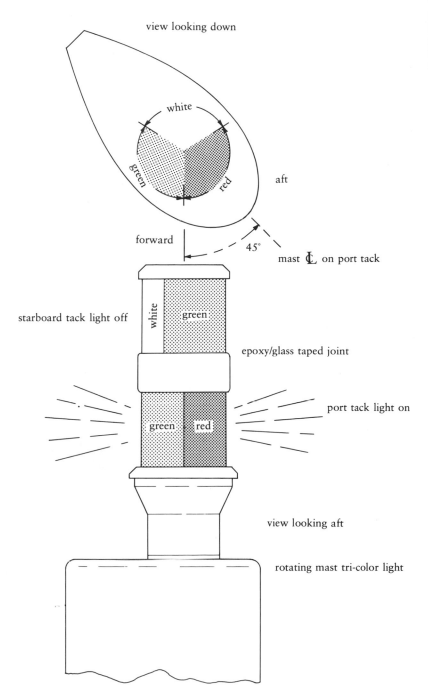

Figure 7-7B.
A scheme for dealing with the masthead tricolor on a rotating mast. The bottom light is turned on for port tack; the top light for starboard tack.

view looking down

white

green

red

aft

forward

45°

mast ℄ on port tack

starboard tack light off

white

green

epoxy/glass taped joint

green

red

port tack light on

view looking aft

rotating mast tri-color light

Figure 7-8A,B.
Rotating mast details.
A) Shroud attachment
at hounds. All wires
terminate on one big
shackle; toggles must
be used at wire ends
to allow mast rotation
without bending and
fatiguing wire. B)
Composite-construction
spreader is removable.

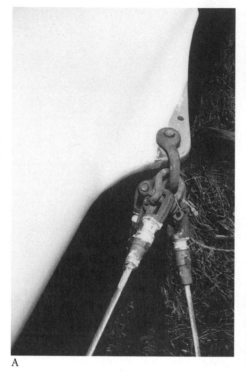

A

B

Figure 7-8C.
Mast base has tiller arm built in to control rotation
angle; composite socket is molded into mast for
freely pivoting mast step.

Figure 7-8D.
Low-friction ball mounted on deck for mast step. Mast
can rotate and be raked without binding on step.

Figure 7-8E.
Rotating mast step
fabricated from
aluminum. Halyards
lead out through base
of mast.

life compared with our first example. The strength of the mast must therefore be related to the righting moment of the boat.

Trimarans have much more stability than monohulls but at least a tri will heel some before reaching its maximum stability; this provides something of a cushion for the mast. Catamarans reach their maximum stability with very little heel, so the mast of a cat must be able to absorb lots of energy very quickly. From the standpoint of rigging loads, a cat is about as close to a block of concrete as a boat can come.

While an unstayed multihull mast must be strong it must also be stiff. A small amount of bend in the mast can be beneficial because it tends to flatten the sail, which is just what you want as the wind builds in strength. But if the mast bends more than a little, the sail starts to lose its shape and thus loses a great deal of drive. This, I feel, is the weakness of the freestanding mast for a multihull. It is extremely difficult to build a mast that is light and has the stiffness required to match the stability provided by the hull.

Juniper's masts, designed for economy, were hollow, hexagonal sections of Douglas fir that were strong enough, but too limber. Up to about 12 knots of wind the sail shape was fine, but just a little more breeze would turn our sails to bags just as *Juniper* was beginning to kick up her heels and go. We could improve sail shape by reefing early, which had the effect of stiffening the mast and flattening the sail again. Double reefed in 30 knots of true wind was always fun: the sail shape was good, the center of effort low, and the sails were far enough apart so that there was little interference between them.

Figure 7-9A,B.
A) *Juniper's* original unstayed rig. Although popular for monohulls, the unstayed rig is seldom seen on multihulls. B) The sleeve-luff sails we developed for *Juniper* worked extremely well and had a clean leading edge.

A

B

Figure 7-9C,D.
C) Standard slab reefing was employed. D) The freestanding rig will never be as powerful as a wire-stayed mast, but it is a fine long-distance cruising rig for some boats.

C

D

Juniper would scream along wonderfully in those conditions. But in light air we always wanted more power, and due to uncontrollable mast bend in medium winds, the power was there but the sail shape to handle it was not.

Increasing the stiffness of the masts by laminating carbon fiber onto them would have been one way to help overcome these drawbacks, but I was eager to try another tack all together and changed the rig entirely.

Although it is not the highest-performance rig for a multihull, the freestanding mast has some real advantages for cruising. If I were embarking on a round-the-world cruise I would seriously consider a rig of this type. If the initial design is good, the freestanding mast is extremely simple and reliable and there are very few parts to wear out. Because there are no shrouds there are few problems with sails chafing, and the sheets can be eased way out when running and broad reaching. With the wide beam of a multihull available for vangs, it's easy to control the sail shape. Reefing while running is easy because the sails can be luffed on any heading; the boat does not need to be turned upwind in a squall to get the sail down. All this results in a very efficient sail plan, ideal for blasting along shorthanded in the tradewinds.

Wood is an excellent material for freestanding masts. After all, trees are freestanding masts of a sort. Wood fiber resists fatigue very well; it is inexpensive and easy to shape. A modest quantity of carbon fiber laminated to the mast will improve the stiffness at some increase in cost. A composite mast of carbon and glass fiber similar to those used in production monohulls could be fabricated for a multihull, but the cost would be high.

A larger dimension, airfoil-shaped mast section that can rotate is one way to improve performance without resorting to expensive, all-composite construction. This will blend the larger mast into the sail to form a very efficient shape.

Designer Dick Newick, having observed the flexibility of *Juniper's* masts, built freestanding masts for his own cruising trimaran, *Pat's,* using this technique. The preliminary indications are very encouraging: The masts bend much less than would round-section masts, thereby preserving the sails' shape. There is an added complication, however: The mast must be able to rotate in its step and in the deck partners. The loads at these two places are lateral rather than axial, as is the case with a deck-stepped rotating mast, which makes the design of bearings more complicated. This problem can be solved with some clever engineering and fabrication but a good solution is likely to be costly.

Because of my experience with *Juniper* and *SIB,* I have had a few requests to design a catamaran with a freestanding rig. So far I have resisted the challenge. Designing a catamaran with unstayed masts stepped on the bridgedeck presents two problems: First is the engineering problem of how to build the supporting structure strong enough to hold up the mast. This can be done, although it may present problems in the accommodation plan. The other and more significant problem seems to be obtaining enough sail area.

In a trimaran or monohull you can use one big (and heavy) mast stepped well forward, or two smaller masts, one stepped forward and the other near amidships. Applying this concept to a large cruising cat, it would be necessary in either case to extend the bridgedeck well forward and make it deep enough to step a mast. However, this solution is likely to cause terrible motion and pounding of the underside of the bridgedeck in a seaway. It seems to me that cats are generally less suited to unstayed masts than are monos and trimarans.

Sails

From a sailmaker's perspective, a significant difference between the sails for a monohull and those for a multihull is that the multihull sails upright in consistently higher apparent wind and therefore needs sturdier sails. Advances in sailmaking technology have enabled very strong and efficient sails to be constructed without the need to resort to such exotic materials as Kevlar or Spectra. Unfortunately, because the general feeling is "a light boat is a tender boat," it often is hard to convince sailmakers without firsthand multihull experience of the need to make sails for cruising multis extra strong. Although a multi can be very light compared to a monohull, it sure isn't tender. It will stand up and sail fast in heavy winds, creating high loads in the sails.

The weight of the Dacron cloth itself should be a little heavier for a multi's sails than would be the case for a monohull's sails, but more importantly, the fibers of the cloth should be aligned properly with the greatest loads. All corners, reef points, batten pockets, and fittings must be stoutly reinforced. If you want the best sails for a multihull, find a sailmaker who is familiar with the genre.

Mainsails

A heavy, slow multihull will have a sail cut similarly to a monohull's since the boat needs lots of power and is not particularly fast. A lighter weight, higher performance cruising multi would benefit from a somewhat flatter sail because it often will be operating at higher apparent winds and closer sheeting angles.

Trimming sails differs little between multi- and monohulls except that the multihull responds more radically to sail trim, whether it is good trim or bad. Light wind and sloppy waves call for the power obtained by increasing the fullness of the sails. Strong winds and high speeds demand flat sails that create lots of lift and little heeling forces.

Full-length battens. Until very recently, full-length battens were prohibited by most monohull racing rules. Consequently they were not used by monohulls either for racing or cruising, although they have been widely used in multihull mainsails for 25 years. Their advantages have become obvious to monohull

Figure 7-10.
High speeds and limited heeling mean multihull sails must be stoutly reinforced, as seen in this mainsail headboard, and constructed of heavier cloth than comparably sized monohull sails. Note two-part halyard, which eases the task of sweating aloft the typically heavier, full-batten multihull mainsail.

cruising sailors (and sailmakers), however, and it now is rare to pick up a sailing magazine that isn't packed with advertisements extolling their wonders.

The long battens improve the sail's shape, and can increase the mainsail's area by supporting more roach, which is the area of the sail lying outside a straight line drawn from head to clew. Full-length battens also prevent the sail from flogging when hoisting, reefing, or luffing, which does wonders for the life of the sail. The addition of lazyjacks eliminates furling, which is another nice thing—particularly for the shorthanded crew.

These advantages don't come without a drawback or two, however. A sail with full-length battens is inherently more complex, and it is essential that the battens and batten hardware be properly constructed. When a sail has significant roach the full-length battens function somewhat like mini-booms; each batten is under considerable compression load from the sailcloth, which pushes the batten forward. In small boats this presents few problems; the plastic end fitting most sailmakers use works well enough. When the sail gets large, however, the batten loads increase and some means must be found to transmit the compression into the mast or sailtrack.

Until recently there were no stock fittings available for this purpose, and most sailors had to improvise with dinghy goosenecks or other modified

Figure 7-11A.
Full-length battens in a
nicely shaped mainsail.

Figure 7-11B.
Full-length battens
must be matched to
the sail and the load;
these are too limber.

A

B

Figure 7-11C.
Effect of broken
battens on a sail's
shape.

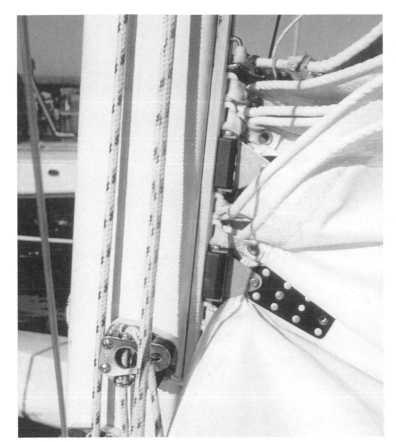

Figure 7-12. Mini-gooseneck batten end. This works well as a slide and can deal with the batten compression load.

universal joints. The recent popularity of full-length battened mainsails for monohulls has provided incentive for manufacturers to develop mass-produced batten-end fittings, like the BattSlide (Sailpower Systems, Inc. 112 Bond Court, Los Gatos, CA 95032) and other systems, so we no longer need home remedies.

The battens themselves often were owner-constructed as well, because off-the-shelf battens either were too flexible or too expensive. The preferred type are rectangular-section tapered wood battens, often made from spruce or Douglas fir skinned with uniglass and epoxy for extra stiffness. These are durable, and can always be had in the right stiffness by adjusting the taper of the wood core or the fiberglass laminate. The cost is low but they take time to make.

Now, however, inexpensive and rugged batten stock is sold by most sailmakers. A common variety is round-section fiberglass batten stock. This and the appropriate end fittings are made by Bainbridge/Aquabatten, Inc. (252 Revere St. Canton, MA 02021), a supplier to most sailmakers. The round

Figure 7-13.
Round, solid fiberglass
battens and end
fittings. A stock item —
rugged, light, and
inexpensive.

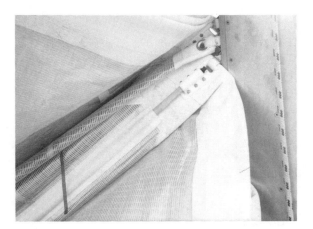 

batten stock does tend to chafe through the pockets quickly if it is allowed to rub on the shrouds, and extra caution or padding is advised.

Another batten recently developed by Rutgerson (distributed by Harken, 1251 E. Wisconsin Avenue, Pewaukee, WI 53072) is made from fiberglass using the same methods used to make snow skis. The resulting battens are fairly light and quite rugged, but are of course quite expensive.

Downwind Sails

Since most long cruises are designed along downwind routes, it is important to be able to rig sails that are effective on this point of sail. Serious cruising monohulls often employ twin poles to wing out jibs or other running sails. The poles are often carried folded up against the mast when not in use—lots of weight, windage, and complication.

A multihull can avoid these impedimentia when running or reaching by putting its great overall beam to work. All that is required is a pad eye and a snatch block, through which the jib sheets are led way outboard—no pole needed. A genoa sheeted this way becomes incredibly efficient. The multihull's inherently great speed often will bring the apparent wind up to the beam—even on a very broad reach. The sails start to "breathe" (all telltales flying), boatspeed builds, and away you go under a very simple and efficient downwind rig.

For sailing directly downwind or reaching in light air, spinnakers can be wonderful cruising sails. A multihull needs no spinnaker pole, and the sail is easy to handle because the boat is easy to steer and cannot start rhythmically rolling out of control. That beautiful invention, the spinnaker sock or squeezer, further reduces the potential for foul-ups. Even without a sock, dousing a chute is easier on a multihull because there is so much more deck on which it can come down.

Spinnakers can be set *sans* poles in several ways, but the most common—and simplest—way is to have both a guy and sheet attached to each clew. Lead the starboard guy to a pad eye on the starboard bow and the starboard sheet to a pad eye at the starboard stern. Rig it the same way on the port side and it's done. To jibe, pull down both spinnaker guys, jibe the mainsail, and sheet the spinnaker in on the appropriate side.

Spinnakers cut for reaching will get the most use on a cruising boat. The apparent wind shifts forward so fast when the boat is headed up from a dead run that a full-cut running spinnaker will have limited utility. Some skippers favor asymmetric cruising chutes, which are jibed by leaving the tack in place, letting the clew out around forward, and sheeting in on the new side. Other sailors favor symmetrical reaching spinnakers that are jibed more conventionally.

A point of debate among multihull sailors is how to sail fastest downwind. In extremely fast boats, like ice boats and high-performance racing multis, there is little doubt that "tacking" downwind produces the best results. By sailing with the true wind about 140 degrees aft of the bow, the apparent wind can be brought well ahead of the beam due to the high boat speed. The

Figure 7-14.
A multihull's wide beam means a spinnaker pole is optional equipment, making the traditionally hard-to-tame sail into one easily handled, even by short-handed crews.

Figure 7-15.
Roller-reefing headsails
make life so much
easier when it breezes
up unexpectedly. (A.
Fitzpatrick photo)

additional apparent wind increases the power to the sails and the boat goes fast enough to offset the extra distance sailed.

A performance cruising multihull probably will go faster by using the same downwind tactics, but the difference is smaller compared with running off "square." However, it is often much more comfortable to sail a series of broad reaches than a dead run. Reaching keeps the breeze moving over the cockpit and generally steering is more fun, which makes it easier to pay attention.

Storm Sails

Any cruising boats that plan to sail offshore will need storm sails or storm reefs in the working sails. Mainsails for multihulls often have a set of very deep reef points just for storm conditions. It is not unusual for this reef to be two-thirds of the way up the mainsail luff. Storm trysails can be used, of course, but it seems far easier and more practical to use the working main (so long as it is adequately reinforced) rather than mess around changing sails in a building gale.

Most cruising boats carry headsails on roller furling stays. Although this makes it possible to reef the jib with ease, it also makes it most difficult to change sails. Sheet leads that work with the jib rolled up into a very deep reef should be available. A jib that can be reduced to 25 percent of its size that flogs itself to pieces because the sheet leads are too far aft is hardly an advantage in a storm.

Cutter rigs have an advantage here; the headsail can be rolled away and a reefed staysail or storm jib carried on the forestay. In addition, staysail cloth normally is selected with heavy conditions in mind, making it better suited to storm conditions than a reefed jib of general-purpose sailcloth.

CHAPTER 8

Auxiliary Power

As was the case with rigs, I can't impart all the existing knowledge on engines. I can, however, shed some light on the ins and outs of how engines relate to multihulls.

Outboards

Nearly all cruising multihulls incorporate some kind of auxiliary power. Historically, outboard motors have been used widely in cats and tris, even in boats of great size. "Compared with inboards," goes the argument, "outboards cost less, weigh less, are easier to install, can be removed easily for servicing, and offer no parasitic drag from props and appendages when retracted."

As with anything related to boats, this issue is not quite so black and white; there are a number of compromises to be made. The good points of outboard motors come bundled with some undesirable attributes as well. To my mind, there are considerable negatives in cruising with outboard power.

The greatest problem with outboard power is finding a suitable way to mount the engine so that the prop is immersed deeply and does not ventilate (either spin free in the air or suck air down to the prop due to the lower unit's shallow immersion) in a chop. With most installations, the engine will power the boat well in a flat calm, but when maximum thrust is most needed waves will likely be present and this may render the outboard useless. In fact in some situations the outboard might be worse than useless because it will occupy the attention of the skipper, who may have other things on his mind.

The type of situation that immediately comes to mind would be when powering out of an inlet or channel. In the shelter of the breakwater everything is fine, but nearing the mouth, the tidal flow turns this into a short, steep, breaking sea. At the very time when power is wanted most the outboard starts to lift clear of the water on every wave, screaming wildly as it churns the air. With surf crashing on the rocks, other boats nearby, and all manner of hellish noises emanating from the outboard, the crew has little time to get some sail up and get the boat moving—not the most pleasant way to start the day. Of course some forethought could have prevented much of this Chinese fire drill, but I have seen this kind of situation develop too many times to think that it is rare.

The second major disadvantage to outboards for cruising boats is that they live their lives exposed to salt spray. Ultimately this shortens the engine's life span and can play havoc with the ignition system. This is especially true in installations where the engine's power head is exposed to the direct onslaught of spray and waves, which can be fierce in a powerful multihull.

Fuel storage and high fuel consumption present yet other problems. Two-cycle gasoline outboards guzzle fuel at about three times the rate of a diesel engine. Ultimately this works against the argument of "lower cost and lower weight" for outboards. And more important, gasoline presents a significant fire and explosion hazard.

As if all these drawbacks weren't enough, there is yet another problem with outboards that many of today's cruisers will be unwilling to overlook: They can't drive such wonderful accessories as mechanical refrigeration, powerful alternators, or desalinators, among others.

Despite all these negatives, multihulls will continue to incorporate outboard motors. Some boats are too small or are not designed to accept an inboard; some owners feel more comfortable with outboards; some applications, such as operation in very shoal water, are better suited for outboard power. Smaller boats benefit from the reduced weight of outboards. Catamarans can attain better maneuverability under power with one steerable outboard on-center than they can with one inboard in one hull.

Four-cycle outboards available from Yamaha and Honda can solve the high fuel consumption problem. Although gasoline remains more dangerous than diesel fuel, most multihulls can find a relatively safe place to store it. Trimarans can mount portable tanks in sheltered parts of the wing or in a vented portion of a crossbeam. Catamarans usually can incorporate a self-venting locker on the bridgedeck and thus keep gas fumes from accumulating.

Bearing all these factors in mind, here are a number of methods that have been used effectively to incorporate outboard motors for auxiliary power.

Outboard Location

Trimarans. Engine location has a great influence on the propensity of the propeller to ventilate. The farther away the engine is from the center of the boat's pitching motion the more trouble you will have.

Trimaran sterns offer a nice, spray-protected location for mounting, but are probably the worst place from the standpoint of ventilation because the stern can move up and down much more than the length of the longest

Figure 8-1A.
Stern-mounted
outboard on a sliding
bracket. Location is
spray protected, but
propeller ventilates in
a chop.

outboard shaft extension. My own 31-foot *Searunner* used a stern-mounted outboard on a retracting bracket. Motoring in a flat calm presented few problems, but once the wind was up the engine was hopeless.

A much better location is alongside the main hull, about a third of the way forward from the transom. This is normally about where the aft crossbeam is located, and this can be used to mount the engine. One problem with this location is that the power head of the engine is exposed to the full blast of water passing through the tunnel. This can be alleviated to a great extent by building a streamlined fairing into the retractable motor bracket. This permits the engine to be lowered to its full depth while shielding it from the onrush of water. A nice example of this technique is shown on Jim Brown's *Scrimshaw.*

One other problem common to this mounting location is that the engine will move up and down in a beam sea as the boat rolls and may ventilate in these conditions. The closer the engine is to the centerline of the boat the better.

Catamarans. Cruising catamarans usually mount their outboards on the centerline of the rear crossbeam. If the bridgedeck is designed so that it is very low to the water at the location of the outboard mount, this method can work quite well (although there are other reasons why a low bridgedeck is undesirable; see Chapter 4). Because the engine is on the centerline, beam seas have less of a tendency to roll it up out of the water, and the normal location of the crossbeam is far enough forward to alleviate some of the pitch-related ventilation.

On cats with higher underwing (bridgedeck) clearance, problems develop when the outboard is lowered on a bracket, which makes it vulnerable to wave action washing through the tunnel. In addition, the lowered engine is largely inaccessible, and that creates difficulties in starting. As in the case of a trimaran with the engine mounted on the side of the main hull, the best solution seems to be the integration of a streamlined fairing into the bracket structure.

Some builders take this a step further and build a *sled*. This amounts to a small boat in itself, which mounts the engine(s) on its stern and is allowed to float on the surface of the water, thereby decoupling the motion of the boat from the outboard. The forward end of the sled is hinged to the boat and the whole business is fully retractable. This system is reported to work very well. I have even seen one inventive cat owner whose sled and dinghy were one and the same.

Integral wells. One other outboard mount to consider is a well built into the hull. This entails building a "hole" in the boat into which the motor can be

Figure 8-1B.
Side-mounted outboard bracket pivots back and up. This operates better in a chop than stern-mounted outboard, but the engine's powerhead is exposed to the full blast of water passing between the hulls.

Figure 8-1C.
Preferred method of side-mounting an outboard. Engine is well-protected by the streamlined bracket. Jim Brown designed and built this one for his well-traveled *Scrimshaw*.

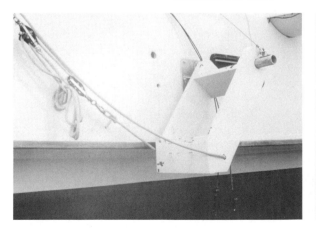

Figure 8-2A.
Typical catamaran outboard installation is straight forward. Note the lines running from the twin rudders of this Gemini to the outboard. This turns the motor along with the rudders, considerably aiding steering. Line is tensioned when outboard is lowered; slack when outboard is raised.

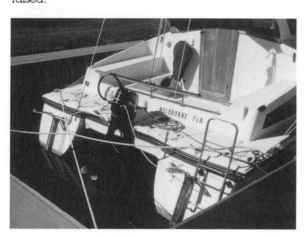

Figure 8-2B.
Outboards have been used on large-scale cats, too. *Skyjack* mounts 65 horses on a retractable bracket.

dropped with the prop protruding through the bottom of the hull. When not in use, the engine is retracted and a false bottom plug dropped into the hole to eliminate the turbulence that would ensue if left open. If properly constructed, the bottom is perfectly smooth with the engine up.

This method has been used most successfully on trimarans. Lately, however, several cats, including the *Banshee* and the updated *Iroquois* from Carlson Marine, have mounted large outboards in purpose-designed wells in the sterns with some success. The high-powered (high gas consumption also, I imagine) craft can even tow water-skiers.

When the appropriate type of outboard motor is employed—one that can blow the exhaust out in the prop wash—there are some advantages to the engine-well approach. For one, the outboard is completely sheltered from wave action, and it is less prone to ventilation because it is mounted on the centerline and can be immersed deeply. Another plus is that it looks nicer not to have an eggbeater hanging off the side of a cruising boat. The downside is that this method cuts into valuable accommodation space, and it can be awkward to retract the motor and close up the hole because the motor has to come up quite high in order to drop in the bottom plug. Oh, if there were only the perfect solution!

With care, outboard installations can be quite successful. But the problem with so many of them is that they contradict the original reasons for choosing an outboard: low cost, easy installation, and light weight.

Inboard Diesels

The vast majority of single-hulled cruising sailboats are fitted with inboard diesel auxiliary engines. There are many good reasons to install a diesel engine in a multihull and fewer reasons than ever before not to. Ten years ago diesel engines were quite heavy, and many designers were understandably unenthusiastic about dropping a big chunk of iron into the bilge of a lightweight flyer. Now, with the advent of the new breed of lightweight, high-speed marine diesels, this situation has changed dramatically. Engine weights are now in the

Figure 8-3A.
Trimaran with outboard well. When sailing, motor is retracted and a plug inserted to fair the hull.

Figure 8-3B.
Retracting the motor (or removing it for service) is eased by a multipart tackle.

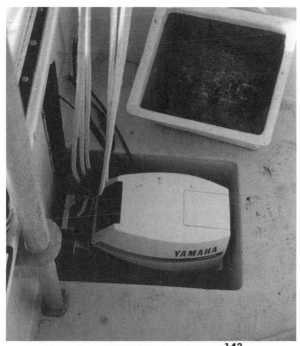

143
Auxiliary Power

Figure 8-3C. Yamaha 4-cycle 9.9 h.p. features a removable twist-grip throttle that can be mounted remotely. This, along with a big propeller and a high-output alternator, make it an ideal outboard for small- to medium-sized multihulls.

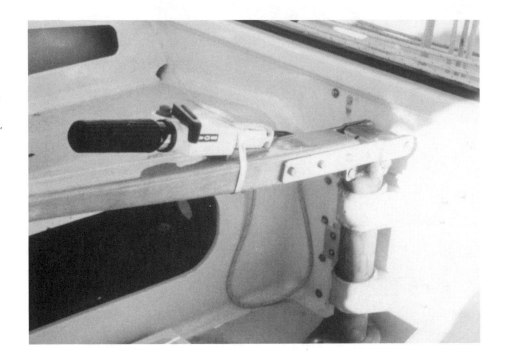

range of 15 pounds per horsepower—even better with turbocharging—and this is quite reasonable when you consider a diesel's low fuel consumption, its ability to drive accessories, and the small horsepower needed to push a multihull up to "get there" speeds.

Multihull Specifics

There are few differences between a ballasted boat and a multihull in the installation of inboard engines, other than the very convenient fact that the engine itself usually can be modest in size and still provide a good turn of speed. Determining boat speed with different power combinations depends on many factors, but as a general rule of thumb a comfortable minimum for a boat intended primarily for sailing is 1 h.p. for every 500 pounds of displacement. A catamaran motorsailer could easily go to several times that horsepower.

Engine location. Engine installation in trimarans is essentially the same as in monohulls. A cruising catamaran, however, has a number of options available. By using a Sonic outdrive leg (see below), the engine can be placed on the bridgedeck. It is also possible to link one engine hydraulically to two props. This permits one engine to be located anywhere in the boat and still drive two propellers. The most common installation seems to be twin engines, however:

one in each hull. Although this is the most desirable way to power a cruising cat, it certainly is not the least expensive.

For catamaran owners who can afford it, a twin-engine installation's widely separated twin screws provide the highest degree of maneuverability attainable under power. The turning leverage developed by the wide propeller separation is incredible; much better than a twin-screw power boat. With one engine in forward and the other in reverse, the boat will turn, and turn fast. You can actually spin the boat in its own length with no forward motion, giving you full control under any conditions. Anyone who has taken a big multihull into the confines of a small yacht basin on a breezy day will appreciate this feature.

As an economy measure, cats sometimes mount only one engine in one hull. There is nothing wrong with this; a very slight imbalance of the helm under power will result but it presents no problem. The weight disparity between hulls can usually be addressed by locating other heavy things, like auxiliary storage batteries, on the engineless side.

Figure 8-4B.
Many larger catamarans, like this Prout Q50, mount a diesel in each hull, giving extraordinary maneuverability. (Photo courtesy Prout)

Figure 8-4A.
Juniper's diesel is mounted below the cabin sole, similar to a monohull.

Outdrive legs. An interesting solution to the engine-mounting problem on a catamaran is a long, retractable outdrive leg. The only manufacturer of which I am aware at this time is Sillette Ltd. of Great Britain (Beverley Trading Estate, 190/192 Garth Rd., Morden, Surrey SM4 4LU England). Their Sonic outdrive leg is standard equipment on Prout Catamarans; it is steerable, retracts, and comes in several sizes to suit larger or smaller engines. This unit allows normal diesel engines, with all their advantages, to be mounted on the bridgedeck, where the engine is easily accessible and out of the accommodations.

Propellers. The Achilles heel of any inboard engine is the system that transmutes engine power into the thrust required to move the boat. Hanging a fixed, two-bladed propeller (or, Heaven forbid, a three-blader) from the bottom of a sleek multihull is worse than dragging buckets behind the boat.

PROPELLERS MOST FOUL

One of my pet peeves is propellers left unprotected by antifouling paint. Anything growing on a propeller blade will dramatically reduce its effectiveness. The slightest slime will knock 10 to 15 percent off your speed under power. The typical jungle growth will take off 40 percent or more. And if there are barnacles, forget it—put on a mask and fins and scrape them off!

In New England, single-hulled boats normally are fitted with huge diesel inboards, which doesn't exactly do wonders for their sailing qualities. A friend of mine bought an older boat that had been repowered with an engine rated at twice the horsepower the boat should require to get to hull speed. To compound problems, the boat had been fitted with a big, three-bladed fixed prop. After owning the boat a few weeks he complained that his boat would barely do five knots under power, and that the prop must be wrong or the engine too small. That the prop might be a ball of weed and barnacles never crossed his mind.

This is the prevailing view: Put in a bigger engine or change the prop if the boat doesn't go fast enough. I expect this is encouraged by the boatyards, who would be just as happy to sell and install a new engine. But there is an easy solution that is so painfully obvious few take the trouble to do it: *Coat the prop with antifouling paint.* The conventional wisdom is that it "won't stick" or that the paint will "wash off" in a short time. But if the antifouling is applied properly this just isn't true.

The method I have used with success is buying the correct primer, such as Interlux "Viny-lux Prime Wash," which is a zinc-chromate primer, and following the directions exactly. This will chemically prepare the metal surface for the paint and allow it to stick. Next, I coat the prop with a hard antifouling paint, like Petit "Unepoxy," and follow this with two coats of the most effective soft antifouling paint. Our prop on *Juniper* has remained clean and effective for more than two years at a stretch when painted this way. Without antifouling paint we must scrub it frequently or performance suffers.

Next time you are wandering around the boatyard, look at the condition of the propellers. I'll bet not one in ten is protected with antifouling.

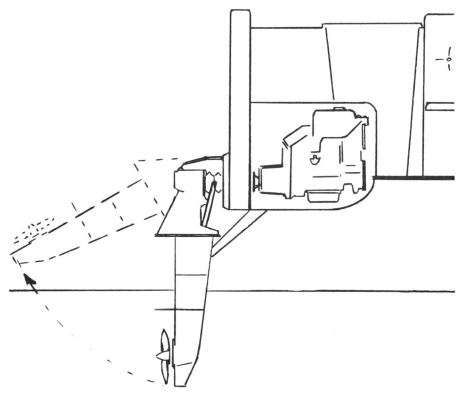

Figure 8-5.
Sonic outdrive leg allows catamarans to mount a diesel engine on the bridgedeck, making it readily accessible, keeping engine drippings out of the boat, and eliminating prop drag while sailing.(Photo courtesy Sillette Ltd.)

The extreme turbulence caused by a fixed prop will reduce the effectiveness of the rudder and make high-speed sailing practically impossible.

Performance sailboats almost uniformly mount a folding or feathering propeller so that the prop causes minimal drag when not in use, and this is even more essential on a multihull. Fortunately, folding and feathering props are reliable, off-the-shelf items, and quite efficient provided they are kept clean (see sidebar).

Prop grounding protection. Most monohulls have a keel or hull that is considerably deeper than the propeller, and this protects the prop from damage when the boat grounds. A multihull with retractable boards and rudders, however, may leave the prop quite vulnerable in a grounding. This should be considered in the design of the underbody, propeller shaft, and struts. By careful juggling of components and possibly the addition of a small deadwood rub strake on the bottom of the hull, it often is possible to obtain some hull protection for the propeller and shaft. If this cannot be done, then it may be wise to consider an extra-stout shaft and strut.

Water intake. Another consideration particular to multihulls is the location of the cooling water intake. While heeling usually will not present a problem in keeping the intake below the waterline, it is possible that pitching or wave action may cause air to be ingested into the cooling line. For this reason it is still desirable to get the cooling intake as low as practical in the hull and away from the transom, where it is more likely to pitch up out of the water.

The Specifics of Multihull Construction

CHAPTER 9

Costs: Comparing Apples to Apples

The yachting press is full of "How to Buy a Boat" articles, many of which provide off-the-cuff rules for determining approximate cost. One of my favorites is that a boat should cost so much per pound—like hamburger. Maybe I should try going into the chandlery and asking for ten pounds of self-tailing winches.

Give up the idea of trying to establish cost by a boat's (especially a multihull's) weight. *Lighter boats usually cost more.* The lightest boats often cost the most; the heaviest hulls often cost the least (steel boats are a good example). Shakespeare said, " . . . all comparisons are odious." They also are tedious and usually inaccurate.

Comparing the cost of monohulls with multihulls in a general way is of little use. The only valid cost comparisons are made between one specific boat and another, empirically taking into account differences in performance, accommodation, or construction.

For a seagoing boat, construction is everything. If poorly or inadequately built, the best design in the world isn't worth the paper the plans are printed on. This has been a problem with multihulls throughout their modern history: a steady stream of shoddily constructed abominations. By and large, one common factor links all these poorly built cats and tris: *Their owners assumed they were cheap boats!* Let me shout it from the masthead for all to hear: *MULTIHULLS ARE NOT INHERENTLY CHEAP BOATS!*

The standard multihull sales pitch, "multihulls are cheaper," has been said so often that many people who know better still say it out of habit. Professional boatbuilders, who have to estimate construction costs accurately if they hope to stay in business, all know that there is nothing cheap about building two or three hulls linked together with intricate crossbeams.

Despite all the evidence to the contrary, however, people in this business still make this claim. Is there *any* truth to it?

A grain of truth, maybe, under certain circumstances. If more than anything else you want to sail fast, you can buy a small multihull with little or no accommodation that will sail at 15 to 20 knots. A monohull that could reach the same speeds would have to be very large and expensive; it also would be a very different sort of boat. Is this a valid comparison? I don't think so. Does it make the multihull "cheaper?" No.

Another expression of the cheap boat hard-sell comes from the manufacturers of some of the more commodious cruising catamarans, who tout their boats as having the "most accommodation for the money." This may well be true. Despite relatively small overall dimensions, these catamarans offer a huge block of uninterrupted volume within a central bridgedeck cabin. Coupled with the living space in the hulls, the habitable space can be enormous. Ipso facto, big interior plus small overall size equals cheap boat. But the all-around sailing performance of these boats often is below that of a comparably priced monohull. Does this mean the multihull is still cheap? It is if you don't value sailing performance. But enhanced performance often is the reason a multihull is chosen in the first place.

"They are cheap because you can build them yourself," is another argument made on behalf of low-budget multihulls. Granted, building your own boat can save you money because you supply the labor—the largest portion of a boat's cost. But this is equally true for any boat, no matter how many hulls it has. Because many monohulls can utilize construction techniques and materials that are decidedly less sophisticated than those necessary for the average multihull, home building a monohull can be even cheaper than building a multihull.

A big, cheap boat would best be built from steel, with a flat bottom and slab sides—something like a barge. Cut a tree for the mast, buy some used sails, and off you go. It's big as a house, strong like bull, and believe it or not, a barge can be made to sail tolerably well by cruising monohull standards. More than a few fancy yachts have been embarrassed by a big, sprit-rigged sailing barge bombing along down the Thames.

The bottom line is that all good boats cost real money to build, usually more money than their owners want to admit. Why? Materials are expensive. Pick up the hardware catalogs, price a piece of stainless steel, or an engine or sails, or quality material of any kind. It adds up fast. A well-built cruising boat, even if you build it yourself, will not be cheap.

A critical mistake often made by first-time boatbuilders, in many cases misguided by their "designer," is to reduce hull construction cost by using inferior materials. Nothing could be worse than jeopardizing the very foundation of your boat by incorporating questionable materials into its permanent structure.

Any part of the boat that cannot be thrown over the side and replaced must be of high structural quality—not necessarily the most expensive, but reliable, proven goods. If you want to save money, and who doesn't, leave off the gadgets. Knotmeters, for example, are expensive and practically worthless for navigation. The dollars saved by this sort of economy alone will pay the difference between exterior- and marine-grade plywood for all but the largest boats.

There is another side to building cheaply: What will this boat be worth when it is finished? The used-boat market has any number of home-constructed, cheaply built boats—both mono and multi—that generally sell below the cost of materials, if they can be sold at all. In contrast, a well-constructed owner-built boat often will sell secondhand for enough money to cover all of the material expenses and allow the owner a working wage for his time.

I have built two cruising trimarans for my own use. The first, a 31-footer, was a smaller boat than I really wanted but I felt that it was as much as I could afford at the time. The boat was designed lightly, and my inexperience led me to substitute questionable materials for various components. Consequently, after years of work I owned a too-small boat of suspect durability—one in which I had little interest in making long-term improvements.

I built my next boat, *Juniper*, with a completely different mind-set. I knew exactly what I wanted—a big, powerful, offshore-capable boat, built ruggedly enough to last my lifetime. All my effort went into constructing the basic platform to meet these needs. To keep down costs, I initially left off all items that were not strictly essential. Sure, we had a few years of Spartan cruising, but at least I felt I had a boat under me that was worth improving.

Every year *Juniper* gets a new goodie or two, and after eight years of sailing she is looking well equipped and finely finished. The alternative was to build much smaller or not as well, neither of which appealed to me. As a basic approach to economical amateur building, I highly recommend taking this sort of long-range view. The payoff comes in the enjoyment of a fine, well-built vessel that requires minimal maintenance.

The Amateur Boatbuilder

Amateur builders, home builders, backyard builders—call them what you will—have been the mainstay of multihull development since the days of Arthur Piver. There are many reasons why individuals build their own boats, but most often it is because they want a certain type of boat and building it themselves is the only way they can afford it. The largest portion of the cost of a custom-built boat is labor; providing this yourself may bring an otherwise unaffordable boat within reach.

The Keys to Success

Building your own boat on your own time in your own shop is one of the great pleasures and challenges available to modern man. A cruising boat is by nature an extremely complex vehicle that incorporates a diversity of systems, and building it from scratch is intellectually stimulating in the extreme. But it is also hard—sometimes very dull—work that occasionally can be totally

Figure 9-1A.
Building your own boat is hard but rewarding work; the long hours often can produce results superior to production-line boats.

Figure 9-1B.
First-time boatbuilders can do beautiful work. The tarp and electrical conduit shelter covering this wood/epoxy *Juniper II* trimaran is one type of easily constructed shelter that works well in most climates. Don't try to build outdoors (unless you live in the desert).

exasperating and frustrating. Building a boat is not for those seeking instant gratification; all benefits are deferred until launch day.

The amount of time you will need to build your own boat depends on many factors, but the successful projects that I know about usually share common elements. To succeed you must:

- *Make time for boatbuilding.* Cruising boat construction is measured in *thousands* of hours. It is difficult to get anything done in an hour or two; real progress depends on being able to work for long periods without interruption. Those who work jobs with rotating schedules that allow them to devote longer blocks of time to the boat do well. If you can get several months at a time to work on the boat, so much the better. Your mental health will depend on seeing progress, and a hired helper often will speed construction far out of proportion to his cost. Some builders carry this a step further and in essence become their own contractors, hiring help as they see fit. If you can afford it, the addition of a qualified boatbuilder and a helper or two can really make a project fly.

- *Have a place to work.* A weatherproof, well-lit shop is critical. Your requirements will depend, of course, on the local climate. Obviously you will need a more elaborate structure in Maine than in Southern California. Looks are not important; I have seen some awfully nice boats rolled out of some very dilapidated buildings. What is important is keeping out the rain and wind and controlling the temperature. Modern boatbuilding materials just do not work at freezing temperatures, nor do fingers. Long, late hours are part of the process, so good lighting will pay for itself in short order. Having enough space to work efficiently also will pay big dividends. A workable shop will constitute a considerable part of the total cost for the project, but as with everything else in boatbuilding, a little money spent now will save much grief later. Do not be tempted to build a boat in the open; progress will slow to a crawl and quality will suffer.

- *Maintain your equilibrium.* Personality plays a great part in determining how long a boatbuilding project will take. One builder may accomplish in nine months what another builder needs five years to do. Everyone has his own idea of what is "good enough." This is one of the beauties of amateur building: You build to satisfy your own tastes. But individuals who worry excessively about every minor detail, often backtracking and redoing things that were fine to start with, are doing themselves no favor. Sometimes you must

The Specifics of Multihull Construction

force yourself to forge ahead and realize that perfection in boats—or life—is an illusive goal.

Construction Materials

Wood/Epoxy

Until recently, all boats and ships were built from wood or plant products. What else is as strong, lightweight, easily worked, and grows all around us in constantly replenishing supply?

As ships became larger and large trees became more scarce, steel gradually replaced wood for large commercial vessels. Because it could be molded quickly and profitably when done on a large scale, plastic quickly replaced wood for pleasure and small commercial boats.

What is wrong with wood? In the traditional form of plank-on-frame construction it results in a heavy (too heavy for a multihull), high-cost, high-maintenance vessel. To achieve substantial durability the timber used must be of the highest quality, and this is becoming more difficult to find in the large dimensions required. There are still traditionally built wooden boats around, but more and more they are the domain of cult groups intent on keeping the old ways alive.

The harbor I live next to has a number of finely built traditional wooden sailboats. Every time I walk into the boatyard another one is being stripped down and painted—year after year, strip and paint, strip and paint. It's as bad as owning the Verrazano Bridge; by the time you paint your way to one end it's time to turn around and start over. If this were the only type of boat I could own I think I would take up golf.

As a quick look around just about any harbor will reveal, most people feel this way about traditional wooden boats. They may be beautiful, but unless you're more into maintenance than sailing, most people now prefer to avoid them. This is unfortunate because there are other forms of wooden construction that are both extremely durable and as low-maintenance as anything available.

By gluing multiple layers of wood together and coating the exposed surface with resins that prevent the absorption of water, a composite material results that has characteristics completely unlike traditional wooden boats. Instead of a basket-work of hundreds of pieces tentatively held together with screws and bolts, the hull of a modern, laminated wooden boat becomes a single unit, with no seams to leak, no joints to work loose, and no fasteners to corrode. Because air and water cannot circulate freely into the cell structure of the wood, rot is effectively eliminated.

Epoxies are by far the most effective resins for gluing wood and preventing moisture absorption. Epoxies are tough and stick well to most materials, including wood. Anyone who has ever tried to fix a broken household item

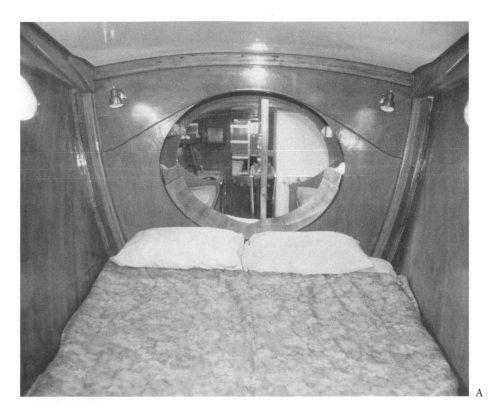

Figure 9-2A,B.
Wood/epoxy
construction produces
a boat that combines
the strength, warmth,
and personality of
wood with the
low-maintenance
characteristics of
impersonal fiberglass.

A

B

Figure 9-2C.
Bridgedeck of a large
cruising cat under
construction using
wood/epoxy.

with hardware store "glue" will be amazed at the ease with which dissimilar materials can be stuck together with epoxy resin.

In the past, obtaining an effective bond with most woodworking glues required that the pieces of wood fit together precisely and be clamped under pressure. Obtaining a 100-percent joint with epoxy requires only that the pieces be in contact. This speeds construction considerably because the fits are less important, and Rube Goldbergesque clamping arrangements needn't be devised for each joint.

The developers of the method, the Gougeon Brothers of Bay City, Michigan, called this wood/epoxy composite construction the WEST System, and now sell a specially formulated epoxy resin and other related products (WEST System, Gougeon Brothers, Inc., P.O. Box X908, Bay City, MI 48707).

The process of epoxy-laminating layers of wood together and coating them with a surface skin of epoxy effectively stops the swelling and contracting that wood undergoes when its moisture content changes. As an engineering material wood has some very desirable properties. Once its disadvantages are overcome, as they are in wood/epoxy construction, the benefits of wood become obvious.

Cost. Since wood really does grow on trees, it is a renewable and energy-efficient resource, generally inexpensive compared with other boatbuilding materials. Lumber of the quality required for laminated construction is widely available. Because big pieces are glued together from smaller pieces the problems of finding large or long timbers are avoided. The laminating process minimizes the effects of a defect (knot, pitch pocket, or grain run-out) that might be in any one piece, thus perfectly clear stock is not required.

Because the inability of air and moisture to circulate into the cell structure makes the wood immune to rot, species of wood that are not inherently rot-resistant (and thus less expensive) can be used. All of these factors combine to make wood/epoxy construction a very practical and economical method for building one-off boats.

Durability. Wood has a very high strength-to-weight ratio, a characteristic that makes it a particularly suitable material for multihull construction. It is possible to build a stronger, lighter boat from wood/epoxy than from any but the most expensive composite materials. In particular, wood excels at withstanding the constant repeated loads that a boat experiences over a long lifetime.

All materials get weaker (fatigue) with use. In the laboratory, materials are tested by stretching and compressing a sample in a machine that accurately measures the load applied and counts the number of cycles before failure occurs. By testing samples over millions of stress cycles, a curve can be drawn to illustrate how a material loses strength with use (see Figure 9-3).

Wood/epoxy composite performs remarkably well under such testing. After

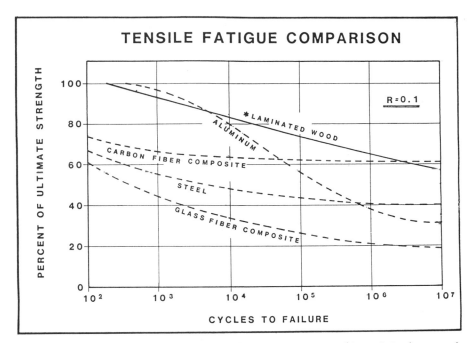

Figure 9-3.
Tensile fatigue comparison of common boatbuilding materials. (Courtesy Gougeon Brothers)

10 million stress cycles, wood retains almost 60 percent of its original strength. By comparison, steel, which is regarded as an extremely reliable structural material, degrades to 40 percent of its ultimate strength, and fiberglass composite, the most common of all boatbuilding materials, is reduced to 20 percent of its original strength.

Wood does not deteriorate from cyclical loading as badly as most other materials and thus does not need to be overbuilt to have a long, useful life. But there is another side to the fatigue curve that is not evident on the chart, and that is how the different materials behave in the real world of salt water. Very little testing has been done on how corrosive salt water affects the endurance of boatbuilding materials, but preliminary evidence suggests that steel, aluminum, and fiberglass fare much worse than wood/epoxy in the marine environment.

Fiberglass has been touted for so long for its low maintenance and great durability that there is a general feeling that nothing else can compare. This is particularly true for modern wood construction, which conjures up images of rotten planks, peeling paint, and leaky hulls in the minds of many who are familiar with traditional wooden boats. "A wooden boat?" people say. "Forget it."

But a well-constructed wood/epoxy boat is extremely durable and as low maintenance as any fiberglass boat. As an example I can cite the maintenance record of my own wood/epoxy trimaran. We launched *Juniper* eight and a half years ago, and have since sailed her to the Caribbean and cruised the East Coast of the U.S. and Canada extensively, from the lower Chesapeake to Nova

Scotia. Except for one winter spent in the tropics and one winter hauled out in a boatyard, *Juniper* remains in the water year round, locked in the ice for a portion of the winter. I have done *all* of the maintenance on this boat so I know exactly what has been done and what hasn't.

MAINTENANCE

The hulls of a well-built boat require incredibly little maintenance. More than 90 percent of the maintenance effort goes into keeping winches greased, engines running, and sails repaired. The hull and deck structure seldom need attention so long as they were built properly to start with. Of course the day will come when the bottom paint is worn off and needs recoating, and the boat must be hauled. What do you do with a boat that is 20 to 30 feet wide?

Haulouts are not really the problem they are made out to be. Granted, the little boatyard you've dealt with for 10 years may be unable to haul a multihull with its small TraveLift, but a little looking usually will turn up a place not too far away.

Boatyards equipped with cranes are a good bet. In a pinch you can always hire one to come to you. Most new multihulls are launched with a crane.

A few *very* wide TraveLifts are around; one near my office can accept hulls up to 40 feet wide. Some boatyards have marine railways that can accept very wide hulls. Look to see where the commercial fishermen haul out.

A big trailer and a launching ramp can handle all but the very largest boats. Most professional boat haulers use slick hydraulic-powered trailers that can slide right under a hull and brace it up in a matter of minutes. Trimarans can be braced more or less like a monohull; cats often can be picked up at the crossbeams or bulkheaded portions of the underwing.

And there is always the beach. You'll need more than one tide to get the bottom cleaned, painted, and dried, but some clever rigging combined with brute force can move quite a large boat up the beach far enough to stay dry. A two-part tackle coupled to a pickup truck could likely pull a 35-foot multihull up a shallow beach. More purchase, obviously, could move a larger boat.

I have her hauled out for a few days every other year for a bottom painting. (I use the multiyear antifouling paints.) A few years ago I repainted the topsides with linear polyurethane (which will hold its gloss as long as fiberglass gelcoat), because the bargain-basement paint I had used originally was fading badly. I have filled a few dings and scratches, mostly caused by other boats (we have been run into twice while at anchor!). That's the hull's complete maintenance record. To this day she has never leaked a drop, except for a drip now and then through the propeller stuffing box. There is no rot. There are no stress cracks; no delaminations; no checks or peeling paint — *anywhere*. The structure is every bit as sound today as the day she was launched. Very few fiberglass or metal boats of equally light weight can claim as much. A wooden boat? Absolutely, if it is a properly engineered, wood/epoxy composite.

Aesthetics. There is another side to wooden boats, both in the shop and on the water. Wood is a wonderful material with which to surround oneself, and it is a wonderful material with which to work. Less toxic or irritating than most components of fiberglass, and without the hazardous gases produced when welding metal boats, wooden construction minimizes the potential health risks inherent in boatbuilding.

Often, during the grind of construction, you'll come upon a magnificent plank, clear of knots, straight grained, a beautifully efficient structural material produced by nature. You stop for a few minutes and count the annual rings—maybe 30 per inch in a ten-inch-wide plank of old-growth Douglas fir. The plank, you surmise, was from a thousand-year-old tree. For one thousand years this wood was part of a tremendous living structure standing hundreds of feet high, constantly flexing and bending, exposed to violent winds, and still it stood. And now you have rescued it from the lumberyard, where its certain fate was to be butchered into a porch floor. Its use now will be dynamic rather than static; it will become part of a crossbeam designed to utilize the fantastic properties of this wonderful material to the fullest. It feels good when you touch it; it smells good when you cut it . . . . Miracle fiber **W** some call it. I don't know anyone who feels this way about fiberglass.

Epoxy. A substantial portion, often as much as 15 percent, of a laminated boat's weight will be epoxy. Epoxy is not particularly wonderful stuff to work with. While it does not smell as strongly as polyester resin, it does have an odor in its liquid state that can bother some people. Liquid epoxy resin—particularly the catalyst—irritates skin, and some boatbuilders develop an allergic reaction after repeated exposure. It is important to work clean when using epoxy. Smart builders avoid health problems by wearing disposable surgical gloves and coveralls, and by using respirators or forced ventilation.

It would be nice to build boats from wood alone, with no chemicals required, but this is the price we pay for high-performance, low-maintenance structures. (Epoxy itself will be addressed in greater detail later in this chapter.)

Figure 9-4.
Chined, sheet plywood construction has been popular for multihulls for years, but the hull shapes that can be produced are limited, the chines create drag-producing turbulence, the framework consumes precious accommodation space, and the "busy" interiors abound with nooks and crannies that are difficult to keep clean.

Sheet Plywood

Sheet plywood is a wonderfully strong and versatile material. A quality marine panel is very durable, free of internal voids, and subject to stringent manufacturing controls that ensure permanent, waterproof bonds between the multiple plies of lumber veneer.

In the early days of multihulls, many designers tried to save their clients money by encouraging the use of common exterior-grade plywood for hull construction. Whether this was a wise practice at that time can be debated, but it certainly isn't a wise practice now. Basing a yacht's very foundation on questionable materials seems quite a gamble. And questionable material accurately describes today's exterior grades of plywood, the manufacturing standards for which have declined substantially over the years.

Marine ply, on the other hand, is consistently high in quality, and consistently higher in price. Bought in quantity, marine ply is about 50 percent more expensive than an exterior-grade panel of the same lumber species. This sounds like a lot of extra money, but in reality it may increase the *total* cost of materials for the boat only five percent—easy to swallow considering the assured quality.

There are places to save money and places to buy quality, even in an economy boat.

Plywood comes in flat, generally 4 × 8-foot sheets. Boat hulls are anything but flat, thus the plywood must be shaped over a framework. Plywood can be bent easily in one direction to obtain simple curvature. Small amounts of compound curvature (curvature in two directions) can be forced into plywood fairly easily, but the plywood will tell you quickly when it can be bent no more. For this reason, most hulls designed for sheet plywood construction are either simple vee-sections or incorporate one or several chines.

Simple vee-section hulls. Catamarans by English designer James Wharram have used the simple vee-section sheet plywood construction for decades. The ubiquitous Wharram cats can be found in most of the world's cruising harbors, and many hundreds, possibly thousands, have been built. The Wharram cats remind many people of the humble Volkswagen bug, not so much in their looks, but in their numbers, raw simplicity, and the dedication of their owners.

Certainly a vee-section hull is easy to build, and therein lies its appeal. It does have some drawbacks, however. The shape is acceptable for long, lightly loaded hulls, but a problem arises in a quest for higher performance or increased payload: The designer can't add volume (displacement) to the hull where it is most needed.

In addition, a vee-section hull has high wetted surface for its displacement, which hinders light-air sailing. Because the distribution of displacement along the length of the hull is less than ideal, problems with hobbyhorsing (pitching) and high-speed sailing can surface.

All this being said, the vee-section hull should not be discarded out of hand. As long as the designer understands and allows for the imposed limitations of the hull form, vee-section designs can produce a perfectly serviceable boat.

Chined hull. By incorporating single or double chines, a simple vee-bottom hull can be substantially modified. If designed carefully, a chined hull can closely approximate the shape of a round-bottomed hull and still be built from sheet plywood. The popular Jim Brown/John Marples Searunner trimarans utilized a double-chine that permitted a fine entry, full midsection, and "U"-section stern. In addition, the Searunners were among the first boats to use fiberglass-taped chines, which allow the builder to round off the "corner" of the chine, lessening their drag substantially.

But fish don't have chines. Ultimately, the most efficient shape for a fast cruising sailboat is a smooth hull free of radical bumps or ridges. And there is another consideration to take into account if you are contemplating a simple sheet plywood hull: resale value. Sad but true, a chined hull says "homebuilt" to a prospective buyer. Even if the boat were magnificently constructed using the finest materials available, brokers and potential buyers almost invariably relegate chined-hull boats to a lower class of yacht.

Compounded plywood. The compounded plywood method is an interesting technique for rapidly constructing beautiful and very lightweight round-bottomed hulls from sheet plywood. By carefully but forcefully torturing large plywood panels, it is possible to force them to assume shapes having considerable compound curvature.

In a nutshell, flat sheets of plywood are scarfed together into two big sheets (one for each side of the hull) the size of the final hull. The sheets are trimmed to the correct "boat" shape, wired or taped together along the keel edge, and spread apart, like opening a book. The two sides are then bonded together down the keel line using thickened epoxy and fiberglass tape. After the rugged keel joint cures, the sides are pulled forcefully toward one another, torturing compound curvature into the plywood skin until it assumes the desired shape. The addition of some frames and deck beams hold things together, and *voilà*: there's your boat.

The innovative Gougeon Brothers have used this technique to build racing and cruising trimarans up to about 35 feet long. It is a method that speaks to the needs of multihull construction; the hulls are light, long, and narrow. Some "eyeball" construction skills are required, but the materials are inexpensive and a hull can be produced in short order.

Figure 9-5A.
Compounded plywood construction in miniature. This model's sides have been bonded together at the keel and spread apart.

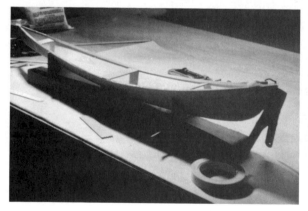

Figure 9-5B.
Hull sides are forced together into deck jig. This action tortures compound curvature into the topsides, making them very stiff and strong.

There are some limitations that hinder this method's usefulness for cruising-size boats. First, because thick plywood is too difficult to compound, there is a practical limit to the size of hull that can be built. I have designed floats for a 42-foot cruising tri using the compounded plywood technique but that is about as big a hull as I am willing to try. Second, there are substantial constraints on the possible shape of the hull: It must be narrow in relation to its length, often too narrow for the desired cruising accommodation. Third, the hull shape is the least predictable of all construction methods, which can create all sorts of problems in building a large cruising boat where many things have to fit into the hull just right.

Molded Plywood

The way to build a laminated wood hull of *any* desired shape—round bottom, flared bows, streamlined topsides and decks—is to erect a framework of bulkheads, temporary frames, and stringers, and cover it with multiple layers of thin planking glued together. This is molded plywood construction, today often called cold-molding. This distinguishes it from the hot-molding process used during World War II, when lightweight boats and airplanes (the British

Figure 9-6.
Multiple layers of diagonal planking held in an epoxy matrix produce a light, very strong boat with a "clean" interior that needs few supporting frames. It does require a fairly elaborate male mold over which to lay up the planks, however, and each plank has a slightly different shape and must be spiled.

Figure 9-7.
Constant Camber
construction forms a
frameless hull from
giant, custom-made
sheets of compound-
curved plywood
buttstrapped together.
It yields a hull with
much the same
advantages as a
diagonally planked,
cold-molded hull, but
eliminates the need for
building an elaborate
plug or individually
spiling planks.

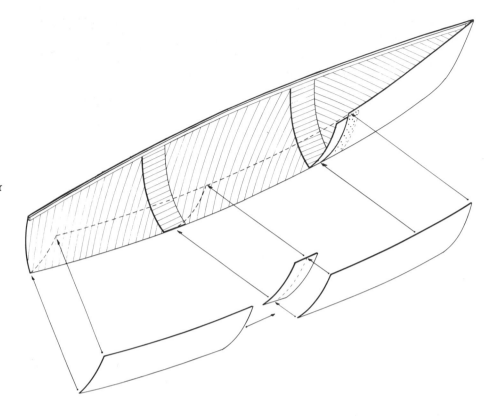

Mosquito bomber, for instance) were made from wood laminated with adhesives under heat and pressure in giant pressurized ovens called autoclaves.

Today's better adhesives eliminate the need for heat and great pressure so the structure can be laminated cold, or at ambient temperature. In order to bend properly over the framework the hull planking normally is laid diagonally over the fore-and-aft stringers. After the first layer of planking is bonded to the skeleton another course of planking is laminated over the first, usually at right angles. A minimum of two layers is required, although more layers are used if the planks are very thin.

When the planking is completed, the exterior surface is faired smooth and, normally, a light layer of glass fabric applied with either epoxy or polyester resin. This skin coat of glass provides a ding- and scratch-resistant surface that can be smoothed for painting. Boats built this way are light and strong; in fact, for many years this was the preferred way to build high-performance airplanes.

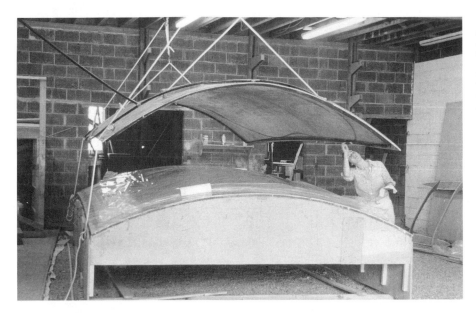

Figure 9-8.
Constant Camber
panel mold. Multiple
layers of epoxy-
saturated diagonal
planking are pressed
to shape using a
vacuum pump.

Constant Camber. Strong and light though it may be, the traditional method of laminating a round-bottomed, cold-molded hull takes a great deal of work. The framework must be lofted and set up; each of the multiple diagonal layers of thin wood veneer must be shaped to fit, spread with glue, and fastened with staples. Because the staples do not apply pressure to the glue joint evenly, the surface usually must be sanded fair before the next layer of planking is begun.

In an effort to devise a faster and simpler method of laminated wood construction, multihull designer Jim Brown came up with the idea of using giant tailor-made sheets of compound-curved plywood formed with regular curvature; that is, the form (or mold) is a portion of a "body of revolution."

Normally the shape of a hull is complex; the curvature differs from spot to spot. This is what complicates the construction process. Jim reasoned that if a good boat could be built from flat sheets of plywood that bore absolutely no resemblance to the final hull, then a better boat could be built from a giant, compound-curved sheet of plywood if its curvature approximated that of the final hull form.

Because the mold used to laminate the custom-made panel has constant uniform curvature throughout its length and width (hence the name Constant Camber), the shape of all the small planks used in the construction of the large panel is identical and the labor of custom fitting each one is avoided. In addition, one mold can form both port and starboard sides of the vessel. Because the curvature is molded directly into the panel, there is little or no need for internal framework to shape the boat, thus avoiding the lofting process

Figure 9-9.
SIB, the first Constant Camber boat, shows the type of long, narrow hull best suited to the method.

Figure 9-10.
Charis II, a Constant Camber trimaran designed by John Marples, shows the variety of shapes that can be obtained using this method.

as well. The entire method was geared toward efficient, low-volume production of simply shaped wood/epoxy hulls. As a boatbuilding method it works quite well, although there are some quirks.

The first of these occurs in the design stage. Because the hull panels are uniformly curved but the best hulls are not, the panels must be "tortured"

Figure 9-11.
This view of the 40-foot *Yanmar Endeavor* trimaran shows strip plank composite construction (using DuraKore strips) prior to application of the outer skin of epoxy resin and unidirectional fiberglass. (Courtesy Baltek, Inc.)

into the desired shape during hull assembly. This torturing can change the shape of the hull for better or worse, and the effects are not always predictable. I was involved in the early development of the Constant Camber method and spent considerable time puzzling over this problem during the design of my own *Juniper*. The only solution I or anyone else was able to come up with was to first build good scale models.

Once the tricks of the Constant Camber trade are learned, fairly accurate predictions of torture-induced changes are possible. But you can never know *exactly* where the hull skin will end up, and this prevents the preparation of accurate drawings for many of the internal components. Builders using any of the several construction methods that involve torturing must have self-reliant, "eyeball construction" personalities, because real precision is not to be had.

Another design quirk of Constant Camber boats is the limitation it imposes on hull shape. There is only so much you can do with a given panel. Long, narrow, double-ended hulls are easy and sweet to build with this method, but it is not always possible to convince the owner to go for a hull as long as it ought to be, and this necessitates trying to obtain shapes that are not compatible with the method. Some designers working with Constant Camber have gotten around this by slicing, turning, and twisting panels, but that seems contrary to the method's intended simplicity. To me, the extra effort far outweighs any benefits.

On the plus side, Constant Camber produces a very high-quality final laminate that normally is thicker than the usual cold-molded hull because the entire structure is self-contained and not shared with an internal skeleton. Thicker skins are tougher, insulate better, and their smooth interior surface is most attractive and space efficient. The frames and stringers common to conventional cold-molded construction can eat up lots of precious volume that could otherwise be used for accommodation in a narrow hull.

Even higher quality laminates can be produced by vacuum bagging. Essentially, vacuum bagging uses the weight of the atmosphere (over 2,000 pounds pressure per square foot) to clamp the lamination together until the glue sets up hard. Briefly, the laminate is laid up over the mold, an airtight sheet fitted, and the air is pumped out with a vacuum pump, squeezing the layers of laminate tightly together.

Vacuum bagging is a comparatively easy process, but it does take some time to set up, and if you lose vacuum during the curing process (a power failure, perhaps), the laminate can be ruined. Vacuum bagging should be considered only by well-organized builders.

Strip Plank Composite

Advantages. Strip planking has been a popular boat construction method for many years. In the traditional approach, narrow, often square-section planks are glued and edge-fastened to one another and to frames that are set up just as for traditional carvel-planked construction. These frames are a crucial part of the hull since they reinforce the planking across the grain, which is its weak point.

The advent of epoxy resins and unidirectional glass fibers (for more about unidirectional glass fiber, see "Fiberglass," below) has allowed a new twist in the strip-plank method that makes it faster to construct, lighter in weight, and, because it eliminates most of the interior framework, more attractive inside.

In essence, strip plank composite is an amalgam between wood/epoxy and fiberglass-sandwich construction. The core of this sandwich is lightweight lumber that carries all the primary structural loads. The interior framework is replaced by millions of tiny fibers in an epoxy matrix spread evenly over both the inside and outside of the wood planking. This forms an efficient sandwich that reinforces the hull shell across the wood grain, protects and stabilizes the lumber core, and carries the secondary structural loads.

Strip plank composite construction has become increasingly popular and respected. The reasons for its popularity are easy to see: It is fast to construct, competitive in cost, and imposes no limitations on hull shape.

The basic procedure is straightforward and involves neither elaborate molds nor the complication of vacuum bagging. Lightweight plywood frames, including the permanent frames and bulkheads required for crossbeam attachment, interior partitions, and sufficient temporary frames to regulate spacing at about two feet, are set up on a building base. Full-length wooden strips (scarfed together from shorter strips) are buttered with thickened epoxy glue, pushed firmly against their neighbors, and stapled to the frames with a pneumatic staple gun. The strength of the unidirectional fiber skins eliminates the onerous task of edge-fastening the strips together with nails or dowels.

The planking procedure goes very quickly. Because it uses lightweight, easily handled materials (the plank stock of a 40-footer, for example, would be about 1 inch wide by 5/8 inch thick) and involves a minimum of fastening; a crew of two or three people can plank up a 40-foot hull in a few days.

When the planking is completed the hull exterior is faired and sheathed with the appropriate fiber laminate. Generally, this is somewhat thicker than needed for a multiple-plank cold-molded hull, but thinner than for a foam-cored glass hull. The hull is then turned upright and the inside fiber laminate applied. Gone are the headaches associated with most forms of one-off fiberglass and tortured wood panel construction methods, which have been compared with trying to frame the interior of a wet noodle: The precisely located permanent frames and bulkheads hold the hull in its proper shape during this operation.

The only extra step required by the strip plank composite method compared with conventional cold-molded construction is sheathing the inside of the hull with fiber. But since the interior of any wood/epoxy hull must be faired and epoxy-coated anyway, this adds little additional work and is more than offset by speed of hull planking and the elimination of molds.

The strip plank composite method produces hull interiors free of stringers, and requires very little additional framing (and most of that can become part of the interior joinerwork). If glass fiber is used for the interior skin it becomes almost completely transparent when properly wet out and allows the beauty of the planking to shine through. In high-stress areas or for the highest performance boats, other high-modulus fibers can be incorporated, such as carbon or Kevlar.

Drawbacks. There are some pitfalls with this construction but these can be avoided relatively easily. The first problem is the need for accurate lofting. If the frames are not cut correctly and set up properly a bumpy, unfair hull will result. Most amateur builders and some professionals do not know how to loft accurately. Fortunately, these days designers can fair hull surfaces using

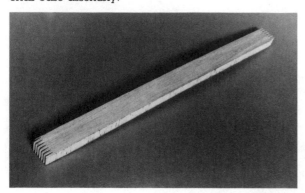

powerful computer programs and print out full-size patterns for all the hull framing. The builder can just lay out a pattern and trace the correct shape onto a frame, quickly producing a dead-accurate frame.

A second potential problem is plank print-through. Some perfectly fair, perfectly glossy hulls eventually will begin to display their plank seams. Structurally this is insignificant; indeed, most foam sandwich hulls have a similar problem. This problem can be cured in the design stage. It is important to use vertical grain lumber for the plank stock; flat-grain stock inevitably will swell unevenly enough to show its seams. It also is important to get the right fiber thickness and fiber orientation on the skins. Lumber cores that are too thick and laminated fiber skins that are too thin will result in dimensional instability.

DuraKore. DuraKore, a new product manufactured by Baltek, of Montvale, New Jersey, has been designed especially for the strip plank composite building method. This prefabricated planking material, composed of thin wood veneer skins sandwiching an end-grain balsa core, is sold in various thicknesses cut to a width equal to 1.5 times the thickness. The ends of the strips are manufactured with finger joints so that planks of any length can be made up simply by brushing glue into the joint and pushing the two mating sections together.

This product came about because, from an engineering perspective, strip-planking lumber should be as low in density as possible so that the hull is as thick as possible for a given weight. With hard-skinned balsa-cored planks (about 15 pounds per cubic foot density, 60 percent of the weight of cedar), hull thickness can be increased without adding additional weight, resulting in a stiffer, lighter hull. At least that's the theory. In practice this material has some disadvantages. There are places where its use makes sense and places where it does not.

Because DuraKore's wood veneer skins are quite thin, and consequently not as strong lengthwise as solid lumber strip planking, it is essential to compensate by using more fiber in the inner and outer composite skins. Because these skins must be continuous, all of the internal framework must be removed, the internal fiber skins applied, and permanent bulkheads installed. This adds an extra step over hulls built with lumber strips.

In areas of the hull with lots of curvature, all strip planking techniques form small, lengthwise ridges or high spots which need to be planed off during hull fairing. With solid lumber this is easy; with DuraKore it can be difficult because only a thin veneer can be planed away before you are into the end-grain balsa, which is not easy to fair. The manufacturer recommends a fairing process that relies on building up the surface with fairing compound rather than taking it down in the ordinary way. Again, this is an extra step.

Perhaps the most effective place for DuraKore in multihulls is in the broad expanse of the decks and underwing panels, where light weight and high stiffness is important, but difficult to achieve without using some form of lightweight core. Because these surfaces normally have little curvature or framing, the construction difficulties previously mentioned will not be present.

Fiberglass

In the 1950s, the combination of stranded, spun-glass fibers and polyester resin laid up in a female mold made the mass production of boats possible, and fiberglass has been the darling of the boat business ever since. There are a great many variations on fiberglass construction, but only a few of them are well suited to the structural requirements of a cruising multihull.

By itself, glass fiber has enormous tensile and compressive strength—far greater for its weight than steel. It is also very economical to manufacture. But there are some subtleties to glass fiber that are not widely appreciated.

Glass fibers. In its virgin state, glass fiber has fantastic strength. In practice, however, every time it is touched or handled during the manufacturing or weaving process it suffers microscopic damage that weakens the fiber significantly. Careless manufacturing or handling can cause a loss of up to 80 percent of its original strength.

The process of weaving glass fiber into cloth or woven roving results in the fibers being bent or crimped. Under tension the fibers want to straighten out, and are prevented from doing so only by the resin that surrounds them. The brittle resins do not do this efficiently, and thus are generally the weak

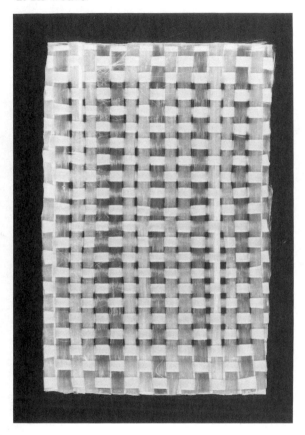

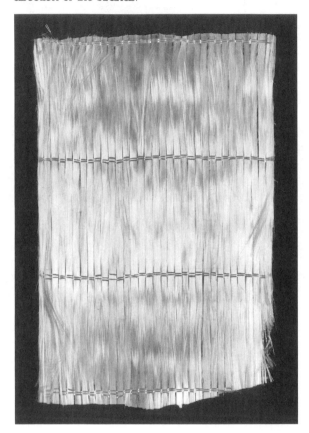

link in the laminate. Scientists use a lot of esoteric terminology to describe what happens at the interface between the fibers and resin, but the long and short of it is that any given laminate is stronger, stiffer, and more durable if composed of straight, uncrimped fibers. This makes non-woven glass fabric the material of choice for a multihull.

This type of glass fabric, called *unidirectional* glass or roving (or uniglass), is widely available at reasonable cost. Unidirectional roving's strength is along the direction of its strands; it has little strength when pulled at 90 degrees to these strands. Finished hull laminates usually consist of several layers of unidirectional roving, with the strand orientation crossing at different angles and aligned with the anticipated structural loads.

To shorten the layup process and eliminate steps in production work, uniglass is also available with two or more layers stitched together one on top of the other. *Biaxial* fabric has two layers of uniglass with fibers crossing at 90 degrees; *triaxial* fabric has three layers of uniglass ordinarily arranged at plus 45 degrees, minus 45 degrees, and 0 degrees with respect to the long axis of the roll of fabric.

In addition to differences in the mechanical arrangement of fibers, there also are different chemical compositions of the glass fibers themselves. *E-glass* is the most common form of glass and generally is considered adequate for most applications. *S-glass* is a stronger, stiffer, and tougher glass, used primarily by the aircraft industry, that is manufactured under more stringent controls designed to avoid unnecessary abrasion of the fibers. The total increase in stiffness of an S-glass laminate compared with laminates using only E-glass can be in the range of 15 percent. As always, of course, the cost is higher—about twice the cost per pound of E-glass.

Exotic materials. The so-called "exotic materials" are really not so exotic anymore—just expensive. In the pursuit of ever-lighter and stronger airplanes and spacecraft, many fibers have been developed that have better physical properties than glass fiber. The most desirable characteristics of a reinforcing fiber are high strength relative to weight and a high modulus of elasticity,

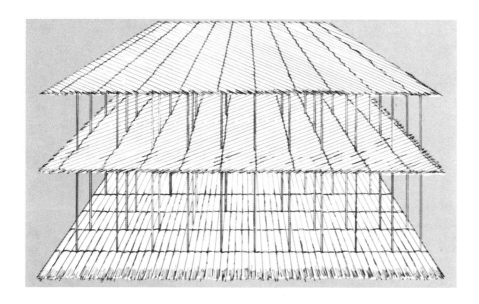

Figure 9-13C. Triaxial fabric, composed of three layers of uniglass stitch-bonded together, produces a laminate that is significantly stronger, yet thinner, than conventional woven roving. (Courtesy Knytex, Inc.)

which means that the material will stretch very little before it breaks. Of secondary importance are resin compatibility, handling ease, toxicity, etc.

- *Carbon fiber/Graphite fiber.* These are one and the same, although there are many different grades. The more expensive ultra-high modulus, high-temperature carbon fiber sells for about $600 per pound! To save an ounce or two in a satellite I suppose it is well worth it. The carbon fiber commonly used in boats sells for about $30 to $50 per pound—still quite expensive compared with most boatbuilding materials.

  Carbon fiber is wonderful stuff. It has exceptional strength both in tension and compression, excellent durability when exposed to repeated loads, it is easy to work with, and stiff as the devil. Racing multihulls use lots of it. A thousand pounds of carbon fiber would be an asset in any boat—if you could get it for free.

  Can its use be justified in a cruising multihull? In small amounts I think so. Because a small amount of carbon fiber can add so much stiffness, this can translate into lighter masts and stiffer crossbeams. Since a pound saved in the mast is worth many saved in the hull, the cost/benefit ratio makes its use there justifiable. Hulls and decks built with carbon fiber will save weight too, but the cost often outweighs the benefits. A better weight-saving technique is to build the interior carefully from lightweight components, and to be more critical about the stuff that piles up in the drawers.

- *Kevlar.* Aramid fiber, trademarked Kevlar by DuPont, finds its way onto boats in some quantity. Aramid costs about the same as carbon fiber. It has some unique properties, not all of which are good for boats. Its tensile strength is terrific and it stretches very little, which is why it is so good for sails and halyards. But as the old saying goes, "you can't push on a rope." If you could, Kevlar would be a terrible choice for rope material because it has low strength in compression.

  Used in a fiber/resin laminate, aramid has a distinct imbalance of tensile and compressive strength. Since both tensile and compressive strains are present in laminated structures, a pure aramid layup is not an efficient structure, unless its use is confined to areas that are largely free of compression loads.

Aramid fabric is used frequently on a hull's inner skin for damage control. The fiber is very hard to tear (tank armor and bulletproof vests are made from it). Under severe impact an aramid-reinforced inner skin may delaminate but it will be unlikely to tear open and admit water.

In the boat shop, aramid can be difficult to work with. Special scissors are required to cut it and it fuzzes up if abraded by sandpaper. Some kayak builders claim that aramid can soak up prodigious quantities of water, making a light, expensive boat into a heavy, expensive boat.

Resins. In all forms of reinforced plastic (fiberglass) construction the tensile and compressive loads are carried by the fibers; these fibers are held together and protected from the elements by one of several types of plastic resin.

- *Polyester resin* is inexpensive and easy to handle, particularly for mass production, and this has made it the resin of choice for production boatbuilders for nearly four decades. Compared with other boatbuilding resins, polyester is moderately strong, although somewhat brittle, and it retains good mechanical properties at the high temperatures experienced by boat decks under a tropical sun. However, gelcoat blistering, or boat pox, a common ailment of fiberglass boats, is directly related to polyester resin's propensity to absorb water. Because customers are justifiably upset if their expensive boat develops a serious case of the pox, there is a gradual shift toward resins that are less permeable.

- *Vinylester resins* were created in the late 1970s for use in composite laminates exposed to high physical loads and chemical attack—exactly the conditions of a boat operating in salt water. The vinyl esters are chemically related to the epoxy group and exhibit the same characteristics of strength, flexibility, and adhesion. Vinylester resins contain styrene (which gives polyester resin its characteristic smell), which reduces the viscosity of the resin and makes it easier to work with than epoxy in a production operation.

  Because vinylester resins absorb little water, they tend to resist blistering. Some of the largest boat manufacturers now use barrier coats of vinylester resin between the gelcoat and the usual polyester resin laminate to prevent water absorption. This an interesting idea, but the laminate is not as strong as it could be with an all-vinylester laminate. Of course the reason, again, is cost. Vinylester resin costs about 50 percent more than general-purpose polyester resin.

- *Epoxy resin* is the strongest and most durable resin available for composite boatbuilding. It has particularly good secondary bond characteristics, of which there are many in a typical multihull's structure. A secondary bond occurs when bonding together two or more fully cured laminated components. Polyesters are not at all good in this application; witness the difficulty production builders have in making a simple hull-to-deck joint fully waterproof and strong. This sort of joint in an epoxy boat is very easily done and perfectly watertight for the life of the boat.

  Epoxies stick well to practically everything—a handy feature for boatbuilding, where strong bonds often must be made between dissimilar materials. With the right surface preparation, aluminum, for example, can be glued to itself, wood, or fiberglass. Secure bonding of component parts and hardware is quick and effective with epoxy.

  Epoxy resins exhibit excellent resistance to chemicals, remaining undamaged by salt water, solvents, fuels, or battery acid. Cured epoxy resin is odorless. A boat built with epoxy resin will not have the permanent "plastic boat" smell that can be so disagreeable in a boat constructed with polyester resin.

  Of course there is no perfect material, and epoxies do have some disadvantages. It is the most expensive resin, costing twice as much as polyester, although in a one-off boat the additional cost is very minor in the whole scheme of things. Many types of epoxy do not perform well at elevated temperatures, although this normally is of no concern except in a dark blue or black hull, which can be heated to 200 degrees F. by the tropical sun.

  A foam-cored glass hull built with epoxy resin should, as a matter of course, be painted a light color. If not, periodic exposure to extreme temperatures likely will cause slight distortion of the surface, resulting in "print-through" of the glass fabric or foam core. In an extreme case, high temperature softening of the resin could result in significant distortion around a highly stressed fitting, such as a chainplate. For this reason, all modern composite airplanes built with similar epoxy resins are painted white or light pastel colors.

Epoxy's strength and bonding tenacity aside, it has a unique characteristic that allows it to do what no other resin can: Polyester and vinylester resins contain great quantities of the thinner styrene, which is the compound that makes "fiberglass" smell like fiberglass. Styrene is crucial to the polymerization of the resin and is mostly used up in the chemical reaction when the resin hardens. However, significant quantities evaporate or "flash off" as the resin cures, and some also remains more or less permanently in the hardened plastic, giving off the characteristic odor. The consequence is that on a microscopic level the cured resin is full of holes.

These holes are too small to pass liquid water, but are too large to prevent water vapor from migrating through the resin. Epoxies, on the other hand, can be formulated to be extremely resistant to the passage of water *or* water vapor, thus protecting the substrate material—whether wood, glass, carbon, or Kevlar—from the moisture damage. This is particularly advantageous in laminated wood construction because wood swells and shrinks considerably as its moisture content changes. This moisture-induced movement is responsible for chipping paint, leaking seams, and corroding fasteners in the old style of wooden boat construction. By stabilizing the moisture content of the laminate all these problems are avoided.

Cored laminates. What about the laminate itself? A laminate of glass fibers and resin can be very strong, but it is also quite flexible. If a solid laminate is constructed sufficiently thick to achieve the rigidity necessary for a hull, it will be too heavy for a performance-oriented boat.

A typical solid fiberglass laminate weighs approximately 100 pounds per cubic foot. To be competitive with other high-performance boatbuilding materials the hull laminate weight must be reduced to about 25 pounds per cubic foot. Solid fiberglass has poor insulative and noise-damping properties and, because it is heavier than water, boats constructed of solid fiberglass will be "sinkers" without the addition of buoyancy chambers or other added flotation.

A solution is to make the fiberglass hull thicker, without adding lots of weight, by laminating a core of low-density material between two faces of fiberglass. This laminate becomes a sandwich of high-strength skins over a core, which has the function of holding the skins apart and resisting the shearing tendency of one skin relative to the other. Structurally, a sandwich laminate is analogous to the common steel I-beam, with the glass skins as the flanges and the foam as the shear web. I-beams work well because the load-bearing material is placed farthest from the center, where it does the most good. But a steel I-beam is all one material; a sandwich laminate comprises several different materials all with different properties, and this complicates the design.

Three types of core materials are commonly used in boat construction: end-grain balsa, rigid PVC foam (Dinvycell, Klegecell, and Termanto are common brands), and ductile PVC foam (Airex and Plasticell). All of these cores have been used in the construction of multihulls at one time or another, and all have their strong points and weaknesses. A laminate designer must take these into account before selecting a certain type of core for a given application. Briefly these are the primary strengths and weaknesses of the common core types:

- *End-Grain Balsa.* Pound for pound (the common variety weighs about 9 to 10 pounds per cubic foot), end-grain balsa is the strongest core in compression and shear, which translates into very rigid hulls. It is also one of the least expensive cores, and it is unaffected by the kinds of temperatures that can make some foam-cored decks undesirably pliable. Balsa is biodegradable and a nondurable species of wood, however; if poorly adhering bonded skins or inadequately bedded deck hardware allows water to seep into the laminate, the balsa can rot quickly.

  Many balsa-cored boats built in the early days suffered problems resulting from the rapid absorption of resin into the end grain of the balsa. This starved the skin-to-core interface of adhesive and affected the strength of the bond between the core and the skin, often resulting in skin delamination and subsequent penetration of the sandwich by water. Because of this the material has had a long-standing reputation for trouble, although I suspect that these problems were more the fault of careless construction than an inherent weakness of the material itself. As long as the material is understood and quality control procedures adhered to, balsa coring should present no significant long-term problems.

  One undesirable feature of a balsa core, however, is that an impact load applied to the exterior skin will be transmitted largely unabated through the core to the inner skin. This may fracture the inner skin along with the outer. Boats with thin-skinned laminates, such as multihulls, can benefit from cores that cushion impact to prevent rupture of the interior sandwich skin. Some types of foam do this well and are preferable to balsa in areas subject to high impact loads.

- *Expanded rigid PVC foams.* These commonly used core materials are available in different densities, with strength increasing with density. Medium-size boats normally use foam with densities in the range of four to six pounds per cubic foot. In areas where through-bolted hardware demands more compression resistance, foam of 10 or more pounds per cubic foot density is used.

PVC foam has the advantage of being non-biodegradable and, due to its closed-cell nature, can absorb little water. While the rigid PVC foams do not provide the exceptional strength in compression and shear of end-grain balsa, they are somewhat stronger in these properties than ductile PVC foam cores (see below). They have good temperature stability and can be used in the deck of a vessel intended for use in the tropics.

One potential problem with the rigid foams is that under extreme loads failure can occur within the foam itself. The primary function of the core in all sandwich panels is to prevent the outer skins from sliding relative to one another. Under high loads, great shearing forces develop between the outer fiberglass skins that can overcome the shear strength of the core, which then would fail with a *BANG!*

More than a few offshore sailboats have suffered massive failures of foam sandwich hull panels due to high slamming loads. The reports of these incidents usually state that the vessel hit something because there was a loud noise of impact. I suspect that many times the noise was the foam breaking within the sandwich panel and not due to the impact of flotsam.

A dramatic loss of stiffness follows a failure in the foam core; often the hull will deflect 10 inches or more in the area of delamination. As if this is weren't bad enough, a damaged foam core is quite difficult to repair. The skins must be cut away, all the foam replaced, and the skins relaminated.

I do not mean to condemn rigid PVC foams; many fine, seaworthy boats have been built using them. But properly engineering the core thickness, its density, and the fiber laminate of the load-bearing skins is crucial to success. Equally crucial to success is very careful construction. All forms of sandwich construction must have structurally effective bonds between the face skins and the core.

• *Ductile PVC foams.* In the multihull, construction weight is especially important. To obtain the most efficient sandwich structure, the correct engineering approach is to use relatively thin skins on a thick core. If normal sailing strains were the only ones that had to be taken into account, the glass skins could be shockingly thin. But it is important to have sufficient skin thickness to resist the high and unpredictable point loads that inevitably come to bear on the hull of a cruising yacht. With this in mind, ductile PVC foam may well be the best choice of core material for multihull construction.

Ductile foams such as Airex look and feel much like rigid foams, but the chemistry is different. The foam is somewhat rubbery; under high load it will yield and deform without fracturing, normally returning to its original shape when the load is removed. This resilience dramatically reduces the possibility of core failure when the outer skin of a thin-skinned boat is deflected by extreme overload, such as a collision or grounding. Compared with end-grain balsa or rigid PVC foam, a sandwich panel incorporating ductile PVC foam can absorb a lot of energy without breaking the core or the inner skin.

To me this looks like the best form of damage control for a lightweight hull laminate. Provided the core is sound, repairs will be confined to the easily accessible skins.

One-off Fiberglass Construction

Amateur builders often build multihulls of foam-cored fiberglass. While this is less common in the United States due to the popularity of wood/epoxy construction, foam/glass is the medium of choice in much of Europe and Australia.

Done correctly, foam-cored glass hulls can be very light and strong—an ideal combination for a multihull. If the engineering is sound and the construction done carefully to minimize excess resin in the laminate, the resulting hulls can weigh less than many forms of wood/epoxy construction. By using high-modulus "exotic" fibers in lieu of glass, laminate weights can be reduced further. Practically all racing multihulls are built this way.

The majority of amateur-built one-off foam/glass hulls are constructed by first erecting a light skeleton of temporary frames covered with closely spaced longitudinal battens. Over this goes foam sheets, which often are screwed to the battens from inside the mold. It may or may not be necessary to heat the foam to bend it over the framework, depending on the kind of foam used.

After sheathing with the foam core, the hull is faired up with putty and sanding blocks and then the exterior fiberglass skin laminated in place on top of the core. When cured, the exterior is faired up to the desired degree of gloss—often a much longer process than it should be—and the hull rolled upright.

So far so good. Now comes the hard part. The temporary skeleton must be removed and the interior fiberglass skin laminated in place. Because the sandwich is only half complete the hull has very little strength and resembles a limp noodle. The hull must be shored up so that it doesn't twist or deform as the interior framing is removed.

Now the inner fiberglass skin is applied. Once the inside laminate is finished, the hull is extremely rigid and will hold its own shape. Permanent frames and bulkheads are dropped into place and construction continues as with any other method.

Compared to wood/epoxy, foam/glass costs somewhat more for materials (in the U.S.A. anyway; places with fewer lumber resources may find less of a difference) and, if you want a nice exterior finish, takes somewhat longer to build. But some sailors prefer fiberglass and others find the potential weight reduction attractive.

There are several snags with the above method and professional boatbuilders often construct one-off foam-cored hulls somewhat differently. To avoid the problems associated with moving around a half-completed hull, they plank the temporary hull skeleton with a complete skin of light plywood or similar material. It looks like a finished hull, but it's just a throwaway "male" mold.

This mold is faired and waxed with mold release agent, then the *inside* skin of the sandwich is applied over the mold. After the resin cures the foam core is bonded to the inside skin, usually being clamped in place with a vacuum bag. After this the foam core is faired up and the outside skin is laminated over the core and faired.

At this point the hull laminate is complete so the hull itself is quite rigid. The mold is still inside and is normally destroyed as it is removed. Because the surface you see from inside the boat was laminated against the mold it is smooth and needs little more attention except for light sanding and paint. Even with the extra step of building the male mold, the pros claim this is a faster method than screwing the foam to the frames and batten molds. I expect they are right but their method requires a lot of manpower if the vacuum bagging operation is to go efficiently.

Production Fiberglass

In the context of production boatbuilding, fiberglass in one form or another is hard to beat. A crew of semi-skilled workers spray gel coat into a "female" mold, laminate the glass/resin to the required thickness, and a few hours later pull out a nearly finished part. Any large-scale boatbuilding operation will employ molds for every component possible, and practically all production fiberglass boats are built this way.

Provided sufficient sales volume exists to amortize the cost of tooling, there is no way to build a hull with fewer man hours. The problem for multihulls, however, is that the market is small (but growing), and the designs evolve quickly. It can cost easily $200,000 to build production molds for a quality, 30-foot cruising multihull, and this does not include funds for design, prototype development, advertising, and promotion. You have to sell a lot of boats to pay for that kind of start-up expense. Often the particular design is obsolete long before the tooling is paid for. Very few builders of production cruising multihulls have been financially successful, and many have gone on to reaffirm one of the basic tenets of the boatbuilding business: "The sure way to create a small fortune building boats is to start with a large fortune."

Figure 9-14.
Production boats are assembled from premolded components. Here, a Privilege 39's deck is receiving hardware before being bonded to the hull at Jeantot Marine's factory in France. (Photos courtesy Privilege Yachting, Inc.)

Aluminum Construction

Welded aluminum is used often in large-yacht construction; indeed, there have been some very large multihulls built of this material. As with all other boatbuilding materials, aluminum has its advantages and disadvantages.

Aluminum is primarily a big-boat material. Excluding small dinghies and runabouts (which can be stretch-formed from single sheets over a male mold), below a certain size, an aluminum boat will be heavier than one constructed of wood or fiberglass. The onset of this threshold is a matter of debate, but I think 50 feet is about the right number. There are several reasons for this.

Aluminum construction is a heavy medium for smaller boats because there is a minimum thickness of aluminum that can be welded efficiently. One-eighth-inch aluminum plate is about as thin as can be welded in a boatshop. A hull of this thickness weighs about 2.25 pounds per square foot when you take the required hull framing into consideration. In contrast, a wood/epoxy or foam-cored fiberglass hull for a 40- to 45-foot multihull will weigh from 1.5 to 2 pounds per square foot.

Insulating materials, which are necessary for aluminum cruising boats to alleviate problems with temperature, condensation, and noise, add more weight. The insulation itself must be covered; these additional steps and materials add still more weight and take more time and energy than one would expect. And most importantly for a cruising multihull, aluminum boats need sufficient flotation chambers to prevent the development of monohull's disease: glug, glug, glug.

Welding aluminum is a more precise and intricate operation than welding steel, adding to construction costs. Also, aluminum reacts chemically with a number of other substances in the presence of seawater. This electrolytic corrosion makes for additional complications in isolating dissimilar materials, and more care must be taken in avoiding dockage areas that may have stray electrical currents in the water.

Some of the early big racing multihulls were aluminum, the French trimaran, *Manureva*, being a good example. This boat racked up a record-setting circumnavigation as well as many impressive transoceanic races, but was constantly falling apart during these exploits. Welds, particularly crossbeam welds, failed often, and the boat and skipper were lost during La Route Du Rhum Race in 1980. No trace of either was found, which is highly unusual for a multihull, and this suggests to me that the boat sank.

This is not meant as a broad condemnation of aluminum as a boatbuilding material, but it is a reminder of the problems associated with welding thin, highly stressed aluminum skins that will be immersed in salt water. The marine grade alloys, like 5086, are highly corrosion resistant and weld better than most other alloys, but the welds are still the weak link.

On the plus side, it must be nice to just weld a pad eye where you want it; the construction, if hard chine, is simple; and since aluminum does not hold paint well you really are better off not bothering with paint at all.

CHAPTER 10

Safety and
Seamanship

⛵

Not all multihulls are safe boats; neither are all monohulls. The responsibility for the safety of any boat is shared among the operator, builder, and designer. In this section we will consider factors that contribute to the seaworthiness of a cruising multihull. It is not intended that this be the last word on the subject, nor is it suggested that commonsense safety features used routinely in monohulls do not apply to multihulls—many of them do.

Controlling Flooding

Collision Bulkheads and Hull Subdivisions

Eventually, any cruising boat worthy of the name is likely to run into something hard enough to open the hull. There are so many logs, lost shipping containers, whales, and other large, unfriendly objects floating around that to assume otherwise is foolish. The most likely places for impact damage are the bows, fins or boards, props, shafts, and rudders. A gushing leak at any of these places must be contained to the smallest possible portion of the hull.

Because large-scale flooding often leads to capsize and sinking, stringent government regulations require commercial ships and fishing vessels to subdivide their hulls with watertight compartments designed to contain flooding from collision damage. Usually done by installing transverse watertight bulkheads at intervals along the length of the hull, this type of subdivision is important for cruising sailboats, too, and it often is used in each hull of a multihulled boat.

A multihull's primary subdivision, however, is multiple hulls. Because it is so unlikely that two or three hulls will suffer simultaneous damage, this longitudinal subdivision offers an important safety advantage over single-hulled boats. The phrase, "don't put all your eggs in one basket" comes to mind.

In most multis, the hull's maximum depth below the waterline is no more than 20 inches. By adding conventional transverse-bulkhead subdivisions to the already lengthwise-divided, slender hulls, flood-prone areas can be reduced to small and manageable segments that will have minimal effect on overall trim.

The first and most obvious location for a watertight partition is a few feet back from the bow. A collision bulkhead here can prevent a big hole near the stem from flooding the hull. Because the water depth in the narrow forepeak can reach a depth of only about 2 feet, the watertight bulkhead need be no more elaborate than a suitable thickness (typically, $3/8$ or $1/2$ inch) of plywood bonded strongly to the hull. An access hole can be cut into this bulkhead so that damage can be repaired. As long as the threshold of the opening is substantially above the waterline, a watertight door probably is an unnecessary refinement.

Another place for subdivision is in the stern of the boat, where it is wise to install a partition forward of an inboard engine that is watertight to a point at least 6 inches above the static waterline. This contains stuffing box and cooling-water leaks, which are fairly common, as well as confine any engine drippings. Similar partitions should be considered to contain leakage from inboard rudder stuffing boxes, or from massive flooding should a rudder be sheared off. Because the area being contained generally is quite small and the hull heels very little, these partitions normally can be worked into the accommodation with little difficulty.

Catamarans deserve special consideration. If one hull is allowed to flood completely, the ensuing dramatic loss of transverse stability could result in capsize. For this reason, it is worth considering adding an additional watertight bulkhead somewhere along the midsection of the hull to confine flooding to, at the most, half the hull. This bulkhead is likely to interfere with the accommodation if it is made watertight up to a point 18 to 24 inches above the load waterline. An acceptable alternative is to have the threshold somewhat above the LWL, and to make provisions to nail or screw a cover over the lower portion of the opening in the event of an emergency.

Trimarans are a little better off in such situations because the flooding of one hull still leaves two buoyant hulls. In addition, most floats contain bulkheads that form part of the crossbeam structure, and these further compartmentalize the hull, prohibiting a complete loss of buoyancy.

There have been cases of near capsize caused by flooding of the leeward float. Normally, this should be quite evident—the boat may become sluggish, the angle of heel will increase, and you should hear lots of water sloshing around. These signs aren't always recognized immediately, however. In this situation the proper response is to get onto the other tack, *fast*. Provided there is sufficient wind, the flooded float will be lifted clear and, assuming the hull was holed, much of the water will drain out.

It is a good idea to have the means to pump the floats from within the main hull. This will allow easy periodic checking, even when thrashing to windward. A good diaphragm-type bilge pump (such as those made by Edson,

Whale, or Henderson) located in the main hull can be plumbed to the float bilges via ¾-inch plastic hose. Add the appropriate valves and one pump can suck water from any number of compartments.

Because the floats of a cruising trimaran are premium stowage places for bulky, wet, and smelly things you would rather not have in the cabin, deck hatches often are fitted. In a fast tri, high-velocity water often sweeps the leeward float deck so these hatches must be strong and watertight.

Finding suitable, off-the-shelf hardware for this type of hatch is not easy. *Juniper* has some beautiful, old-fashioned bronze icebox latches (I rescued them from a junk heap) that are perfect for the job: they operate easily, lock positively, and are designed to compress a gasket, which stops the small leaks. Unfortunately, I have never seen anything like them for sale. Most other tris either use regular production-made deck hatches or homemade hatches that use heavy-duty turn pegs to lock down a gasketed hatch cover.

Buoyancy

A multihull should not sink, *ever*. Its structure should contain ample flotation so that no matter what happens—right side up, upside down, or riddled with holes—there is no way she will head to the bottom.

"Just" floating is not good enough. If filled with water, a boat with only a minimal amount of buoyancy would be completely awash, making living inside or even on top impossible. For the highest degree of safety in the event of capsize or massive collision trauma, the boat's inherent buoyancy should be enhanced wherever possible by using thick, lightweight hull and deck skins, sealed buoyancy chambers, and, if practical, buoyant masts.

Wood/epoxy multihulls have a density approximately half that of seawater. This means that for every pound of hull, deck, and crossbeam structure there is ½ pound of built-in flotation. Calculating the built-in flotation of foam- or balsa-cored fiberglass boats is a little more difficult because the core thickness significantly influences the density. Generally speaking, thin-cored balsa structures are less buoyant than wood/epoxy, and thick foam-cored hulls are more buoyant. Single-skin fiberglass and aluminum hulls are sinkers, and need ample added flotation to compensate for the inherent lack of buoyancy.

Often, additional flotation is readily available by simply sealing hollow crossbeams or other structural components. Some designs can achieve great buoyancy by doing this. The sealed upper box-beam portion of *Juniper's* crossbeams provides 8,000 pounds of positive flotation. If capsized, she will float very high in the water, and the water level in the main cabin will remain knee deep (or less), dramatically improving her inverted habitability.

If capsized, a trimaran has the built-in advantage of the airlock within the floats. Since there are no through-hull fittings and the only openings are in the deck, the floats will not flood. This results in tremendous reserve buoyancy without having to do or add anything.

Catamarans, with their broad bridgedecks, can achieve lots of buoyancy through the use of thick-cored decks, which have the further benefits of increased strength and insulation.

To help locate habitable parts of an inverted hull, some effort should be made to determine an offshore cruising boat's approximate inverted waterline. This is not easy to do accurately, but only a rough approximation is needed. For instance, you know that if capsized the decks will be immersed. If there is, say, 700 square feet of deck area, and each square foot provides 1 pound of flotation, the deck has 700 pounds of buoyancy.

Make a rough guess at an inverted waterline, and figure the buoyancy contribution of any immersed portions of the hull. Add the effects of sealed crossbeam chambers, airlocked hulls, or other sources of buoyancy, and you have an approximate buoyancy number for the inverted boat.

Now total the weight of all the parts of the boat floating above the water. If this figure is greater than the buoyancy number then the boat will float lower in the water than you assumed. Remember that equilibrium is always a condition of floating; the weight of the portion of the boat above water will always equal the buoyancy of the part of the boat below the surface. Some back and forth calculating will yield an approximate equilibrium waterline location; extreme accuracy is neither necessary nor possible considering the nature of the problem.

In all probability the boat will not sit level fore and aft, which means that one end of the boat is likely to be much drier than the other. This is the place to locate survival accommodations and gear. Dense objects like engines, batteries, aluminum spars, and above-water tanks have the most influence in pushing the hull lower. And large sealed chambers, like those commonly employed in crossbeams, have the greatest effect in lifting the hull. If your boat, like many, has the engine and batteries located well aft and has substantial buoyancy chambers in the forward crossbeam, then it is a sure bet that the stern will be lower in the water than the bow. In this case the best place to consider locating survival accommodations is forward in the hull.

Of the 12 cruising multihull fatalities known to have occurred in the Atlantic Ocean that could be attributed to capsize (including one outright sinking), 11 deaths occurred aboard designs that made heavy use of single-skin fiberglass construction. To compensate for the lack of inherent buoyancy in the structure, builders often install *flotation chambers,* which are sealed portions of the hull. If the boatowner has not violated their watertight integrity in a quest for more storage, these chambers may well prevent actual sinking. But to float a capsized boat high enough to provide a habitable interior, the buoyancy chambers need to be located up high in the boat, preferably at deck level. This is not always done because it would interfere with the accommodation, and consequently many single-skin fiberglass cruising multihulls float poorly.

This contrasts markedly with typical racing designs (and most one-off cruising designs) which, due to their low-density construction materials, float very high if flooded or capsized. Despite many more capsizes of racing multihulls compared with cruising multihulls, fewer fatalities have resulted, which suggests to me that more effort should be made to ensure that cruising multihulls not only float, but float well enough to offer a safe survival platform.

While on the topic it seems fair to mention that, at least in recent years, most multihull racers are much better prepared to deal with misfortune than the average cruiser. The racers leave port intending to push it to the outer limits, and they prepare for the possible consequences with collision bulkheads, ample flotation, survival suits, and secured emergency equipment.

Cruisers seldom prepare to this extent. Certainly most cruising sailors don't run the same risks as transatlantic racers and needn't prepare so thoroughly. But cruising sailors making long offshore passages *are* exposed to significant risk and should prepare as well as the racing sailors.

Capsize

Lest you get the idea that all multihull sailors are haunted by the specter of capsize, I should point out that I have never capsized a boat larger than 16 feet and have never felt I was near capsizing a cruising cat or tri offshore. But capsizes do occur, and the offshore cruising sailor should be aware of factors that enhance or detract from a multihull's capsize resistance, how to handle a boat in danger of capsizing, and what to do if capsize should occur.

That a multihull can be capsized and not self-right is *the* argument against them. If there is any reason that most cruising boats are not multihulled it is the subtle, sometimes irrational, fear of being turned over. I still fear this every time I set out on a long passage. Capsize would be no fun to say the least, and very likely I would lose my boat, which would break my heart. But a measure of fear is a healthy thing. Fearless people often lead abbreviated lives. However I may fear it, I don't *worry* about capsize, because I know that our choosing to build a multihull exposes my family to no more risk than if we had fashioned the same pile of material into a single-hulled boat with a ballast keel.

Most cruising is done in protected waters in which capsize is highly unlikely. Most sailors of cruising multihulls need never confront the conditions that could cause an out-of-control capsize. But regardless of the type of boat they own, all mariners like to feel that their vessels can withstand the worst conditions.

Capsize is a problem, and like any problem it at least can be minimized if not actually solved. The first task is to understand the dynamics of the problem. Once the causes are known it is possible to present solutions that reduce the risk.

There are two forms of energy that can cause a capsize: wind energy and wave energy. Of these, wind is the most commonly encountered force that could overturn a boat. Fortunately, wind capsize is the most easily avoided.

Wave capsize is far more complex and potentially more dangerous. Waves of great destructive force seldom are encountered, but when they are your counter-measures are limited. Of course wind and waves nearly always are present in some combination, and one may augment the other in a detrimental way.

Wind-Induced Capsize

A multihull can be sailed over in flat water. This is a pure and simple wind-induced capsize, which is fairly common among small beach catamarans and daysailers. It is much more difficult to capsize a cruising-size boat from wind action alone. Since a boat's righting moment (the force that resists heeling) increases by the fourth power of the increase in size, and the sail's heeling force increases only by the third power; bigger boats proportionately are much more stable. For instance, if a 15-foot boat is scaled up to 30 feet, it has 16 times more hull stability with which to resist 8 times more heeling force from the sails. If it took 20 knots of wind to capsize the smaller boat it would take 28 knots of wind to capsize the larger one. (A 28-knot wind has twice the kinetic energy of a 20-knot wind; Force = $\frac{1}{2}$ mass $\times$ velocity^2.)

But no matter how big the boat may be, unless it is terribly under-canvased, there will come a point when sail must be reduced to stay upright—nothing new here. The important thing to remember is that you have complete control over the amount of exposed sail and its attitude to the wind.

For most cruising multis sailing to windward under full sail, wind capsize

Figure 10-1.
Thrashing to windward. Knowing when to reduce sail is the key to eliminating the risk of wind capsize.

becomes a possibility between 25 to 40 knots true wind. As long as sail is reduced or sheets eased, no problems can arise. In fact, the cruising sailor normally will want to shorten sail *long* before the danger of capsize just to slow the boat and reduce the heaving motion caused by leaping over waves at high speed.

Minimizing the risk of wind capsize. There is no excuse for a cruising cat or tri being capsized by wind alone; it happens only rarely, and usually from gross negligence. Sailors new to multihulls, doped by the speed and accustomed to sailing at single-hull heeling angles, have a near monopoly on the few wind capsizes that occur. An experienced multi-mariner hears all kinds of alarm bells long before the weather hull of his cat (or main hull of his tri) lifts clear of the water.

In strong gusty winds, a cruising multihull should be sailed with ample stability held in reserve to deal with gusts. This is done by trimming sail safely for the gusts and sailing between gusts with less sail than optimum. This points up one important difference between sailing a monohull and a multihull: *The monohull reefs to suit the lulls; the multihull reefs to suit the gusts.*

As an analogy, I can only point out that people routinely behave this way when they drive a car. You do not careen down a busy street at 80 m.p.h. just because the car can *go* 80 m.p.h.; you have to exercise control over the power plant. Simply put, there are times in a cat or tri when you must reduce power!

A boat's design has a large influence on its ability to stand up to heavy winds. Certainly width helps. Wide boats have higher static and dynamic righting moments and resist the heeling forces of the wind better than boats with less overall beam. Many other factors, such as hull shape, distribution of hull volume, crossbeam shape, rudder type, and keel type and location, also come into play when resisting wind forces. Because it is so important that the helmsman be able to retain control of the boat at all times, all of these components must work well together at the outer limits of the performance envelope.

In particular the design of the sail plan and the deck layout play an important role. Obviously a tremendous sail plan can overpower a boat at even modest wind velocities; a minute sail plan, on the other hand, could not capsize the boat except in hurricane-force winds. Either extreme should be avoided for enjoyable and safe cruising. Provision should be made for reefing sails efficiently, keeping in mind that sail plans need to be reefed in a balanced way so that the center of sail area remains near the longitudinal center of the boat. A sail plan that is unbalanced when reefed may make tacking impossible.

Sheets need to be close enough to the helmsman so that they can be released quickly in an emergency. Small multihulls need some form of quick-release cleats, although self-tailing winches usually are fast enough. All of these things are basic, commonsense features, but unfortunately common sense has been superseded largely by "marketing" during this decade, and the sensible things often take a backseat to the amenities.

Automatic sheet releases. Some people advocate automatic sheet releases for multihulls to prevent capsize from wind gusts. While this might be a good idea for singlehanded ocean racing, where the boat is sailed hard with no one on deck, it seems unnecessary in a cruising multihull. I have never seen anyone use them for cruising, and I would be reluctant to have them on my boat for fear of an accidental release. If someone were in the way or had a hand or foot tangled in the sheet as it released a very serious injury could result. A cruising multihull is *always* sailed well below the threshold of wind capsize. If it is being pushed to the limit for some reason the only appropriate response is to have a crew member riding shotgun on the sheet, ready to ease it at the first sign of trouble.

Hot-rodding. After a boat is launched, *you* are the primary variable in coping with wind capsize. You must know the boat and how hard you can push it, and there is no way to learn this other than sailing hard and observing.

On a windy day in protected waters, with a capable crewman hand-tending the sheets, try hot-rodding the boat to its limits. Take it easy at first; get the feel slowly, then begin to push it until a hull starts to fly (the windward hull of a cat or the main hull of a tri), if you can! The boat will be moving *fast,* the wind howling in the rigging. Experience the feel of the helm, note the angle of heel, see how far the leeward hull bow is immersed. Then *never drive the boat so hard offshore!*

Wave-Induced Capsize

At the risk of restating the obvious, the ocean's surface consists of nothing but waves, millions of square miles of waves, each a store of energy absorbed from the incessant winds. Great winds produce great waves but, despite their size, they're not always dangerous. They can become so, however, if opposed by strong ocean currents, or if they travel over shoals or banks that block the wave's underpinnings, causing them to topple over, releasing in just a few seconds an enormous amount of stored wind energy in a burst of fast-moving, turbulent water—a breaker.

Any boat, or even a small ship, that remains beam-on to large, heavily breaking seas is asking to be rolled over. The only way to prevent this sort of capsize is to have sufficient dynamic stability available in the hull form to resist the overturning force of the jet of water expelled by the wave. No matter how many hulls your boat has, avoid lying beam-on to large breaking seas.

Wave Impact
Some very interesting research has been done to discover exactly what contributes

to wave-capsize of monohulls. Much of this research was prompted by the carnage of the infamous 1979 Fastnet Race. Of a fleet of 303 boats (all monohulls), 163 either were knocked down past 90 degrees or capsized completely; 15 lives were lost and 136 crewmembers had to be rescued by outside agencies.

Extensive studies, done both in the United States and in England, were detailed in *Seaworthiness: The Forgotten Factor,* by C. A. Marchaj, and "The Final Report of the Directors of the Joint Committee on Safety From Capsizing," sponsored by the U.S. Yacht Racing Union and The Society of Naval Architects and Marine Engineers.

A major thrust of this research was to find out exactly how the dynamics of a breaking wave overturn a (single-hulled) boat, and what, if anything, can be done do improve a boat's resistance to "wave-impact" capsize. Model boats were tested in a large tank equipped with a computer-controlled wave generator. A scale breaking wave of the type found in deep water was formed, and the model boats repeatedly were capsized while precise measurements were taken.

The results were surprising. It has long been known that big boats are

Figure 10-2. (opposite page)
Comparative Roll Moments of Inertia.
Experience has shown that a cruising cat's wide beam makes it extremely resistant to wave impact capsize. One possible explanation for this good behavior is the very high roll moment of inertia inherent with the catamaran's widely separated hulls. To illustrate this point, compare a monohull and a catamaran with identical rigs (Cat A). The monohull's rig represents about 65 percent of its total roll moment of inertia. On the cat, the same rig provides the same amount of inertia, but this represents a much smaller portion of the total because the hulls, which are spaced far from the roll axis, contribute so much more inertia than the monohull's hull or ballast.
The monohull can only rotate around an axis that coincides with or is very near to its centerline plane. But a multihull exposed to wave impact is likely to rotate around the leeward hull (if it is fully buoyant), or around an axis that is off the centerline plane. This can contribute even more roll resistance, as shown by Catamaran B.
A further benefit to having large amounts of roll inertia within the hulls accrues if the boat is ever dismasted in heavy weather. Without rigs, Cat A has 3.9 times the roll moment of inertia of the monohull; Cat B has 8.7 times the roll moment of inertia. By contrast, the dismasted monohull loses 65 percent of its roll moment of inertia.

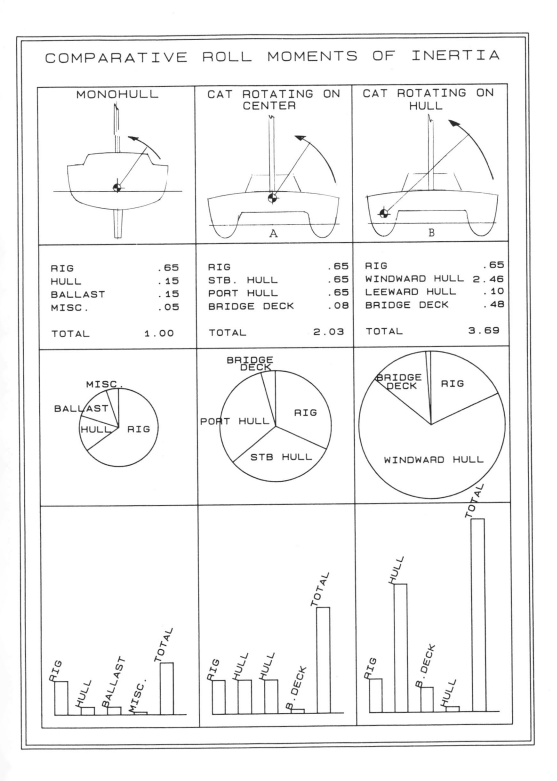

COMPARATIVE ROLL MOMENTS OF INERTIA

	MONOHULL	CAT ROTATING ON CENTER	CAT ROTATING ON HULL
		A	B

MONOHULL		CAT ROTATING ON CENTER		CAT ROTATING ON HULL	
RIG	.65	RIG	.65	RIG	.65
HULL	.15	STB. HULL	.65	WINDWARD HULL	2.46
BALLAST	.15	PORT HULL	.65	LEEWARD HULL	.10
MISC.	.05	BRIDGE DECK	.08	BRIDGE DECK	.48
TOTAL	1.00	TOTAL	2.03	TOTAL	3.69

more capsize-resistant than small boats; common sense, experience, and the statistics of capsize in the Fastnet race bear this out very clearly (all of the boats experiencing loss of life in the 1979 Fastnet were under 28.9 feet). But no one had ever established exactly why this was so.

Roll moment of inertia. Big boats have much greater static stability (the force needed to heel the boat on her side in flat water), and this generally was assumed to be the basis for their increased safety. However, the model tests showed very clearly that a boat's ability to resist breaking wave capsize is a function of its dynamic stability, specifically the *roll moment of inertia.*

This is a big term and needs explaining: Pretend you are holding a 10-foot-long broom stick in front of you horizontally; attached to the middle of the stick are two 5-pound weights. Try to tilt the stick quickly, as if it were the deck of a boat heeling to a wave. You have just applied energy to the stick, and the stick absorbed the energy by moving quickly.

Now slide the weights out to each end of the broomstick. You have not changed the total weight of the broomstick nor have you changed its center of gravity (balance point), but you *have* increased its roll moment of inertia. Now try to heel the stick quickly. It responds more slowly. More energy and more time are required to effect the same motion as before—we have increased the roll moment of inertia.

A wave breaking on the side of a boat imparts energy to the boat. If the boat has a small roll moment of inertia, it takes a small amount of energy to turn it over. If the roll moment of inertia is larger, it takes more energy to capsize it. A yacht's roll moment of inertia is the sum of the individual roll inertias of all the component parts of the boat. The roll moment of inertia of each individual part is a product of its mass (weight) multiplied by the distance of the mass from the roll axis, squared. This means that the greatest increases in roll moment comes from spreading weight as far from the axis of rolling as possible.

The model tests showed that a monohull's ballast keel makes only a minor contribution to the roll moment—about the same as the mass of the hull. The lion's share (often 60 percent or more) of the roll moment of a single-hulled yacht is contained within the mast. This becomes obvious when you consider that the weight of the rig is far removed from a boat's roll axis, and the distance from the rolling axis is the most heavily weighted term of the equation.

Many boats were dismasted during the 1979 Fastnet Race. Contrary to popular belief, with their rigs gone the boats became *less* resistant to capsize by successive waves, and many were rolled repeatedly after dismasting. As a result of this research, the Joint Committee on Safety From Capsizing made some interesting recommendations to improve capsize resistance. The most important of these recommendations is: "1. The most significant contribution to the resistance to wave-induced capsize would be to increase the roll moment of inertia of yachts. Of the practical means of achieving this, the most promising is a moderate increase in the scantlings of masts/rigs, because the mast is the single largest contributor to the roll inertia. . . . "

Increasing the roll moment of inertia is the single most effective way to prevent wave-induced capsize! Since the rig's weight represents such a large portion of the total (in a monohull), increasing the scantlings (weight) of the mast and rigging will add to the roll moment and, more importantly, reduce the chance of dismasting, which can lead to a catastrophic loss of roll moment. (Of course there are good reasons for not increasing mast/rig weight willy-nilly: Increasing weight aloft can aggravate pitching in a multihull, and aggravate pitching *and* rolling in a single-hulled boat.)

Another important conclusion from this research is that increasing the size of a boat, as measured by the *combination* of length, beam, and mass, greatly increases the roll moment of inertia, which substantially decreases the likelihood of capsize. But length alone is an insufficient indicator of capsize resistance. Since the roll moment is the product of mass times distance (squared), a long, narrow, very light-displacement hull (such as a ULDB) can have a much lower roll moment than a boat of the same length but of more conventional form. It is important to realize that two boats of the same length can have substantially different roll moments and therefore one may be much more capsize resistant than another.

What implications do these studies have for the design and handling of multihulls offshore? We now understand that one of the primary forces resisting breaking-wave capsize is the roll moment of inertia. This confirms several widely held beliefs regarding multihulls: Big boats (as measured by a combination of length, mass, and overall beam, i.e., their roll moments) are more wave-capsize resistant than smaller designs; and catamarans, because their major hull mass is spread farther apart, can have the largest roll moments and therefore are the least likely to be rolled over by a breaking sea. Hugo Meyers, the late catamaran designer and mathematician, maintained this position for years based upon his mathematical analysis of wave capsize. (There are other significant capsize-resisting forces in the multihull that are not present to a great extent in the single-hulled boat, such as the roll-damping effects of widely separated hulls and the absence of large keels that often cause a "tripping" motion.)

Although the scale model research has yet to be carried out on multihulls, it seems that any cruising multihull will have a very high roll moment of inertia compared to a monohull because the weight of the hulls is located so far from the axis of roll. Remember, the most effective increases in roll moment are gained by spreading the mass of the boat as far as possible from the rolling axis (the fore and aft centerline).

A further implication for the offshore multihull sailor is whether a temporary increase in the roll moment, say through the use of water ballast placed near the rail, might add to the capsize resistance of a cat or tri in danger of being flipped by breaking storm waves. Research is sorely needed in this area.

Countering Wave Capsize by Design

Control. Compared with a monohull, a multihull has greater potential for minimizing the impact of breaking seas for a very simple reason: control. A well-designed, sea-going multihull can be steered easily at high speed without developing the rolling and steering problems common to monohulls that often lead to broaching. And it is broaching before a wave that often sets the stage for disaster.

As we saw in Chapter 1, single-hulled boats can and often do develop serious control problems due to excessive rolling. Many causes accentuate rolling: the pendulum effects of the ballast keel; the rudder forces needed to counteract the yawing induced by the force of the sails displaced from the centerline of the heeling boat; wave patterns that induce a rhythmic roll; aerodynamic forces of the sails that have been shown to be self-exciting. If the rolling gets out of control, steering can become difficult or impossible, likely resulting in a broach, knockdown, or capsize. But a multihull suffers from none of these problems. She can be sailed faster, longer, without loss of control and the associated risk of broaching before a breaking wave.

Size. A boat's size is extremely important in determining its degree of wave-capsize resistance. This is borne out not only by gut feeling, theory, and tank tests, but by the frequency of wave capsize in less-than-severe sea conditions of small boats (mono and multihull), in the 20- to 30-foot range.

Fact: Bigger boats are harder to turn over. An *offshore* cruising multihull ought to be as large as practical. Every sailor will have his own idea of what is big enough, tempered by the restraints of expense, crew size, and anticipated use. But within each individual's range of constraints it will be beneficial to maximize the size of the boat, even if this means simplifying some other portion. Since capsize must be avoided in a non-self-righting boat, size becomes an important safety consideration to sailors who plan on frequent offshore voyaging.

In 1989, an adventurous Swedish couple sailed their 15-foot monohull, *Bris,* across the Atlantic to New England. According to owner/builder Sven Lundin, he and Olga had a very easy trip: They only capsized three times.

Bris is an interesting boat—small, rugged, and built to be rolled over. I stood on her decks at the dock and was impressed by the ease with which she heeled to my slightest shift of weight. It doesn't take much of a wave to capsize a boat of this size; she either must be self-righting or very easily righted by her crew.

Remember, the requirement for self-righting is in direct proportion to the risk of capsize. A multihull of *Bris's* approximate interior space and payload capacity would be many times more stable and *might* cross an ocean without capsizing, if the weather holds, but the risk of wave capsize would be high. For offshore cruising in this size range, a self-righting *monohull* would be safer than a multihull.

Increasing boat size reduces the risk of wave capsize, eventually reaching a crossover point where a multihull's advantages outweigh its risks. A

Figure 10-3.
Relationship of reported catastrophies to FDS (fully developed sea), wind speed, and boat size.
This figure has been compiled from data of actual monohull capsizes, and was published in the Final Report of the Committee on Safety from Capsizing. It illustrates the increase in capsize resistance with increasing boat size for single-hulled boats. It is reasonable to assume that a very similar, perhaps even more pronounced, relationship exists for multihulls.
An interesting, although troubling, revelation from this graph is the occurrence of capsizes and knockdowns in considerably less than severe conditions. The region of Beaufort Force 8 conditions (34 to 40 knots) is marked on the chart; obviously, the smaller boats are encountering much difficulty.
(Courtesy USYRU/SNAME)

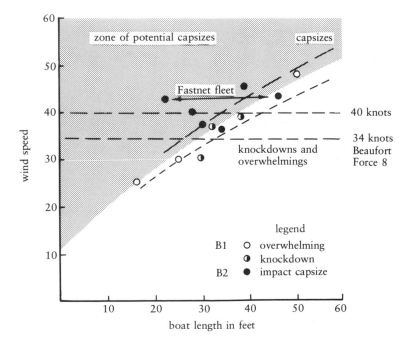

19-percent increase in a yacht's size doubles its stability; doubling its size increases its stability 16 times. This relationship of stability to size is crucial for non-self-righting cruising boats. If they must be as capsize resistant as possible and if size is such a major factor in determining a vessel's stability and capsize resistance, it stands to reason that increasing size increases safety—much more so than in a self-righting boat. Arguably, there is a minimum "safe" size for offshore-sailing multihulls, below which the risk of capsize is too great and outweighs any possible benefits the boat may offer.

What is the minimum "safe" size for a multihull sailing frequently offshore? This is a tough question. Many factors combine to determine a specific boat's capsize potential. I have written before that 35,000 foot pounds maximum static righting moment seems to be a sort of transition area above which substantial resistance to capsize occurs. This number, however, is a completely empirical "gut feeling" based on the observed frequency of wave capsize encountered by small multihulls. Personally, I feel much better about sailing offshore when the boat is around 40 feet long, with a maximum static righting moment nearing 100,000 foot pounds.

If a potential client walks in the door and tells me he wants a transocean-capable cruising trimaran I tell him that it ought to be about 40 feet long, minimum. The minimum size cat could probably be a little shorter. *I* would not be happy with a smaller boat; how can I expect anyone else to be?

Sailing along shore, coastal cruising, and short hops (a few hundred miles) offshore—the type of cruising done by *most* sailors—is a completely different situation, and smaller boats can be entirely suitable and safe for this purpose.

I am not the only multihull sailor who feels that 40 feet LOA is an approximate lower limit for a safe multihull offshore in heavy weather. Lock Crowther, the well-known multihull designer and sailor, made some interesting observations after the 1988 'Round Australia Yacht Race, in which competitors saw consistently bad weather, with winds ranging from 30 to 90 knots. As they rounded Tasmania, all of the boats in the fleet (monos and multis) used drogues and sea anchors at times. The winds were so fierce for so long that Crowther, in an article in *Multihulls* magazine, reported that, "It was amazing how the crews became used to the extreme winds; 40-knot winds are terrible conditions for most racers, but these sailors said they felt like partying and lying around in the sun on deck when the winds dropped to this degree. . . . The general consensus amongst the multihull competitors was that 40 feet is the absolute minimum multihull size in this type of sea conditions." (Courtesy *Multihulls*)

A cruising sailboat's size largely determines what degree of "bad" constitutes a threat of capsize. A very small boat may risk being rolled in moderate gale conditions; the crew of a much larger boat may become concerned only by hurricane-force storms. Statistically, the frequency of encountering dangerous wave-capsize conditions decreases with increasing boat size, but statistics are small comfort when faced with threatening seas. Every boat that spends much time at sea eventually will encounter waves that threaten the vessel's safety.

Tactics for Avoiding Capsize

Faced with heavily breaking seas that threaten the vessel's safety, a sailor really has only four possible alternatives:

- Lie ahull or heave to.

- Keep sailing, doing your best to retain control and steer around the worst waves.

- Turn downwind and use a drag device to slow boat speed, prevent surfing, and aid steering.

- Stop the boat completely using a specialized sea anchor.

Lying Ahull or Heaving To

Lying ahull, a favorite storm tactic among monohulls, means that all sail is struck and the boat left to her own devices. Most boats will turn broadside to and drift with the wind. Lightweight boats easily drift at speeds of 2 knots, and some multihulls may double that rate. Obviously, drifting this fast requires searoom to leeward, which limits lying ahull's applicability.

In less than severe conditions, lying ahull is reasonably comfortable for the crew. If conditions worsen, however, a boat lying broadside is extremely vulnerable to breaking waves, and their violent impacts make resting below impossible.

Even with ample searoom, lying ahull as a survival tactic seems risky. At best, expect structural damage or stove-in ports; at worst, things might get very, very wet.

The primary factor that determines a boat's ability to resist being rolled over by the impact of large waves is its roll moment of inertia. Catamarans, which often have very high roll moments of inertia, generally are more successful at lying ahull in severe conditions than trimarans.

Heaving to is a time-honored tactic for dealing with heavy weather. Essentially, the helm is put down, sail area sharply reduced, and the forward sail sheeted aback (hauled up to windward). A boat hove to will head up and bear off repeatedly, and this generally will keep the bow pointed more toward the wind and waves than when lying ahull, reducing the amount of hull exposed to breaking waves.

Heaving to works well with some hull and rig combinations and with others not at all. Try your own boat in moderate conditions to see how it reacts. Generally, two-masted boats with a relatively large underwater lateral plane apply the tactic most successfully. Our ketch-rigged *Juniper* heaves to well in moderate conditions by dropping the mainsail, sheeting a reefed mizzen flat and backing the small jib, although I have yet to try it in a storm offshore.

Sloops or cutters may be hove to by backing the jib in the traditional manner, but many lightweight multihulls are likely to be unsteady while hove to—alternately accelerating, rounding up, and stopping. This may be safe enough but it will not be restful.

Either of these tactics, lying ahull or heaving to, can be employed any time you have searoom to leeward. But continuing to lie ahull is probably not a good idea if waves are breaking against the hull so hard that substantial quantities of water are coming on deck or if the boat is being pushed to leeward more than a few feet. In this case, heaving to will turn the bow up into the wind and minimize the wave's impact. This seems preferable—at least until the breakers start to push the boat backwards with enough velocity to threaten a broach in reverse.

Keep Sailing

Although the natural inclination when faced with extreme conditions is to drop all sail and take to your bunk, continuing to sail has several advantages over lying ahull: A boat with some headway can punch through the waves and avoid the worst breakers; in good hands, it can absorb a tremendous amount of punishment. A boat moving slowly into the seas presents less surface area to be pounded by waves than one lying ahull, and is less likely to be capsized.

During the 1981 TwoSTAR, a two-handed transatlantic race, racing super-sailors Rob James and Chay Blyth, aboard the Shuttleworth-designed trimaran *Brittany Ferries GB,* encountered a storm five days into the race. They experienced a frightening near-capsize while lying ahull and decided that it would be much safer to get some sail up and continue sailing to windward.

Before 01.00 we were headed to a north-west course as the storm raged from the west. Down to storm staysail and deep-reefed main we were still making good ground to windward even though the seas were building up to an enormous size. At daybreak we could see how bad the weather was—the wind was over 50 knots with waves up to 30 feet. To steer in these conditions one had to try to luff up into the waves and bear away rapidly on their peaks in order to slide down the back face. The danger arose when the trimaran got knocked off the wind and suddenly accelerated from a comfortable 7 or 8 knots to 15 or more. At this speed one could do a lot of damage taking off over the top of a wave. The secret was to stay slightly free, hitting the waves fast but at a wider angle, until a gap to windward presented itself. Then a sharp luff back to close-hauled would bring the situation back under control again. It was nerve-wracking and the slamming over the waves, despite careful helming, was enough to send the off-watch crewman off his bunk and into the cabin roof.

Not long after dawn the reefing leech line broke; the only way to reeve a new one was to lower the mainsail. With it down we lay ahull reasonable comfortably and actually chickened out of getting under way again. Two hours later the wind shifted to north of west and we wore around to the other tack. Suddenly, a large breaking wave approached and started to lift the windward float. We had raised the centerboard so the boat slid sideways as intended but not before she'd been lifted to a 45-degree angle. This was pretty frightening and stupid; we immediately realized that with way on we would have climbed the wave instead of being nearly rolled over by it. We instantly started sailing again.

No sooner were we under way than it struck us what a mistake it had been to stop at all. The broken leech line had put us into a position which we were too lethargic to reverse. The only good aspect was swearing to each other that we would never stop again—whatever the weather. *Brittany Ferries* seemed to be standing up to the punishment very well—no structural damage or movement whatsoever, so it would be easier in future to force ourselves to push on. (From *Multihulls Offshore,* Rob James, Dodd Mead & Company, 1983, Courtesy The Putnam Publishing Group and A & C Black Limited.)

What conclusions can we draw from this experience? On this day, *Brittany Ferries* sailed 230 miles through the water, making good 170 miles toward her destination—talk about the ability to slug it out to windward against 50-knot winds and 30-foot seas! But Blyth and James were racing to win (they did win), and were able to push the boat and themselves to their limits. A cruising sailor, on the other hand, most likely would have tried running off or lying ahull, as *Brittany Ferries* did. However, both these tactics may well have led to being rolled over by a very large breaking wave.

As a cruising boat storm tactic, "keep sailing," while effective, has its limitations. Sailing in severe conditions is hard on the crew; it is difficult to sleep, eat, navigate, and stay alert. A small crew of ordinary humans *will* be worn out quickly and be unable to function at the level required.

Sailing to windward in storm conditions requires skill and concentration. If the conditions are so bad that you must dodge the worst waves continuously, it will be impossible to sail in the dark effectively—a significant problem since it is dark 40 percent of the time.

Running Off

Sailing a multihull downwind is life at its best. But as wind and waves build higher and higher, speed may increase to an uncomfortable or even dangerous level as the boat surfs on giant waves. With a boost from gravity as the boat sails downhill on the face of a large, fast-moving wave, sailing speed can increase to extraordinary levels.

Ocean waves move at a speed proportional to their wave length. A fully developed 14-foot wave from a Force 6 wind will be moving a maximum of 25 knots. It is not unusual to be able to surf on a wave of this size for half a minute or more. Large storm waves can travel 35 to 40 knots! Surfing on waves of this size is just too nerve-racking to bear, with loss of control becoming a real possibility. Most cruising multihulls become difficult to control over about 20 to 25 knots and may broach or spin out.

Of course whether or not the boat surfs depends on how much sail is up: less sail means it takes more wind or steeper waves to begin surfing. If surfing begins to tire the helmsman or to interfere with the sleep of the off watch, tuck in a reef, roll up some jib, and things are quiet again. But in storm-force winds, the hull and rig may present enough windage to accelerate the boat to surfing speeds even though all sail has been furled. This is when things get hairy, and you need some way to put on the brakes.

Drogues. The time-honored method for slowing boats is to trail long lines astern, often tipped with a length of chain to keep them submerged. Towing 400 feet of anchor rode can produce a surprising amount of drag, and it will slow the boat—some. But a full-blown storm will require more drag than the line can provide, and other objects often are added to increase drag. One simple, cheap, and effective drag device, or *drogue,* is a discarded automobile tire. It can't break, it adds lots of drag, it's always available for the asking, and it can double as a fender if necessary. (Paint it white or it will mark up your topsides.)

An anchor rode works well to attach the drogue. Simply unshackle the anchor, wrap the anchor chain around the tire, and shackle the chain back on itself. Of course the rode should be shackled to the chain through a good splice over a metal thimble, and care must be taken to avoid chafe.

One approach advocated frequently is to run two warps to the drogue, one from each quarter, thereby forming a bridle. Because you can steer the boat by varying the tension on the bridle lines, this greatly enhances directional control. There is a problem, however: Two separate lines running to the tire will tend to twist together for most of their length unless a very efficient swivel is used at the tire. A ball-bearing swivel is the only type likely to work well enough to be worth the effort, and they are not easily found in the large size needed.

If only a conventional galvanized steel swivel is available, or if no swivel is used, the bridle lines usually will twist together to within about 75 feet of the stern. This doesn't seem to cause a problem or significantly reduce the "bridle effect," so I prefer to run only one warp to the tire and bend on another line, forming a short bridle about 75 feet long. This conserves warp, allowing the drogue to be trailed farther astern.

Adequate separation between drogue and boat is critical. If the tire is exactly one wave length behind, both the boat and drogue will be on the crests of two different waves at the same instant. As the boat begins to surf ahead the tire will surf as well. The pull of the warp tends to pull the drogue *out* of the wave — just when you need its drag most—and both boat and tire go careening down the faces of two different waves.

The solution is simple: Pay out more line to move the drogue back a half-wave length out of sync with the boat. When the boat is on the crest the drogue is in the trough; the warp has to pull the tire *through* the wave rather than out of it.

Keep in mind that as a gale progresses the waves build in size and *increase in length*. It will be necessary to adjust warp length to keep the drogue about half a wave length out of step with the boat. If you run short of line in very large waves you probably could shorten up enough so that the drogue was positioned one half wave length behind rather than a wave length and a half, but the drogue will not be as effective.

A multihull's wide overall beam allows the bridle lines to be widely separated, and this very effectively holds the boat on a steady course, normally self-steering or requiring only minimal tending. If the bridle lines are led through snatch blocks on the stern quarters and then to large sheet winches, the boat can be steered quite effectively by adjusting the bridle. This can serve as emergency steering if the rudder fails, often allowing the crew to retain enough control to get just about anywhere, albeit at a slower pace.

The situations best suited for running off with warps and drogues are:

- Racing: When high downwind speeds begin to create control problems and reducing sail is not acceptable, a drogue may add control without diminishing speed excessively.

- Cruising: In gale conditions, when you want to and can make progress toward your destination but do not want to surf on large waves, or if you feel uneasy about controlling the boat. Also, a small drogue may be helpful when running a severely breaking inlet.

- In the event of rudder or steering system failure.

The Seabrake. In our era of high technology, the time-tested tire drogue now has some sophisticated competition from purpose-designed devices such as the Australian-made *Seabrake.* (Seabrake International, 225 East Boundary Rd., East Bentleigh 3165, Victoria, Australia.) Originally conceived to prevent broaching in monohulls rather than surfing in multihulls, the fundamental requirements are sufficiently similar so that the Seabrake has been used successfully for both purposes.

The Seabrake is cone-shaped with turbulence-generating slots in the after portion, and comes in two versions to accommodate different sizes of vessels. The larger design has specialized slots that open at a pre-adjusted setting to create more drag. As the boat starts to broach, the drag automatically increases at the right instant and yanks the stern back into line. The smaller unit, suitable

Figure 10-4.
Far more attractive than a worn-out tire, the Australian-made Seabrake is an effective drag device that permits running off at higher speeds.

for vessels up to about 35 feet, is simpler, of heavy plastic without moving parts.

The Seabrake and its cousins are sharper looking and easier to stow than a couple of nasty old tires. They likely would permit running off at higher average speeds because the drag is somewhat controllable, extra drag being applied only when needed.

Problems with running off. Boats have been capsized by waves while running off towing warps and drogues, so it seems that, as a survival tactic, this method has its problems. While it may check your speed and minimize the chance of broaching before a wave—a primary cause of rolling over—the drogue does not provide sufficient force to pull the boat out from a huge breaking wave that overwhelms the vessel.

Running away from storms presents several other problems. It often forces you away from your destination. The skipper, reluctant to give up hard-won miles, may procrastinate until his crew becomes dangerously fatigued. Because of the boat's comparatively easy motion when running off, the crew may favor it even though it may expose them to more risk than another tactic.

If there is land or shoals to leeward, running off may not be an option. You may need 200 miles or more of searoom in a storm of any duration. In cyclonic storms, like hurricanes, running can bring you into the most dangerous part of the storm. Know your position relative to the storm center before deciding to run off.

In a cyclonic storm, the storm center is to your left when the wind is square on your back. You should always be able to tell the approximate direction of storm travel by referring to the typical storm track in that area *and* the change in wind direction during the previous few hours. Plot the storm's position along with yours on a chart; if you are ahead and to the right of the storm center you are in the "dangerous quadrant," and the storm will tend to suck you into its path and into the most violent weather. Make progress to windward or stop, don't run.

Remember, in the Southern Hemisphere cyclonic storms rotate clockwise instead of counterclockwise, so all these instructions should be reversed. With the wind at your back the storm center is on your right side; if you are ahead and to the left of the storm you are on the dangerous side.

The capsize of Gonzo. One sunny day in early October, 1982, my wife Kate and I sailed *Juniper* out of Nantucket Island harbor on our way south for a winter of Caribbean sailing. We had friends and family to see along the way, and had a beautiful beam reach for the first 100 miles toward Long Island Sound. As we sailed, the wind backed steadily from south to southeast then to east, always increasing in strength.

Finally at anchor in Oyster Bay, New York, a full-blown nor'easter kept us behind our books for the better part of two days, unwilling to venture a dinghy ride ashore in the wind and rain—friends and family to see or not.

It was a typical October depression, formed off the Georgia coast by the cold continental air of autumn drawing energy from the summer-heated water along the coast. These storms normally proceed up the eastern seaboard, intensifying and slowly curving offshore, usually reaching gale force at Cape Hatteras, and sometimes building to near hurricane force by the time they are off Cape Cod.

This particular storm was especially intense. Back in Nantucket, the few boats remaining on their moorings were driven ashore. A Russian freighter bound for Canada from Cuba took refuge from the heavy seas by anchoring in the lee of the island. Fifty miles to the east, the Coast Guard cutter *Unimak* "reported seven men injured early Saturday after a wave swept over the deck of the ship. The cutter reported that 'a solid wall of blue water' crashed over the ship, sweeping a man overboard. . . . The force of the wave broke one crew member's leg; another suffered serious head injuries. Both were airlifted off the cutter by a Coast Guard helicopter." (*Nantucket Inquirer Mirror*)

Offshore, in the teeth of the storm, was the 50-foot racing trimaran, *Gonzo,* designed, built, and sailed by Walter Greene of Falmouth, Maine. Walter has more multihull racing miles in his wake than any other American, and competes in the most challenging offshore races. When asked how many times he has sailed multihulls transatlantic, he hesitates and says ". . . more than 15; it takes too long to count them all up."

This October, he and two crewmates were sailing to France for the start of the Route du Rhum Race, which is a singlehanded race from St. Malo, France to Guadeloupe in the West Indies, a distance of about 4,000 miles. They never made the start. Walter's account of their experience holds many lessons and insights for the sailor intent on improving his chances of surviving the worst kinds of storms.

We didn't pay a lot of attention to the weather here before we left. I talked to a weather guy and he was not too concerned about things, so we left and sailed pretty much due east—not making much northing. Usually when I sail to Europe I like to sail east for awhile before turning toward the north. It puts you in the Gulf Stream where it is warmer, and keeps you off the shallow water of the Grand Banks, which I like to avoid.

So we were in the Gulf Stream, about due east of Provincetown, Mass., and the wind came around to the east and just started to build. We had on a delivery mainsail (no full-length battens) and a roller-furling jib. We reefed the main and rolled up the jib; then we double-reefed the main and set a staysail. Soon we were down to main only and then switched to staysail only. We were still beating to windward at this point, but the conditions were bad and getting worse.

I was just trying to get to the start of the race without breaking anything, so we were not going to push it too hard. The wind was gale force, and the boat was climbing over the seas and falling off the other side, BANG. And then two minutes later it does it again, BANG. I said to the helmsman, "Can't you make it not bang?" But he said "I can't, I'm too tired." Eventually we got tired of pounding against it—the wind went up even more and we took the sails down.

Mike Birch [a well-known multihull racer] had sailed this same boat across the North Atlantic the previous November on his way back from the finish of the 1981 TwoSTAR Race. He said he had run before some really big seas and dragged some junk off the back, and the boat had been great. I thought "I want to see this boat doing that"—not that I felt I really had to do it, but I wanted to see what it was like.

We turned downwind at about four in the afternoon and ran off to the west or southwest as the storm continued to build. After a while we took the anchor line—probably 200 feet of ¾-inch nylon—put some big bowlines in a bight in it and tied some other junk to it like sail bags—four sail bags I think—and added some anchor chain to drag it down into the water. We cleated this on the stern of the main hull without a bridle. It really didn't stop us but it let us slide along pretty nicely; it was very comfortable.

We felt we had to hand-steer the boat. I took turns steering with Nye Williams, who is a good helmsman. There were three of us on the boat but the other guy was not an experienced helmsman, so Nye and I steered all that night, sailing straight down the waves. The drogue kept us from surfing; I don't think we ever went more than 12 knots. The waves were not breaking too badly at this point, but I feel that you get a false sense of security running.

We ran all night, we got real wet, the inside of the boat got wet. Two or three times at night the boat got out of attitude so that things that had never fallen off shelves in two previous Atlantic crossings were jumping off onto the floor—it was heeling and banging around quite a bit. Every now and then a breaking wave would come over the cockpit.

We thought running off like this was not a bad thing to do—that it was working—but although we hadn't capsized yet and we had seen some pretty awful waves, we decided during the night it certainly was possible that we could, so we nailed the EPIRB [Emergency Position

Indicating Radio Beacon] into one of the lockers, took out the survival suits, secured the portable VHF radio in its metal box, and taped some flashlights into the bilge so that if we went upside down we could find them. The three of us weren't changing sails or anything, just steering, eating, and sleeping, so we had plenty of time to get things prepared.

In the morning I was steering the boat downwind when a big wave took the boat and just crashed over my head. The next thing I know I am swimming in the ocean. I had on a life vest but no harness; I don't think we had worn harnesses for about 12 hours because both the guys said they'd rather not be strapped in if the boat were to capsize. Anyway, the wave washed over my head and I thought I was being washed away from the boat, but the boat capsized at the same time. I swam around the underside of the crossarm and pulled myself up on top. There were port holes into the cabin and I could talk to my crew, who handed me a saw so I could cut a hole to get in. You'd be surprised how fast you can cut a hole under those circumstances.

The Coast Guard cutter, *Fearless,* (that picked us up) had been within 100 miles of us the night before, and they told us the biggest seas they measured that night were 53 feet high. They said the wind didn't blow over 65 knots, but we were in an area where there was current going against the wind and that helped screw the sea up. I have been in storms that have blown harder and longer, but none of them built up a sea like this one.

In retrospect I should not have run off. Probably it would have been better to sail under bare poles, close reaching. Or I would park it, lay ahull—do anything but run. Now, if I were in that situation again I'd put out a sea anchor over the bow on some sort of bridle. I should have done that in *Gonzo,* but I didn't have a sea anchor then. And the cobbled-together drogue we did use didn't last; the stuff we tied to it slowly disappeared during the night, either getting wiped off or ripped up.

Today we have good sea anchors. I've got two built by Shewmon, plus a drogue, and they can pull the boat through the worst waves. A sea anchor will stop the boat and the drogue will let it move a bit. I'd be inclined to set the sea anchor over the bow and have the boat held more or less stationary. The important thing is to break through a breaking sea without being thrown by it—you need to be physically pulled through the breaking sea for a few seconds, and that takes a sea anchor. You can go backwards some, the tether line can stretch, and that is OK. The first part of the breaker is what turns you over. If the breaking wave can't start rolling the boat over, you'll be safe.

Part of the problem with running is that you are already moving, very much at the mercy of the wave. You can say, "Well, I can steer by hand," but you really can't—you can't do much of anything when you're overwhelmed.

The interesting thing about the capsize was that there were three of us on the boat, all awake. I thought the boat turned over forward; the other two guys thought it turned over sideways. The point is it's hard to tell what is happening when a big wave comes and covers you up with water. You can't tell which way to push the tiller; by that time you are long out of control. If we had been in a monohull in the same situation we would have come up with no stanchions, no cabin trunk, no rig; we would have been hurting bad, too.

For a boat that sails across the Atlantic and stuff like that I'd recommend a sea anchor, something big and strong. Before the crew gets too tired to make good decisions, get the sea anchor over the side. A lot of times you just have to be relaxed and wait the sea out. If you try to force things by saying "we have to be somewhere by tomorrow morning," you are just asking for trouble.

For sure a cruising multihull is a hell of a lot safer than a racing boat: It has weight and inertia. This idea that the lightest weight multihull is the safer boat is bullshit as far as I'm concerned. The heavier multihull is safer, as long as it has reasonable beam, enough flotation, and enough volume in the hulls.

Much useful information can be gleaned from Walter's account of *Gonzo's* capsize. As a cruising sailor I'm a little surprised that they departed New England for Europe in October. No matter what sort of boat you have, leaving at that time of year seems imprudent. Be that as it may, a storm of that intensity, blowing against the Gulf Stream current, must certainly have created some vicious seas. Without the effects of current it takes a Force 11 storm a full 24 hours and 300 miles fetch to build waves up to the 53-foot height measured by the nearby Coast Guard cutter. Adding 2 to 3 knots of current setting against these waves would cause them to steepen and break severely in a much shorter time frame.

Dealing with this sort of storm successfully requires two things: having a storm tactic proven to prevent wave-capsize, and knowing when to employ it. In 1982, the time of this capsize, the parachute sea anchor (see below) had yet to become a well-known storm tactic and *Gonzo* did not carry one. Instead, Walter elected to run off stripped of sail, trailing a makeshift drogue. With the benefit of 20/20 hindsight, obviously this was not the best thing to do.

Whether another storm tactic would have prevented capsize in conditions this severe can never be answered with certainty but there is some reason to believe this capsize could have been avoided.

The Parachute Sea Anchor

A recent development proven highly effective for riding out dangerously breaking waves is "anchoring" the boat bow-on to the seas using a parachute-like sea anchor. The large sea anchor, attached to the vessel with a long nylon tether, provides enough drag to stop the boat from drifting, and more importantly, it can pull the boat head first through an enormous breaking wave without allowing a capsize roll to begin. I have only seen one published report of a multihull capsized while riding to a parachute-type sea anchor, despite some horrendous storms. And in this one instance of capsize there was a problem that kept the sea anchor from opening properly.

A large parachute sea anchor will virtually stop a boat, effectively "anchoring" it in deep water. Of course the boat and parachute will move together at the speed of any current, but this is practically negligible compared to the boat's rate of drift hove to or lying ahull. Running off under storm jib and trailing a drogue, the boat might travel 100 or more miles in a day, often in the wrong direction or toward a lee shore. The maximum daily drift for a boat lying to a parachute sea anchor seems to be in the range of 5 miles. The Cassanovas, early developers of the system (see below), reported losing no more than 15 miles during a 36-hour period.

Cruisers familiar with the para-anchoring technique become very fond of it and frequently deploy the para-anchor in moderate conditions. If the wind

Figure 10-5.
A modern sea anchor is a multihull's best survival tool. All boats traveling offshore should have one aboard and the crew should be familiar with its deployment and recovery. (Illustrations and instructions courtesy Para-Anchors International)

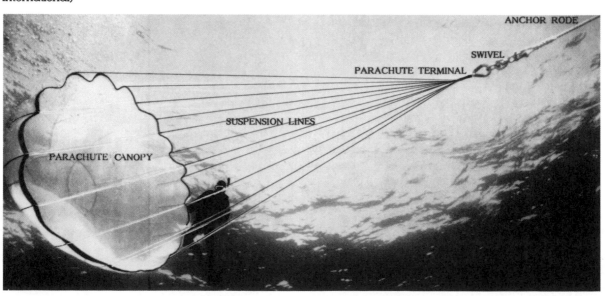

ANCHOR RODE

SWIVEL

PARACHUTE TERMINAL

SUSPENSION LINES

PARACHUTE CANOPY

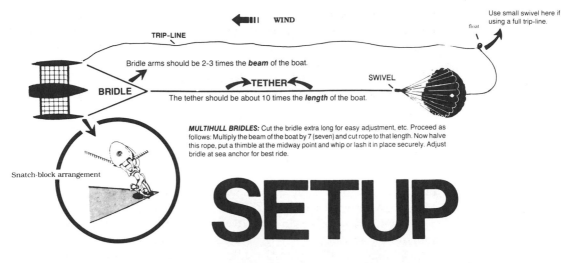

WIND

TRIP-LINE

Use small swivel here if using a full trip-line.

float

Bridle arms should be 2-3 times the **beam** of the boat.

TETHER

SWIVEL

BRIDLE

The tether should be about 10 times the **length** of the boat.

MULTIHULL BRIDLES: Cut the bridle extra long for easy adjustment, etc. Proceed as follows: Multiply the beam of the boat by 7 (seven) and cut rope to that length. Now halve this rope, put a thimble at the midway point and whip or lash it in place securely. Adjust bridle at sea anchor for best ride.

Snatch-block arrangement

SETUP

A full trip-line should be kept fairly taut at all times, **in other words NO EXCESS SLACK HANGING DOWN IN THE SEA TO FOUL WITH RODE AND SEA ANCHOR**

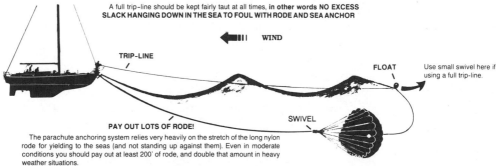

WIND

TRIP-LINE

FLOAT

Use small swivel here if using a full trip-line.

SWIVEL

PAY OUT LOTS OF RODE!

The parachute anchoring system relies very heavily on the stretch of the long nylon rode for yielding to the seas (and not standing up against them). Even in moderate conditions you should pay out at least 200' of rode, and double that amount in heavy weather situations.

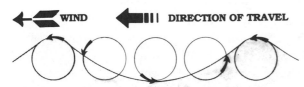

WIND   DIRECTION OF TRAVEL

TROCHOIDAL WAVE THEORY, (from the Greek *"TROCHOS"*, meaning *"WHEEL"*). The diameter of the "wheel" is equal to the height of the wave. The period of the wave determines the time it takes for the wheel to make one revolution. The approximate rate at which the water molecules rotate at their orbital (surface) velocity can be determined by dividing the circumference of the wheel by the wave period.

INCORRECT RODE LENGTH *(TOO SHORT)*: Molecular rotation downwind on the crest and the corresponding rotation upwind in the trough cause the boat and the parachute to momentarily diverge (move apart). Note also how the inadequate rode length causes the sea anchor to interfere with buoyancy of the yacht as well, *ALL IN ALL A POTENTIALLY DISASTROUS SCENARIO.*

INNCORRECT RODE LENGTH *(TOO SHORT)*: Molecular rotation upwind in the trough and the corresponding rotation downwind on the crest cause the boat and the parachute to momentarily converge.

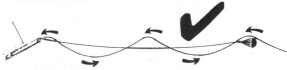

CORRECT RODE LENGTH: The long rode leaves the boat free to rise/move/rotate with the seas, and by stretching acts as a "buffer" to absorb much of the peak divergence loads; notice how the rode has been finely adjusted so that the boat and the sea anchor are rotating in unison on their respective waves.

is contrary or the crew excessively tired, a nice time out can be had while the boat bobs at "anchor." If repairs need to be made to the vessel, especially aloft, riding to a para-anchor will be the easiest way to effect them.

Commercial fishermen increasingly use para-anchors to maintain station over deep-bottom fishing grounds, to provide a comfortable resting period between haul backs, and to ride out severe weather. Monohull cruisers are employing the para-anchor system more and more, but their inability to affix a wide bridle to their hull makes sea anchoring in storm conditions less effective than it is with a multihull.

John and Joan Cassanova have advocated the use of para-anchors for many years, and used this technique with great success during their circumnavigation, via Cape Horn and the Roaring Forties, aboard their 38-foot Horstman-designed trimaran *Tortuga Too*.

The Cassanovas began experimenting with sea anchoring by using surplus military parachutes, finally settling on a 28-foot diameter canopy attached by a very long nylon warp to a bridle rigged from their trimaran's float bows. They also rigged a trip line to ease recovery of the chute. Before getting into the specifics of para-anchoring, it's worth reading their firsthand account of what it is like to be sea-anchored in a severe storm.

. . . we were sailing in a high latitude Southern Ocean gale, one that arrived on the back of another low pressure system. These two storms averaged winds up to Force 11-12 which, after blowing for several days, created some of the highest seas ever witnessed by us. *Tortuga Too* was tethered from the chute when an enormous mountain of water rose before her bows, with another wave riding piggyback upon the first. This top wave began to well up, then roll over in gallons of green water, and break in truck-size foamy crests. It was the type of wave which pitch-poles yachts in these oceans—the type which every voyager sailing in the high latitudes fears.

While we watched, horrified, through the wheelhouse windows, this monster welled up for a second time, curling over as if breaking on a beach, then roaring in foamy masses on top of *Tortuga Too*, covering deck and wheelhouse, before running off into the sea once more. We were so shaken by this experience that it seemed an eternity before we regained our composure to check the boat's condition, but she was all right. In fact *Tortuga Too* recovered faster than we did. There was no structural damage. She had returned to her original position of facing the storm and was already climbing the next wave.

We want to stress here, that no vessel—multihull, monohull, or freighter—could have survived such a sea unless tethered with a long line from a sea anchor. Again, it was one of those waves impossible to sail over.

Later, in another storm, the Cassanovas reported that:

> By early morning light, the winds had worked their way around to the southeast and blew with a vengeance. The barometer now read 960 millibars [28.35 inches], the lowest reading during the whole voyage. The boat continued to climb oncoming seas, lifting a hull now and then, to make room for huge cross waves. Each one grew and formed giant breakers that rolled over into yards of foam. As the wind increased, these breakers began to blow off and away, until the ocean around us was white. This was the full force of the storm as it thundered and rumbled over us. The noise was terrifying. Minutes later, a glance at the anemometer told us that the gust needle was stuck at 100 m.p.h.! After eight hours of this punishment we woke up to the fact that the parachute was doing its job: the boat was still upright, there was no damage to the structure, and we were alive! (From *The Parachute Anchoring System,* Joan Cassanova, Chiodi Publishing, 1982.)

Not all sea anchors are created equal. In 1974, as I was about to leave for the Caribbean on my 31-foot trimaran, a well-meaning friend gave me a "sea anchor" that he had carried on his boat for some time but had never used, although he thought having one was a good idea. Two weeks later, faced with strong head winds and big seas, it seemed the time to give it a try. This "sea anchor" was a small ex-military drogue chute (used to pull the big parachute out of its pack) about 3 feet in diameter. I set it over the bow on a 100-foot tether, and it worked—sort of.

Although the sea anchor did not have enough drag to bring the trimaran completely facing the wind, she was relatively steady, pointing about 40 degrees off the wind. The motion was somewhat jerky due to the short tether line but, compared to the boat's motion before setting the sea anchor, it was reasonably comfortable below.

After a few hours the motion seemed to be getting worse, and the boat began jumping around as it was slammed broadside by wave crests. I checked the tether line and found it had little drag, so I pulled in the chute and found it in shreds. Conditions were far too rough to resume sailing to windward in the wee hours of the morning, so we were forced to run off in the wrong direction using a tire drogue to check our speed and limit our negative progress.

Unfortunately, this has been the type of experience with "sea anchors" most often reported in the primary offshore sailing books. Because of this, sea anchors often are regarded with suspicion. Victor Shane of Para-Anchors

Figure 10-6.
Not all sea anchors
are created equal.

International, Inc., a maker of large, effective sea anchors, has researched this phenomenon:

> How did this body of prejudice against sea anchors come into being? The term "sea anchor" itself appears about 36 times in Adlard Coles' *Heavy Weather Sailing;* in most every instance of attempted use the results being dismal. Closer examination, however, will show that in each and every instance the term is misapplied to a small, "admiralty pattern cone," probably about 21 inches in diameter.
>
> Why anyone would refer to a 21-inch cone as a "sea anchor" instead of referring to it as a "drogue" or a "drag device" is beyond me. . . . Indeed, it seems to me that throughout the entire litany of seafaring legend and tradition, the term "sea anchor" is used synonymously with midget cone devices! (From *Drag Device Data Base,* by Victor Shane, 1988, available from Para-Anchors International.)

A sea anchor must be *big* enough to prevent the hull from moving through the water, otherwise the boat will not face the wind and waves but will lie at an angle to them. Exactly how big is big enough depends on the type of boat and the construction of the sea anchor. Opinions differ among manufacturers and users, but what else is new? The Cassanovas used a 28-foot-diameter military surplus parachute. Their rule of thumb is that the chute's diameter roughly should equal the multihull's beam.

Two of the major manufacturers of parachute-type sea anchors (Shewmon, Inc., 1000 Harbor Lake Drive, Safety Harbor, FL 34695, and Para-Anchors International, Inc., P.O. Box 19, Summerland, CA 93067) have done extensive drag testing of their products and find that a sea anchor, if designed and built from the outset as a sea anchor, can be much smaller in diameter than a military surplus parachute and yet have the same drag.

Purpose-built sea anchors also are much stronger than surplus military chutes, which were designed to float a 180-pound soldier carrying 100 pounds of equipment to earth—*not* to pull a 6,000-pound boat through a 15-foot high wall of white water. A 40- to 50-foot cruising multihull typically requires a modern sea anchor of anywhere from 8 to 18 feet in diameter, depending on the specific boat and type of sea anchor. Go by the manufacturer's recommendations for your size and type of boat.

The tether line from boat to sea anchor is another hotly debated topic. Each proponent prefers his own system of shackles, line types, and retrieval systems. They all agree on one thing, however: the tether line should be *long*. Daniel Shewmon, of Shewmon, Inc., suggests 20 times the maximum wave height—which could run into an awful lot of line in a severe storm. The Cassanovas write that the minimum tether line should be 10 times the boat's length—certainly within the normal range of ground tackle rode carried aboard. Victor Shane of Para-Anchors recommends a minimum scope of 300 feet, or 12 times the boat's length up to a maximum of 600 feet.

Extensive information is available from the manufacturers on rigging, deployment, and use of sea anchors. It makes good reading.

The tactic of choice. As a survival tactic, the para-anchor has more advantages than any other technique. It can pull a boat *forward* through a wave that might otherwise start to roll it over. Its low rate of drift means that it requires practically no sea room, making it the only reasonable alternative if caught on a lee shore in a deadly storm. The comfortable motion of a boat riding to a sea anchor allows the crew to rest and regroup until conditions get better.

With so many advantages and no serious disadvantages, the decision to deploy a sea anchor becomes almost a non-decision: Go ahead and do it. If you are tired and the weather is sloppy, ride to the sea anchor and get some rest. If the weather worsens you are all set to ride it out comfortably; if it improves you can start sailing again after a decent meal and a good night's sleep. As your mother said, that never hurt anyone.

Dealing with Capsize

Although it's unlikely, multihulls *do* occasionally capsize, just as monohulls do occasionally sink. You can make either situation more bearable by adequate preparations.

In his book, *The Case For The Cruising Trimaran* (International Marine Publishing, 1979), multihull pioneer Jim Brown detailed many sensible techniques for coping with capsize. Unfortunately this book is out of print, but the preparations Jim outlined are, for the most part, inexpensive and easy to do. Some things have changed in the last 10 years, however. The following section parallels Jim's recommendations, with an additional ten years' perspective.

Habitation Potential

All capsize preparations hinge on one question: Is your boat habitable upside down or will it sink or float so low that you must rely on a life raft?

If your boat is unable to float substantially above water, either when upside down or right side up and severely damaged, she is non-habitable, and you must rely on a life raft or a dinghy for post-disaster living space.

How high must she float to be habitable? You need a place where the crew can get up out of the water and stay as dry as possible—a minimum vertical interior height of 3 to 4 feet of consistently dry space. The lower the water level in the habitable part of the boat the better. Lightweight multihulls with lots of flotation placed high in the boat may have water levels within the cabin that are knee deep or less, yielding a semi-comfortable "home" in which to await rescue.

The Life Raft

If the interior is uninhabitable, or if the boat can sink, then a life raft or similar vessel must become "home." The self-inflating life raft is the cornerstone of sinking-boat survival. A multihull that is not capsized-habitable also will need to carry a good raft since it will be the primary source of shelter.

In my opinion, the life raft ought to be called a "death raft," "last-glimmer-of-hope raft," or some other sobering name designed to dissuade sailors from entering one until all other alternatives are gone. Given a choice between treading water or entering a life raft, I'll be happy to crawl into a raft, thank you. But if the choice is between a floating boat and a life raft, I'll take my chances with the boat.

Life-raft survival is terribly difficult. They capsize easily, they're small, wet, uncomfortable, and *fragile*. The food, water, medical supplies, tools, fishing equipment, signaling apparatus, and clothing or survival suits that you will want *and need* for survival under anything but the most benign circumstances are unlikely to be in the raft.

Because the crew seldom enters the raft with more than their clothing—often not even that—the "sinker's" life raft must be a self-contained module that can at least partially provide all critical supplies and equipment. Read any account written by life-raft survivors and you will see that the standard equipment packed inside the raft is inadequate for long-term survival. (A recent well-publicized case of a couple's ordeal aboard a life raft showed their single most important piece of equipment was a hand-pump operated desalinator. So much for the biggest problem all shipwreck survivors face: "water, water, everywhere and not a drop to drink.")

This lack of necessary survival equipment is not the raft maker's fault. It is just not possible to fit sufficient life-support materiel for several people into a package compact enough be tolerated on deck.

Commercially available life rafts are designed to fulfill the needs of typical cruising boats—sinkers. In a sinking vessel, the raft must separate quickly from the mothership, which otherwise would drag it to the bottom, and become the crew's sole means of survival.

For multihulls with insufficient flotation to provide a habitable interior, the life raft has a substantially different role to play. The theory is for the crew to move into a raft tethered to their inverted vessel. By this means they have access to critical equipment and supplies, and enjoy a symbiotic relationship of raft to mothership.

Nice theory, but it has been tragically unsuccessful. Not only is the raft vulnerable to chafe from the boat, but the tether itself often chafes through or pulls right out of the raft, which then drifts away with its occupants aboard, their essential supplies still aboard their capsized "mothership."

Standard life rafts are not designed to be tethered to a boat floating awash. If your multihull cannot be made to float high enough to offer reasonable survival habitation and you have no choice but to enter a raft, you must devise a way to keep it with the boat. Your life will depend on it!

Remember that a breaking wave will hardly move the capsized boat but will try to carry away the raft with enormous force. Have the raft manufacturer install specially reinforced *multiple* attachment points, and attach the raft between the inverted hulls using three or four stout tether lines. Store these with the raft, made up and ready to go.

A "floater's" life raft should be manually operated. An automatic ejection/inflation feature may cause it to inflate beneath the boat and be caught or damaged in the process.

Because the raft will not drift away, you need not store the large quantities of food and water in the raft since these will be available from the mothership. Instead place more emphasis on protection from hypothermia by having appropriate clothing or wet suits packed within the raft. Have a mask and fins aboard to ease entry into the mothership until you can devise alternate entry methods.

The case for no raft. I carried a life raft aboard my first trimaran, but the more I thought about it, the more sense it made to have a mothership that provides for you well enough to eliminate the need for a life raft. At the risk of heresy, *Juniper* carries no raft. She is her own "life raft"—200 times more stable, 25 times larger, and with more critical water, food, tools, and equipment packed away than you could ever hope to carry in a dozen inflatable rafts.

Once, when forced to carry a borrowed raft to comply with racing rules, I had a chance to digest the emotional security of its presence. Instead of offering peace of mind, I found it only to be heavy, hard to stow, in the way, and a general threat to a much more practical and proven *multihull* survival tactic: staying with the boat.

Other sailors may be less pessimistic about "life" rafts and prefer to have them aboard, even if the boat is a high-floating habitable type. If the same precautions are taken against separation from the mothership, there is nothing wrong with having a raft aboard a capsize-habitable multihull. It could come in handy if you have, say, a major fire aboard. Just remember its limitations and avoid the temptation to emulate the crew of "sinkers" and abandon ship.

The Inverted Home

A far better alternative to living in a tethered life raft is to have a multihull that maximizes the survival potential of the inverted interior. Some designs will float so high that they will have extensive dry areas within the boat. These can house sleeping platforms or hammocks that will enable long-term, relatively comfortable survival.

Just a few weeks ago, a newspaper story came over the Associated Press news wire from New Zealand about a capsized trimaran that washed up on the island after drifting for *four months!* The crew was in such good shape—physically and emotionally—that the authorities at first suspected a hoax. No one could believe they could be so healthy after such an ordeal!

I can believe it. Certainly 118 days of drifting is no day at the beach—it comes close to breaking all other records for shipwreck survivors—but to walk ashore in such good condition that your truthfulness is questioned? That is something.

How did they do it? Well, the skipper, John Glennie, had enough multihull experience to know that his boat was his best life-support system available. In his own words:

> Just before we left, one of the wives came to the boat and asked where was the life raft. I said I didn't believe in life rafts, that they are the most dangerous things you can carry on a multihull. I claim you should always stay with the boat. It's the largest platform and far superior to any raft. (Courtesy *New Zealand Yachting* Magazine)

Toward a more habitable interior. Before setting out on an extended voyage, you will need to address some important practical considerations for dealing with capsize that can ease life considerably in an inverted multihull:

- *Prevent diesel fuel or gasoline from spilling into the cabin and rendering it uninhabitable.* A normal fuel tank installation, with filler cap on deck and vent pipe leading overboard, should not pose a problem, but every installation should be examined with the possibility of leakage in mind.

- *Spilled conventional batteries can emit poisonous gas.* Replace them with sealed batteries or the new gel-based batteries, like the "Prevailer" batteries available from Survival Technologies Group. Failing that, ordinary lead/acid batteries should be readily accessible so they can be deep-sixed.

- *Protect fresh water from loss or salt water contamination.* You should be able to close any on-deck fill or vent pipes from inside the hull. If there is any doubt, a 5-gallon jug of fresh water can be tied into a convenient location.

- *Store medical supplies and food in such a way that they remain dry and cannot be washed out of the hull in the first minutes after capsize.* Obviously, lockers that can open on their own will disgorge their contents onto the cabin's ceiling. The large quantities of water sloshing around will tend to pull things toward open hatches, essentially sucking vital supplies out of the boat. At least some storage lockers should have positive latches to hold their contents in place. Once the situation within the boat stabilizes, food and medical stores can be reorganized.

- *Provide for resting or sleeping places within the hull.* Often the crew finds the underside of berths or the cockpit a suitably large and flat place to stretch out. Identify these places beforehand, then make some effort to minimize or eliminate framework or stiffeners that would make sleeping on the underside uncomfortable. Consider having special hammocks aboard which could be strung up inside the hull, or have a plan to improvise them from between-hull netting or sailcloth.

None of these preventive measures are terribly expensive or difficult to accomplish. As always, the hardest part is facing squarely the potential for calamity and *doing* the simple things ahead of time to make coping with capsize easier. In the unlikely event of disaster you will be prepared.

An interesting idea that would ensure relatively comfortable habitation within a capsized boat would be to completely bail out the hull or a portion of the hull. Considering the low hydrostatic pressure on the deck openings, it out of the cabin. Obviously this technique could not be applied to every multihull, and retrofitting an old one may be difficult, but for a new boat (especially a small one) that will sail frequently in exposed offshore waters, it would be something to consider in the design stage.

Because of the airlock in a trimaran's floats, the main hull ordinarily will float very high, affording a reasonably habitable interior—even without taking extra measures to achieve high buoyancy. Catamarans, on the other hand, seldom will have airlock in the hulls due to a variety of through-hull openings. Unless countermeasures are taken, the hulls will be deeply immersed, with the bridgedeck cabin completely submerged and useless for accommodation.

For these reasons the cruising cat, especially, may want to incorporate a section of the hull that could be partitioned off from the rest and pumped dry. If this section were forward, its watertight bulkhead could serve both as an upright collision bulkhead and to partition off inverted survival accommodation space.

For the coastal or waterway cruiser this kind of preparation may well be superfluous, but the long-distance multihull cruiser will enjoy great peace of mind because he knows that he is prepared to deal with the worst. Survival is almost a sure bet as long as he stays with the boat.

Tools and survival equipment. In the event of capsize or practically any other calamity, access to basic hand tools and signaling devices will be vital.

- *Locate and secure the boat's tool box where it cannot be washed out of the hull.* Carry duplicates of certain basic tools, (keyhole saw, hammer, nails, pliers, Vise-Grips, screwdriver, and self-tapping screws) in a waterproof container that can be securely tied into the boat to prevent loss. Make sure you have waterproof flashlights securely stored. Cyalume light sticks, sold in many hardware stores, are a good emergency item.

- *Pack flares and smoke signals in their own waterproof box tied to the boat.* The fisheries supply house where I bought my flares packed them in a gasketed metal "ammo box," which seems like just the right container—after all these things are explosive!

  The Ocean Racing Council (ORC) requires that boats participating in offshore races carry a combination of SOLAS- (Safety of Life at Sea Convention) approved parachute flares, handheld flares, and smoke signals. A cruising boat can benefit from the same equipment. These items cost considerably more than the ordinary marine store distress signals, but you get what you pay for. If you ever *need* to fire a parachute flare it might as well be the brightest, highest flying, and longest burning flare you can buy.

• *Tie your EPIRB (Emergency Position Indicating Radio Beacon) into the boat so that it cannot be washed away.* Check the battery's expiration date, and carry a replacement if you're going out on an extended cruise. EPIRBs are usually, but not always, effective in soliciting assistance. There are so many false alarms due to the vast number of EPIRBs in use that occasionally a real distress signal goes unnoticed.

• *Carry a handheld VHF radio.* These have proven invaluable in many instances. Many brands are on the market, some are quite water resistant, although a heavy-duty waterproof pouch probably is essential to ensure its performance if fully immersed in water.

These radios have surprising range considering their comparatively meager 5-watt output. I have spoken clearly to ships that were nearly out of sight. (Actually my wife did the talking; it is amazing the way a woman's voice will elicit all sorts of weather information from the watch officer of a passing ship on a dark and lonely night.) Alkaline batteries give longer "playing time" than the rechargeable NiCad battery packs. Several changes of batteries could be worth their weight in gold. Several electronics supply specialty shops carry small solar battery chargers designed to recharge the small NiCads used in these sets.

• *Carry a good radar reflector.* Merchant ships rely on radar to spot other vessels. A boat in distress that presents a strong radar echo will be "seen" better this way than by any other means. This is especially true at night or in rain, snow, or fog.

During the Second World War, downed airmen in rafts flew kites with attached radar reflectors to make them more visible to shipboard radar. This seems worthwhile trying today, although it would take significant preparation or some clever on-the-spot kite making. A more practical method would be to erect a temporary "mast" by lashing together booms, oars, fishing poles, or anything else that can get the reflector up as high as possible.

• *Consider having survival suits aboard for all crew members.* These bulky, insulated, one-piece hooded suits (resembling deep-sea diver's suits) are the single best way to conserve body heat. Without a survival suit your life expectancy fully immersed in warm water is a matter of hours; in cold water, little more than a few minutes. Their built-in flotation chambers give you a reasonable chance of survival, at least for a day or two, even if your boat sinks, taking your raft down with it. A floating boat in conjunction with survival suits gives the crew a fortified chance of dealing with just about anything that may come along.

Survival suits are expensive ($300 to $500) and bulky to stow, but for offshore sailing in temperate and cold waters they are proving to be the most significant piece of safety equipment developed in a very long time. The decision to buy survival suits for use in a multihull would swing on the type of boat, the frequency it is sailed long distances, and the climate and water temperature of your cruising area. Practically all commercial fishermen now carry survival suits, but at this writing few cruisers routinely carry them. I am willing to bet this will change in the next decade.

Emergency access hatches. The rules for multihulls racing offshore often require an "escape hatch" to be fitted in the hull topsides so that the crew can get in and out of a capsized hull without diving beneath the boat. Given the frequency of racing boat dumpings, this is a sensible idea. But a cruising multihull is a different animal altogether, and a hatch of this type may or may not be advantageous.

If capsized, the crew of a non-habitable multihull will want to get out—and may need to get out in a hurry—if the boat floats so poorly that airspace inside is problematical. On the other hand, the crew of a habitable multihull will want to stay inside; there is no reason to "escape."

The single biggest problem with hatches fitted in the hull topsides is that if the boat is inverted the hatch normally will be too low to the water to be useful. While a topsides hatch may provide an easy path for initial entry or exit, at least in a habitable multihull, a better long-term location for a hatch is up high, where waves can't wash into the hull and a crewman can keep watch for rescuing craft. This "high" hatch invariably will be made with a saw and the built-in topsides hatch probably will not be used.

Built-in capsize hatches can be useful in certain situations:

- •If the boat is small and frequently voyages offshore (i.e., has a higher-than-average capsize risk).

- •If the companionway hatches are especially inaccessible when capsized.

- •If the hatch can be located near the galley it makes an incredibly convenient way to get ice and groceries aboard directly from the dinghy. This may sound frivolous but this is probably the only way this hatch will ever be used.

Capsize Aftermath in Real Life

Earlier in this chapter, we left the story of Walter Greene's capsized trimaran *Gonzo* hanging just as Walter was describing how he got back into the boat in the minutes following capsize. The measures Walter employed after the capsize were basically sensible and appropriate; similar techniques have worked well for others.

Gonzo had no escape hatches fitted; the racing rules didn't require them then. I think in a way a hatch in the hull topside, [like those required by the offshore multihull racing rules] is a bad thing because when the boat is inverted the hatch is low. Sawing a hole worked well, but we cut the hole too near the water and every wave that came along came pouring through the hole. We eventually plugged it up satisfactorily, but you really want the hole to be as close to the bilge as possible. When the boat is upside down you want the hatch right in the top of the boat.

We moved into the aft part of the boat, and Nye Williams got out the EPIRB and rigged it up. The main storage batteries gave off a small amount of gas for about five minutes, and you could feel a little bit of 12-volt running around in the water, so we cut the cables and chucked the batteries, as well as a generator set. We had lots of tools, which really came in handy.

The EPIRB was switched on at nine in the morning; we spent all day in the boat. During the night (it got dark around five o'clock) we always had one guy on watch and the other two sleeping. We all had been wearing survival suits ever since the boat capsized. Although they were wet inside when we put them on, they kept us warm anyway.

Survival suits are a pain in the neck to move around in because they are so bulky. They have clumsy, diver's-type mittens, but you still can eat an apple or a candy bar well enough, and you are not doing much at this point anyway; there's no rush. I would never trade survival suits for anything else: You are sure to stay warm in them and that is the most important thing.

The next morning we heard a plane. Nye stuck his head out and saw it, so we shot off a flare and the plane came by and wagged its wings. We got out the portable VHF radio, tried channel 16, and I could talk to the pilot instantly. (The plane was a U.S. Navy Submarine-Hunter which had been directed to us by the EPIRB.) A portable VHF radio is a lot more valuable than a bunch of flares if you're in trouble. The pilot said there was a ship about 50 miles away which would be here in three hours, and he would keep flying around until the ship arrived. So we hung out, waiting, occasionally talking to the plane.

It was still blowing 30 to 35 knots, and there still were big seas running—20 feet or more—when the ship arrived, a huge tanker, the *Getty California*. I talked to the skipper on VHF, and he said they would come up alongside and then we should climb up the boarding ladder. I said "this isn't going to work," but he said he had no boat that he could launch, and this was the only way.

He maneuvered the ship toward us, and when it was about 75 yards away the crew threw us a bunch of heaving lines with monkey's fists on the ends. We were meant to jump in the water and swim over to the ship, but we didn't feel too confident—sometimes the man at the other end of the line would let go. So they made another pass and came by very slowly at about 2 knots. That ship drew a lot of water—about 40 feet. It was more like a seawall than a ship; it didn't bounce around at all. He drifted down on top of us but we still couldn't manage to get aboard, so they drifted off to try again.

Eventually he came at us straight upwind, and the bulbous bow hit us right in the middle of the float. That was the end of that hull, it split in two. Then *Gonzo* lifted up so high on a wave that we could look down on his deck; there was just a little bit of water between us and the deck of the ship; on the way up his anchor went through part of the boat.

We jumped off the boat and swam away, holding onto the end of a long line, trying to get away from the ship. Eventually I got back on what was left of *Gonzo* and called the captain on the VHF. "This isn't going to work," I said. "Don't come near us again!" We were wet, tired, and hungry but at least we weren't dying, not at all. But we sure could die in this kind of rescue attempt. The ship's captain said, well, you know it's hard to make a recovery at sea and he wasn't set up for it. The pilot came back on the radio and said there was a Coast Guard cutter on the way, about four hours off, so we just waited for them.

The cutter arrived—not a real big one, about a 240-footer. We spoke on the radio, and they said they wanted to come straight upwind, right at us. They would lay their bow up next to us, just to leeward a bit, and send over a horseshoe sling, like they use to lift people up to a helicopter.

So they brought their bow up to us and threw the sling over, and they hauled us up by hand, one at a time. The captain of the cutter backed down slightly as they pulled the man up to keep him from being pounded on the ship. Their technique worked very well. They were so much better than the merchant ship that, if you ever get in this situation, it is well worth waiting for the Coast Guard.

The tanker's captain could maneuver it very well, but it was just too big to pick us up. One of the problems was that the crew gets running along the deck of a 1000-foot ship, trying to help, but they can't communicate with the bridge and vice versa so no one really knows what is happening. It's not really their fault; it's just not something they're trained to do.

Gonzo's crew took the trouble to prepare for the worst by securing essential equipment such as flashlights, EPIRB, VHF radio, and tools, and making ready their survival suits. Assistance was fast in coming due to the EPIRB, but it was a mixed blessing. Any pickup at sea by a large merchant vessel is extremely dangerous; several fatalities have been caused by people being smashed against the hull of a rescuing ship. As Walter Greene said, "We were tired and hungry but not in imminent danger of dying, except by the ship trying to save us."

It is a sad fact that many fatalities ensue during premature or reckless abandonment of the vessel. During the 1979 Fastnet Race, many deaths and injuries occurred because the crews were too eager to leave their boats, which they imagined were about to founder. Actually, of the 24 yachts abandoned only 5 were lost, and 1 of these sank while under tow. In a multihull capsize, the first rule of survival is *do not leave the boat until pickup is an absolutely sure thing.*

Righting a Capsized Boat

Considerable ink has been expended on the topic of self-righting (righting the boat without outside assistance) a capsized multihull. Some success has been achieved with scale models and small boats with self-righting features, but to date there has yet to be a multihull of any size righted by her crew in the ocean after a real capsize. In my opinion it is unlikely to happen with any of the current schemes scaled up to cruising-boat size.

The basic problem is the boat's enormous stability—even upside down and full of water—which requires a tremendous amount of energy to overcome. Of course the boat's inverted stability can be decreased. If the boat and its contents were designed to be almost neutrally buoyant, so that if capsized it would be completely submerged but not quite sunk, then the self-righting system need only overcome the frictional forces of turning the boat in the water. A powerful man wearing swim fins and scuba gear could push it over.

The trouble with this idea is that the crew would drown or be forced into the life-or-death raft long before the idea could be put into practice. Great inherent buoyancy is so important for a multihull's ultimate survival that it seems terribly dangerous to reduce or eliminate it in favor of an unproven righting system.

While self-righting will continue to intrigue some sailors, it seems to me that if there is any *practical* chance of sailing a multihull home that was capsized offshore, it will hinge on being able to use effectively the outside help that invariably comes along.

The only easy and consistently reliable way to right a large capsized multihull is "the end-over-end, tow-over method." Briefly, a stout line is attached with a bridle to the bows of the boat and lead aft over the bottom of the hull to the assisting vessel. As the line is pulled, the drag of the rig plus the capsized boat's sterns digging into the water begins a somersault that rotates it back upright. Sounds too simple to be true, but it works.

There have been several cases of rescue and salvage craft trying to lift a capsized multihull over sideways with cranes and other brute force techniques; with few exceptions these methods fail and severely damage the capsized boat in the process. When the salvage crew is convinced to try the "tow over," they're invariably successful.

My first experience with the end-over-end technique was when a 23-foot day-racing trimaran overloaded with loaded sailors capsized in a squall outside a harbor in which I was anchored. I was concerned for the well-being of the drunken sailors, and jumped into the only available "rescue craft" in sight, a 9-foot dinghy with a 6 h.p. outboard. When I arrived on the scene, all five of the crew were attempting to right the boat by standing on one float and pulling lines attached to the main hull. Their combined weight could barely rotate the boat 30 degrees from horizontal; obviously, this was not going to work.

I explained the tow-over procedure and we quickly fastened lines to the bows, lead them over the stern of the tri, and thence to the dinghy. I gave a half-throttle pull and the boat started to rotate upright immediately. I was surprised; I knew the method worked, but I didn't realize how small a pull actually was required.

Naturally a larger boat will require a greater pull, but pull normally is no problem for the sort of vessel likely to arrive on the scene after an offshore calamity. If the tow-over bridle can be installed and the captain of the assisting vessel convinced to try the method, a successful recovery is well within reason. Being prepared for an "assisted self-righting" is the only way I can conceive a realistic chance of sailing (or being towed) home after an offshore capsize.

Of course there are problems involved with this system. The two biggest ones seem to be bailing out the righted boat and whether the capsized vessel's

Figure 10-7.
Tow-over techniques
for assisted self-righting.

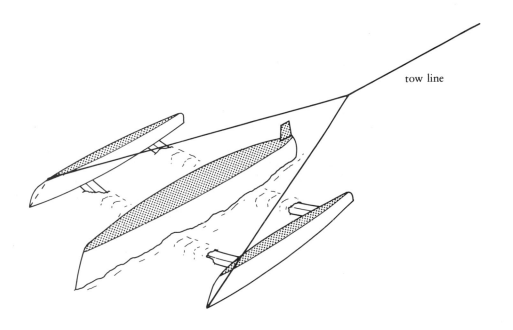

tow line

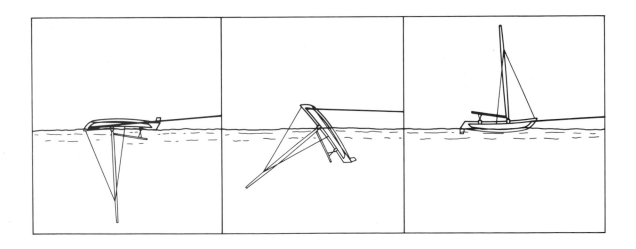

crew is physically and emotionally able to hang in there long enough to effect the righting once assistance is at hand.

Re-righting a capsized multihull is not going to be an easy or automatic task, but I think, if any effort is placed into the self-righting basket, it should be done with outside assistance in mind.

Man Overboard!

Man overboard is so common and so deadly that it needs to be addressed in the design of a cruising boat. As mentioned in Chapter 1, the U.S. Coast Guard's accident statistics for 1983-87 attribute about 80 percent of all reported deaths within U.S. waters on single-hulled auxiliary-powered sailboats to falling overboard.

Intuitively you would expect that a very wide boat that heels little—a multihull—will pose less risk of falling overboard than one that sails at a 30-degree angle and can roll right over onto its side during an unintentional jibe. The statistical evidence, scant though it may be, seems to confirm this. Of the multihull-related fatalities occurring in the Atlantic Ocean, only 14 percent were due to man overboard. It takes only a small leap of logic to conclude that there is considerably less risk of someone falling off a multihull.

On the downside, if someone *does* go over the side of a multihull, there are at least two reasons why they are less likely to be recovered successfully: First, the multihull will probably be going faster than a monohull, and this certainly can work against a person that falls in the water. It has been shown that the larger the separation between the swimmer and the boat, the more difficult the recovery.

The second reason is that multihulls often have greater freeboard than monohulls, and this can make getting a person back aboard more difficult even if contact is made. Extensive studies have been done expressly to help overcome the problems of separation and recovery, and the resulting methods, the *quick-stop* and the *lifesling,* are highly pertinent to multihull sailors.

But the big issue is staying on the boat in the first place. This means solid footing and avoiding on-deck acrobatics. Monohulls often seem to have very cluttered decks, possibly to give the crew something to hang on to when the boat is on her beam ends. In a boat that heels little, this kind of clutter seems more of a detriment than an asset.

For a multihull, I prefer decks that contain a minimum of surprises and things to trip over. Areas that are frequently walked on, particularly crossbeams and their fairings, need to be designed with nearly level surfaces wherever possible. Some boats that are beautiful to look at can be next to impossible to walk over. Assume it is 2 a.m., raining, and you're trying to cross 25 feet of deck with a 35-pound anchor in your arms, the chain and rode dragging behind you. Now reconsider the lovely curves of the decks and crossbeams.

Multihulls often cover open horizontal spaces between hulls with safety netting. These nets must be strong and properly looked after; details are given below. Lifelines and safety harnesses, employed as they would be in a monohull, add further protection against going overboard.

Man-Overboard Recovery

It is one thing to do what you can to prevent man-overboard from occurring and quite another to recover a person in the water. Spurred by a number of fatal accidents, the Seattle Sailing Foundation and the Sailing Squadron of the U.S. Naval Academy have each conducted considerable research into appropriate methods for recovering a person who has fallen off the boat. These methods are described in detail in the publication *Recent Progress in Man-Overboard Recovery*, (USYRU Publications, Box 209, Newport, RI 02840). The basic highlights of the methods developed are presented below.

Extensive research at the U.S. Naval Academy has proven the effectiveness of the *quick-stop method* for man-overboard recovery. Every extra foot that the boat travels (think fast-sailing multihull) after a crew member falls into the water diminishes the chances of successful recovery. Quoting from *Recent Progress in Man-Overboard Recovery,* "In short, the hallmark of the quick-stop is to reduce boatspeed immediately by reducing the driving force from the sails, thereby making the boat stay closer to the victim and maintaining superior visibility."

The process of achieving the quick-stop is ruthlessly simple: "If sailing close-hauled or on reaches, the boat is, at once, *headed into the wind* or beyond, without altering sheeting, except possibly to take in slack. The sails will go aback, the boat will slow, and the turn is continued before the wind, when the headsail can come down or not, depending on the contemplated recovery method. At this point the boat is still quite close to the victim. She has not gone far because her speed has been killed quickly."

This is quick, easy to remember, and effective. As a first step in man-overboard recovery this seems the most worthwhile method for multihulls.

Once the boat is stopped or slowed the problem becomes making contact with the victim and getting him back aboard. The Sailing Foundation has developed a workable method for small crews that would not otherwise have the manpower available to muscle a person aboard. The technique is to "tow a floating object, such as a life-ring buoy, tethered to the boat with a floating line; and by sailing around the victim, making contact after the manner employed in picking up a water skier who has fallen."

Experimentation has shown that the best "floating object" to tow is a horsecollar-shaped combination life vest and lifting sling. This enables the person in the water to be buoyantly supported and lifted aboard without the need to transfer from a life vest into another type of lifting sling. The developed "horsecollar" has become known as a "lifesling," and is available commercially from many marine suppliers.

The basic recovery procedure goes like this:

- Kill headway using the quick-stop method and release the lifesling overboard.

- Sail circles around the victim, towing the lifesling, until contact is made.

- Head into the wind and drop the sails.

- Haul the victim alongside, preferably on the windward side, from amidships to the quarter wherever there are available cleats and winches. Pull up on the tether line, with winch assistance if necessary, to get the victim's head and shoulders out of the water, and cleat it. The victim is safe now.

- Hoist the victim up over the lifelines or rail. In a monohull this often is accomplished by fixing a halyard to the sling portion of the lifesling and using the halyard winch or a sheet winch to hoist the person aboard.

  This system should work equally well for a multihull, but some minor alterations should be considered.
- The floating line joining the lifesling to the boat should be longer than standard to compensate for a multihull's increased speed and turning radius. The Sailing Foundation suggests a minimum of 150 feet; I think this should be increased to 200 feet minimum for multihulls.

- Minimize boatspeed once the victim is in the lifesling. If the victim is towed too fast he could drown. The Sailing Foundation recommends he face backwards in the sling if breathing is difficult. It is doubtful that the victim would be able to turn around in the sling once moving through the water more than 2 knots, so extra effort must be made to check boatspeed.

- In rough weather, a trimaran's float will be moving up and down with some velocity. If the victim were pulled alongside the float he could get conked in the head and be seriously injured. The better place to haul him aboard would be the main hull.

- Many multihulls have raked transoms with built-in steps; this provides an ideal place to hoist the victim aboard and should be considered in the location of the hoisting apparatus.

To compare the quick-stop technique with more conventional man-overboard recovery methods, i.e., launching a man-overboard pole and/or life ring, the Naval Academy Sailing Squadron performed 167 trials of launching this equipment. In 11 percent of the trials, major foul-ups were recorded, unduly delaying launch. The average time for the successful launching in the remaining 149 attempts was about 17 seconds. A boat traveling 10 knots will go 287 feet in 17 seconds, severely diminishing the odds of successful recovery. Rather than getting sidetracked trying to get all the usual man overboard equipment over the side, *stop the boat instead!* Worry about equipment after stopping.

One interesting, but expensive, high-tech solution to the quick deployment of man-overboard gear is a radio-activated system that automatically releases the life ring and pole. Sold by Survival Technologies Group (101 16th Ave. South, St. Petersburg, FL 33701), this system includes a water-activated device worn by crewmembers which sends a signal to the package of man-overboard gear and a small explosive charge releases it from its mount! For the less Star-Wars minded, Survival Technologies also has quick release but manually operated man-overboard modules, called "M.O.M.'s," that seem to be popular.

Safety Nets

Many cats and tris cover the open spaces between hulls with safety nets or trampolines. It is essential that this important piece of the boat be selected with care and maintained properly. Rob James, a prominent multihull (and monohull) racing sailor, was lost overboard and died because a rotten safety net tore away.

Netted areas are lightweight and cannot pound the wave tops, and they are great places to throw a muddy anchor, stow the dinghy, or take a spray bath in the tropics. Properly installed, nets are very strong and can safely hold quite a few people, but they do wear out eventually and must be replaced.

Chafe is an important problem to guard against, especially around the perimeter of the net where it attaches to the hulls. Whatever system is used to fix the net in place, it must be absolutely smooth and free of hard edges or it will chafe through quickly.

The other significant problem with nets is damage from sunlight. The sun destroys plastic. Since all of the desirable net and trampoline materials are various forms of plastic, it is important to select a type that is ultraviolet resistant. Failing that, find a way to protect the vulnerable material from the harmful effects of the sun.

Polypropylene is a strong, lightweight, and inexpensive plastic used often for fish nets. It also is available as 2-inch wide flat webbing made into specialty nets for multihulls by outfits like the Mare Company (P.O. Box 9104, Marina del Rey, CA, 90295). Polypropylene has terrible UV durability. Unprotected, its life span in tropical sun is measured in weeks. Black polypropylene has much greater UV resistance; apparently the black pigment limits the penetration of the harmful rays. Any polypropylene safety netting other than black is potentially dangerous.

Nylon and Dacron are other likely candidates for nets. Both of these are substantially more durable than polypropylene, but still suffer from photodegradation (sun damage). Unprotected, they will last only two to three years. But unlike slippery polypropylene, nylon, and dacron can be coated with any number of paint-like compounds that will keep the sunlight out of the fiber and add enormous longevity to the net.

On *Juniper,* I installed a knotless variety of commercial nylon fish net I saturated with black polyurethane paint. After six years of use some fading was apparent on the upper surface of the net. Fearing that the sun was weakening the fibers, I flipped the nets over to reveal the jet-black underside. I expect they will be due for replacement 10 years after installation—four to five times longer than unprotected fiber would have lasted.

Anchoring

Put three cruising sailors together in the same room for an hour and the conversation invariably will center on anchors for the last 55 minutes! And a hot conversation it will be, as in, "How could you possibly like that piece of !@%&#¥! anchor?"

When cruising, your home and possessions as well as your own physical well-being literally hang on the end of a rope. Often a cruising boat will spend 10 or more hours at anchor for every hour spent under way. Life at anchor is a most important part of any cruising boat and needs to be considered in its design.

Multihulls generally are good boats at anchor, for a number of reasons. Because there is no lead keel hanging from the bottom to impart a pendulum effect, multihulls don't develop the rolling motion from a small swell on the beam typical of most monohulls.

This may seem like a minor point, but many anchorages (especially in the tradewinds) are located in the lee of small islands. A large ocean swell usually wraps around the ends of these islands and comes up along their lee side, approaching anchored boats on the beam.

For those aboard an anchored multihull, the swell is barely noticeable—the boat will bob up and down slightly. Nearby monohulls often will roll severely —not because the swell is big, but because its period closely matches the boat's own period of roll. Like a child on a swing, just a little push at the right moment builds considerable motion. Maybe this is something you get used to, but I prefer not to bother. And I have had many beautiful anchorages to myself because they were too rolly for everyone else.

A multihull's typically shallow draft also is an enormous asset when anchoring. Not only are more harbors available from which to choose, but the best protection and the best holding ground usually is in the shallowest (and frequently least crowded) part of the harbor. Anchored in shallow water, great scope can be gained on the anchor without the need for lots of swinging

Figure 10-8.
Most multihulls are
well behaved at
anchor. This is *Juniper*
riding out Hurricane
Gloria in 1985.

room. When faced with an approaching storm these options may provide salvation.

It is also very convenient to have your choice of storm-survival tactics unlimited by deep draft. For instance, the entrance to many well-protected harbors and hurricane holes are obstructed by shallow bars or reefs. Sometimes a shoal-draft boat may be able to take shelter on a very shallow bank since the height of waves is limited by the depth of the water. Even if there is no other protection, anchoring in gale force winds is not too bad if the water depth is only 5 feet. I have used this technique in the Bahamas when confronted by a fast-moving cold front that left us insufficient time to get into a land-locked anchorage 60 miles away.

The meaning of anxiety can be fully defined by the situation that so often happens when cruising: You have managed to squeeze into the only decent anchorage around; the weather is going from bad to worse; chop is building within the anchorage; a short distance off your stern is a rocky shore—much too nasty for an unintentional landing.

As the wind velocity passes 25 knots, most of your neighbors begin to sail some distance to either side of their anchors. You sit and watch as a large cruising boat runs off to starboard at 3 knots, only to be brought up short by the anchor and yanked back around to resume her journey to port. "I wonder how long that will go on before the anchor breaks loose?" you ask yourself.

Your multihull is riding on the biggest, most trustworthy anchor you own;

the narrow hulls slice through the anchorage chop, and there is little motion or noise below. But the wind continues to rise, and now you, too, are beginning to sail back and forth on the anchor, describing giant arcs around the little, not always completely reliable chunk of steel lying (buried you hope) on the bottom.

Every forced tack strains the anchor rode and threatens to break the anchor loose. You sit a while longer watching the compass—30, 40, 50 degrees from the wind you sail, exposing all the topsides to the full force of the wind. There is no room to drag; can you trust this bottom if the wind increases further? What to do?

The Bridle

Simple: Put the multihull's wide beam to work for you. By rigging a simple bridle, the pull of the anchor line can be spread athwartships 12 feet or more. As soon as the boat starts to sail off to one side, all the force of the anchor line turns the boat back head to wind. Sail off to the other side and the same thing happens—sailing at anchor is stopped dead.

In storm conditions, a bridle using the boat's full beam will limit anchor sailing to 10 degrees or less either side of head to wind. This reduces windage, and eliminates the excessive strains placed on the anchor by forced tacking.

At risk of further exacerbating tensions between proponents of multihulls versus monohulls, we multihull fans gain another important advantage from our easily anchored craft: entertainment. I suppose I should not advertise this side of my personality, but often, while swinging from her bridle in the smooth, shallower parts of harbors, *Juniper* provides a comfortable platform from which to view the shenanigans of our single-hulled cruising compatriots in their battle with the elements—their boats pitching and rolling, finally dragging anchor, their often partly clad and always irate crews having to get under way, shouting and cursing, awaiting the inevitable line in the prop. Not that this sort of thing never happens to multihull sailors; it's just that a cat or tri offers more opportunities to avoid anchoring woes.

It is most convenient to anchor a trimaran by a single rode running from the main hull's bow. If the wind pipes up and sailing around the anchor becomes a problem, it is an easy matter to bend on a short line to the anchor rode (use a prussick knot or a rolling hitch), slack off the main rode so that the knot is near water level, bring the bridle line over to the float, and cleat it. This forms an off-center bridle, but this poses no problem, with the possible exception of real storm conditions, when the maximum separation of the bridle lines is desirable. In this case the main anchor rode can be led to the other float or another bridle line bent on.

Catamarans can use the same procedure, but it is more easily done because the forward net and crossbeam allow easy access all the way across the boat. Incidentally, if a cat has its anchor roller placed somewhat off-center, riding on one anchor is more stable because the boat will sail off to one side and stay there rather than sail back and forth.

Ground Tackle

I prefer 3-strand nylon anchor rode with about 25 feet of chain on the end connecting it to the anchor. All-chain anchor rode is becoming increasingly popular with cruising monohulls, and has the advantage of requiring less scope, but this can be a weight burden for a multihull: 200 feet of 3/8-inch chain weighs 350 pounds compared with 28 pounds for an equal length of 5/8-inch nylon line, which has similar strength.

If you plan to use a parachute sea anchor or another type of drogue you will need to have this long 3-strand nylon rode aboard anyway, so all-chain anchor rodes are redundant aside from their substantial weight penalty. It is almost impossible to row out an anchor with an all-chain rode in the dinghy, a critical safety feature for self-reliant cruising.

As suggested previously, the choice of anchor itself is largely personal—and heavily laced with emotion. I am not fool enough to make any suggestions beyond the following:

In my experience the weight (or size) of a multihull's anchor should be about the same as would be used on a monohull of the same length. The notion that multihulls somehow require only tiny anchors has no credibility with me.

The Danforth-type anchor has amazing holding power for its weight and is an excellent multihull anchor. If you can get it buried in mud or sand and do not swing over it and pull it out backwards or foul the crown with the rode it will hold the boat through almost anything.

But struck by a squall, if the anchor breaks loose, a lightweight multihull with boards retracted can drift sideways fast enough to actually "fly" it through the water, its large flukes serving as wings. I don't mean dragging across the bottom looking for a place to lodge, but skimming over the bottom without a prayer of finding a home. The solution is to have enough chain on the rode to keep it down on the bottom or let out additional scope, momentarily letting the anchor fall to the bottom.

On Invincibility

No person is immortal, and no vessel that has ever put to sea is invincible. But by eliminating ballast, the multihull sailboat successfully eliminates one of the greatest threats to mariners—sinking—and gains a number of highly desirable traits in the bargain: increased performance, seakindly behavior, and shallow draft. In addition, a multihull's wide decks and high stability provide a safe and secure working area for the crew, sharply reducing the threat from the greatest killer on the water: man overboard. The price we pay for all this

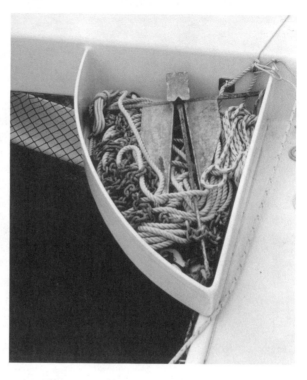

Figure 10-9.
Multihulls offer a variety of easily accessible storage areas for ground tackle. *Juniper* stores hers in trays just aft of the forward crossbeams; others use wicker baskets or built-in lockers.

is high inverted stability. If capsized, a multihull will *stay* capsized. Obviously, avoiding capsize is paramount.

To start with, the offshore sailing multihull must incorporate features that minimize the risk of capsize: size, overall beam, hull volume, sail plan, and deck layout all contribute. Strong but lightweight construction methods that incorporate large amounts of buoyancy within the structure ensure that the boat always floats high enough to afford adequate shelter for the crew—even if capsized or severely damaged. Collision bulkheads and hull subdivisions minimize loss of stability from flooding. *Any* boat can be holed by striking the floating objects that increasingly litter our oceans, and this is a frequent cause of capsize or sinking among ballasted boats. The multihull is equally susceptible to collision damage, but *it won't sink.*

Beyond this, the risk of capsize can be significantly reduced by the way a boat is handled. All sailors must know the limits of their boats; a multihull is no exception. Multihull sailors need to discard the "pedal to the metal" attitude that prevails among ballasted boat sailors. Like the electric golf cart, the cruising monohull can't go fast enough to cause much trouble. But like a gasoline-engined go-cart, the cruising multihull most definitely *can,* and the multihull sailor must know when to reduce sail and slow down.

In severe weather, when there is a risk of wave-impact capsize, the prudent multihull sailor will employ recently developed handling techniques, such as

Figure 10-10.

the para-anchor, that allow the crew to rest comfortably and safely until the weather improves.

Again, no boat is invincible. The sea being the sea, any boat can capsize. But unlike the monohull, the multihull and its contents remain afloat to shelter and assist the crew. Basic preparations prevent the loss of critical supplies. We have learned through the hard experience of others that many simple things can be done to greatly improve the comfort of the crew while they await assistance. As a survival platform, an inverted multihull has shown itself to be infinitely preferable to an inflatable raft.

Is a well-designed, built, and sailed multihull invincible? No. Seaworthy? **Yes!**

A Catalog of Production Multihulls

Although this list is far from complete, it does provide a representative sampling of available production multihulls sufficiently diverse to suit almost any taste—ranging from the elegant simplicity of the Wharram 28 to the spacious opulence of the Privilege 48 and Prout Quasar 50 Espace.

CLYDE CATS

Cheetah

Length overall: 26'0" (8.00m)

Beam: 20'0" (6.11m)

Draft: 30" (0.75m)

Sail area: 485 sq. ft. (43.7m²)

Displacement: 1,980 lbs (900kg)

Designer: John Shuttleworth

Clyde Cats Limited
McAllisters Boatyard
Sandpoint, Dumbarton G82 4BG
Scotland

The Cheetah is a diminutive high-tech speedster, constructed of unidirectional and woven roving E-glass, vacuum bonded to a PVC foam core. The removable bridgedeck is reinforced with unidirectional carbon fibers, and she features a rotating aluminum mast and self-tacking jib. Auxiliary power is supplied by a bridgedeck-mounted outboard.

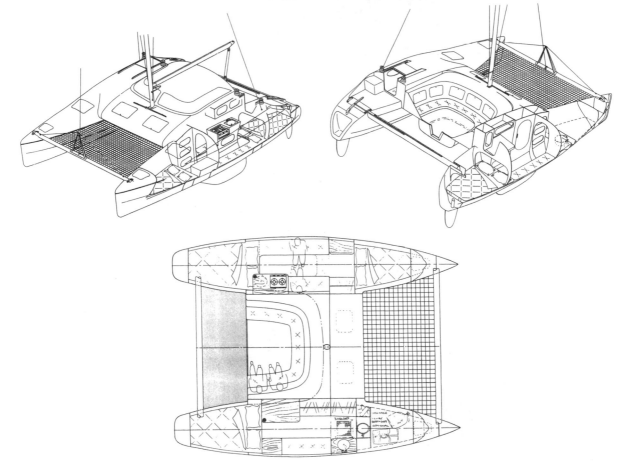

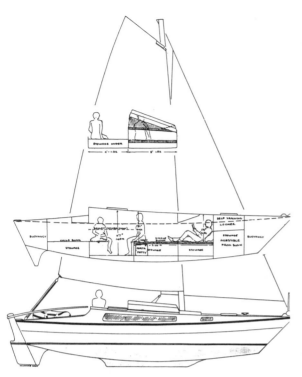

WHARRAM DESIGNS
Tiki 28

Length overall: 28'0" (8.53m)

Beam: 16'3" (4.95m)

Draft: 2'5" (0.74m)

Sail area: 330 sq. ft. (30.7m²)

Displacement: 1,500 lbs (680kg)

Designer: James Wharram

James Wharram Designs
Greenbank Road
Devoran
Truro, Cornwall TR3 6PJ
England

Over the years, James Wharram probably has sold more boat plans to home builders than any other designer; now he has a production boat. Based on his popular Tiki 21 camp cruiser, the Tiki 28, constructed in marine plywood and epoxy, provides extra accommodation with a cleverly engineered poptop bridgedeck cabin. The boomless rig features a sleeve-luff sail supported by a short Dutch-style gaff which adds extra area while keeping the center of effort low. An easily accessible outboard supplies auxiliary power.

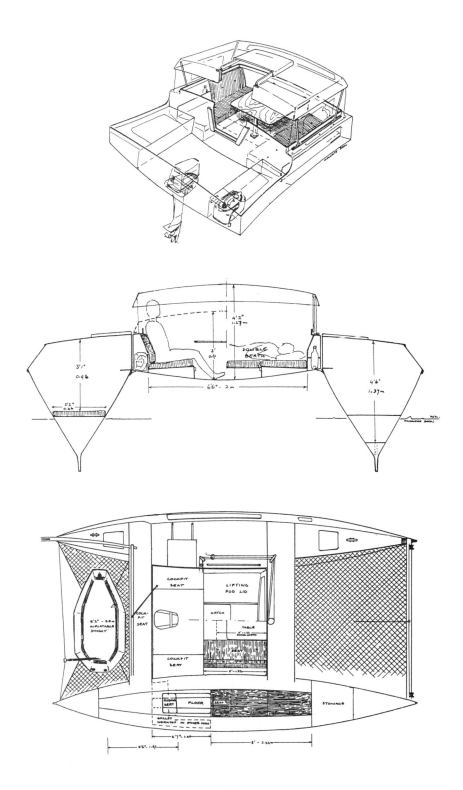

HEAVENLY CRUISING YACHTS

Heavenly Twins 27

Length overall: 27'0" (8.1m)

Beam: 13'9" (4.19m)

Draft: 27" (0.68m)

Sail area: 400 sq. ft. (36m²)

Displacement: 6,000 lbs (2600kg)

Designer: Pat Patterson

Heavenly Cruising Yachts Ltd.
East Harting
Petersfield,
Hants, GU31 5LT
England

The Heavenly Twins, which offers lots of accommodation in a very small hull, has been around quite a few years, and at least one Twins has circumnavigated. This new updated model is stretched a bit and offers more interior headroom than the original. Several choices are offered for auxiliary power: an outboard mounted in a well in the central cockpit; two 10 h.p. Yanmar diesels; or one 18 h.p. Yanmar with twin hydraulic drives. The same builder also produces two larger versions, the Oceanic 30 and 33.

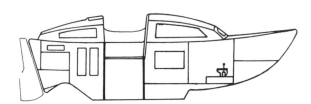

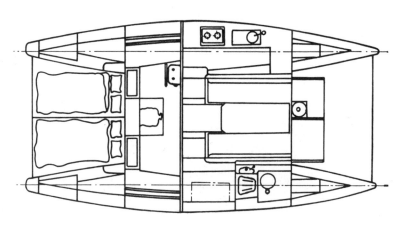

CORSAIR MARINE

F-27

Length overall: 27'1" (8.25m)

Beam: 19'1" (5.82m)

Draft: 14" (0.36m)

Sail area: 446 sq. ft. (41.3m²)

Displacement: 2,600 lbs (1180kg)

Designer: Ian Farrier

Corsair Marine, Inc.
150 Center Street
Chula Vista, CA 92011

The latest model in Ian Farrier's popular trailertri line, the F-27 can go from trailer to sailing in less than an hour, and can be folded up while afloat to make narrow slips accessible. Construction is a high-tech laminate using double-bias S-glass, Kevlar, and carbon fiber vacuum-bagged onto a PVC foam core. An outboard in a well just abaft the cockpit supplies auxiliary power. The F-27 is developing a reputation on the race course, and at least one has crossed the Atlantic.

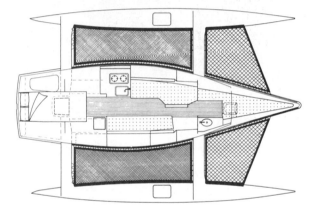

CARLSON MARINE
Iroquois Chieftain 32

Length overall: 32'0" (9.75m)

Beam: 13'4" (4.12m)

Draft: 18" (0.46m)

Sail area: 483 sq. ft. (44.87m²)

Displacement: 6,800 lbs (3085kg)

Designer: Rod McAlpine-Downie/Carlson Marine

Carlson Marine, Inc.
1231 Commercial Drive
Schererville, IN 46375
Dealer: World Catamarans
2631 Flamingo Lane
Fort Lauderdale, FL 33312

A stretched version of Rod McAlpine-Downie's famous Iroquois, winner of the rugged Round-Britain Race and the Crystal Trophy, the Iroquois Chieftain features integral outboard wells that house twin 90 h.p. Yamahas, yielding speeds under power in excess of 20 knots. She even can tow water-skiers!

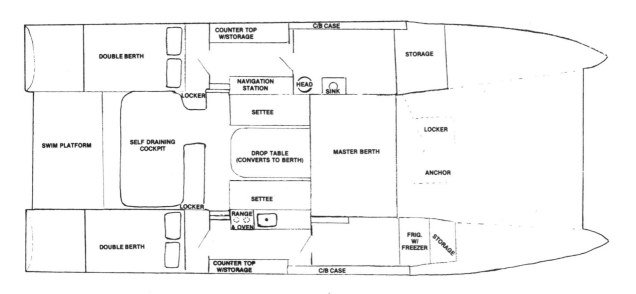

FOUNTAINE PAJOT

Maldives 32

Length overall: 32'0" (9.90m)

Beam: 17'5" (5.30m)

Draft: 3'0" (0.90m)

Sail area: 592 sq. ft. (55m²)

Displacement: 6,000 lbs (2700kg)

Designer: Joubert-Nivelt

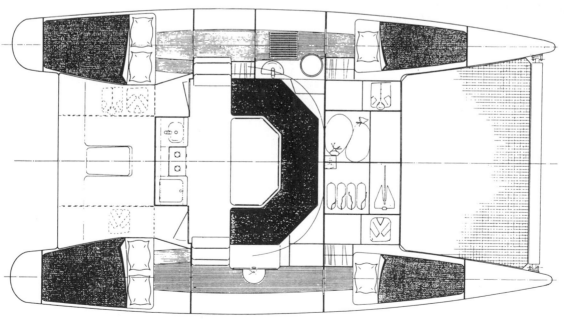

Fidji 39

Length overall: 39'0" (11.8m)

Beam: 21'0" (6.4m)

Draft: 3'0" (1m)

Sail area: 807 sq. ft. (80m²)

Displacement: 12,000 lbs (5400kg)

Designer: Joubert-Nivelt; Interior by O. Flahault

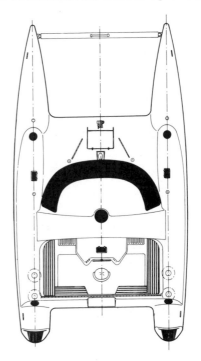

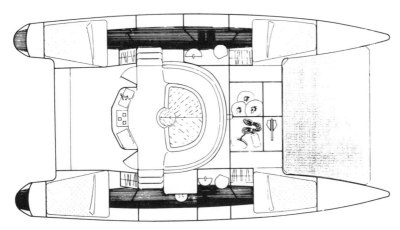

Casamance 45

Length overall: 45'0" (13.90m)

Beam: 23'0" (6.90m)

Draft: 4'0" (1.20m)

Sail area: 1,023 sq. ft. (95m²)

Displacement: 18,000 lbs (8100kg)

Designer: Joubert-Nivelt; Interior by Mario de Bosset

Fountaine Pajot
Zone Industrielle
17290 Aigrefeuille
France
U.S. Dealer: CataMarine, Inc.
43 Edgewater Road
Hull, MA 02045

France's Fountaine-Pajot produces performance-oriented cruising boats with "designer" interiors. Construction is of double-bias roving over closed-cell foam. The Maldives 32 features a bridgedeck cabin "poptop" to increase galley headroom and ventilation. Auxiliary power is by a well-mounted outboard abaft the cockpit. The Fidji 39 and Casamance 45 utilize twin diesels for auxiliary power.

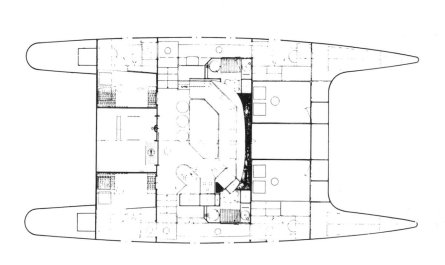

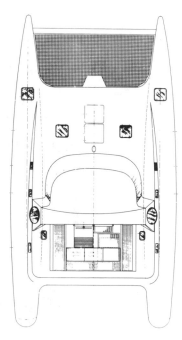

PROUT CATAMARANS
Event 34
Length overall: 34'0" (10.36m)

Beam: 15'8" (4.8m)

Draft: 2'8" (0.83m)

Sail area: 565 sq. ft. (72m²)

Displacement: 8,800 lbs (4000kg)

Designer: Prout Catamarans

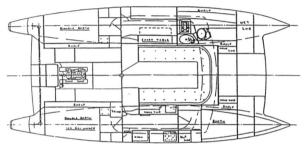

Snowgoose 37 Elite
Length overall: 37'0" (11.3m)

Beam: 16'3" (4.95m)

Draft: 2'8" (0.85m)

Sail area: 700 sq. ft. (412.3m²)

Displacement: 11,500 lbs (5216kg)

Designer: Prout Catamarans

Quasar 50 Espace

Length overall: 49'0" (14.7m)

Beam: 23'5" (7.13m)

Draft: 3'5" (1.04m)

Sail area: 1,190 sq. ft. (111.52m²)

Displacement: 19,000 lbs (8550kg)

Designer: Prout Catamarans

Prout Catamarans Ltd.
The Point
Canvey Island
Essex SS8 7TL
England
U.S. Dealer: Prout U.S.A.
1208 Shore Road
Baltimore, MD 21220

Prout, the world's oldest and largest builder of production multihulls, offers a wide array of cruising boats. Construction is of molded fiberglass. Auxiliary power on the Event 34 and Snowgoose 37 Elite is by bridgedeck-mounted diesel driving a steerable, retractable outboard leg. The Quasar 50 mounts twin diesels in the hulls. Also available from Prout, but not shown, are the compact Sirocco 26 sloop, and, for power-cruising devotees, the Panther 44 Royale power catamaran.

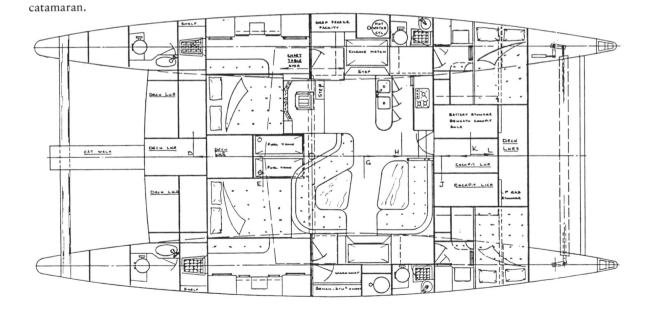

OHLALA CORPORATION

Edel Cat 35

Length overall: 35'0" (10.6m)

Beam: 19'10" (6.0m)

Draft: 2'10" (0.88m)

Sail area: 720 sq. ft. (67m²)

Displacement: 7,000 lbs (3150kg)

Designer: Marc Edel

Ohlala Cat Yachtvertrieb
Robert-Koch-Str. 6-8
D-2000 Norderstedt
Germany
U.S. Dealer: Ohlala Corporation
P.O. Box 1158
St. Petersburg, FL 33731

The Edel Cat 35 comes in two versions: the standard center cabin version, and the Cabrio, which replaces the bridgedeck cabin with a giant convertible top. Both boats are constructed of fiberglass, with Divinicell foam-core reinforcement in the bows, deck, and keel. A retractable outboard motor supplies auxiliary power.

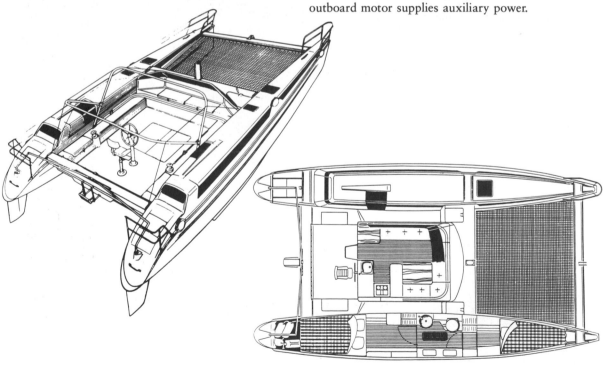

JEANTOT MARINE
Privilege 39

Length overall: 39'4" (12.10m)

Beam: 20'8" (6.32m)

Draft: 3'4" (1.01m)

Sail area: 933.5 sq. ft. (86.80m²)

Displacement: 12,400 lbs (6000kg)

Designer: Jeantot Marine/Eric Lefeuvre

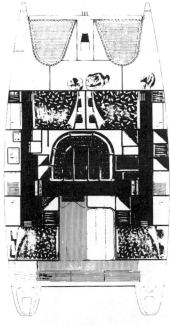

Privilege 48

Length overall: 48'9" (14.85m)

Beam: 26'5" (8.05m)

Draft: 3'11" (1.20m)

Sail area: 1,313 sq. ft. (122m²)

Displacement: 22,000 lbs (9900kg)

Designer: Jeantot Marine/Marc Lombard

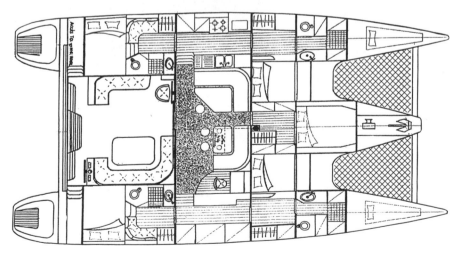

Privilege PC 40 Power Cat

Length overall: 39'4" (12.00m)

Beam: 21'8" (6.6m)

Draft: 3'3" (1.0m)

Power: Twin 150 h.p. diesel (200 h.p. optional)

Displacement: 17,632 lbs (8000kg)

Designer: Jeantot Marine/Marc Lombard

Jeantot Marine
Blvd de L'Ile Vertime
Les Sable D'Olonne 85105
France
U.S. Dealer: Privilege Yachting
Suite 1040
3650 Silverside Road
Wilmington, DE 19810

Solo 'round-the-world racer Philippe Jeantot, in collaboration with Rene Bernard, produces the luxurious line of Privilege cruising cats. Construction is of vacuum-bagged foam-cored fiberglass, selectively reinforced with Kevlar. Auxiliary power is by twin diesels mounted in the hulls. Also available is the Privilege PC 40 Power Cat.

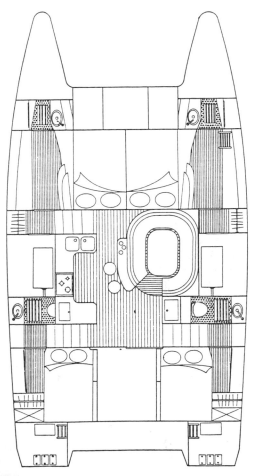

A Review
of Multihull
Designers

For any number of reasons, many people would prefer to build their own boat, or to have one custom built. Here is a list of other well-known yacht designers who have designed cruising multihulls and who have stock designs for sale. There are other multihull designers that specialize in small boats or large racers; these have been omitted from the list.

U.S. and Canada

Vince Bartolone, 3345 Newport Blvd. Suite 208, Newport Beach, CA 92663

Jim Brown, Box 550, North, VA 23128

Rudy Choy, 677 Ala Moana, Suite 918, Honolulu, HI 96814

Cross Multihull Designs, 4326-M Ashton Street, San Diego, CA 92110

Robert Harris, 1656 Duranleau Steet, Vancouver, B.C., Canada V6H 3S4

Ed Horstman, P.O. Box 286, Venice, CA 90291

Kurt Hughes, 612 1/2 West McGraw, Seattle, WA 98119

John Marples, 4530 Firmont Drive S.E., Port Orchard, WA 98366

Dick Newick, Box 2525 RR #1, North Edgecomb, ME 04556

Chris White Designs, Inc., 48 Bush Street, South Dartmouth, MA 02748

Australia and New Zealand

Lock Crowther Designs, P.O. Box 35, Turramurra, NSW 2074, Australia

Tony Grainger Yacht Design, P.O. Box 212, Kingscliff 2487, Australia

Simpson Design Multihulls, Box 2, Hemmand -Q 4174, Australia

Malcolm Tennant, 45A Forest Hill Road, Henderson, Auckland 8, New Zealand

Europe

Lars Oudrup, Hessgade 40, DK 5500 Middlefart, Denmark

Derek Kelsall, Sandwich Marina, Sandwich, Kent CT13 9LY, England

John Shuttleworth Yacht Designs, The White Cottage, Marks Corner, Newport, Isle of Wight, PO30 5UD, England

James Wharram Designs, Greenbank Road, Devoran, Truro TR3 6PJ, England

Woods Designs, 6 Elm Park, Southdown, Millbrook, Torpoint, Cornwall, PL10 1Hd, England

Joubert/Nivelt, L'Aubrecay, 17138 Piullboreau, France

Eric Lerouge, 122 Rue Gambetta, Urqueville, Nacqueville, France

Two Designs from the Author

29-foot Cruising Cat (Design #127)

Length overall: 28'10" (8.8m)

Beam: 17'0" (5.18m)

Draft: 15" (0.38m)

Sail area: 410 sq. ft. (38.13m²)

Displacement (fully loaded): 3,500 lbs (1590kg)

Designer: Chris White

A central feature of this design is the large sheltered cockpit. While sailing, the crew is protected by a wrap-around windshield; at anchor, a snap-on cockpit cover turns the cockpit into a main salon, complete with dining table and panoramic view. The sailplan is set up for single-handing, with a self-tacking jib and single-line-reefing mainsail. A vertically retracting, centrally mounted rudder is easily adjusted for shoal draft by the helmsman, and is directly in the propwash from the 4-cycle outboard, which improves maneuverability under power.

This catamaran can accommodate up to five in one double and three single berths. Construction is of strip-plank composite or foam-cored fiberglass.

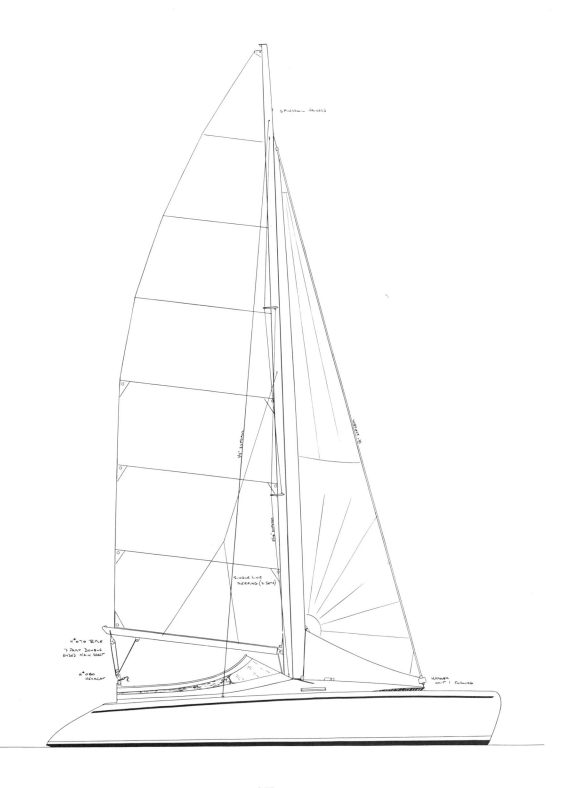

257
29-foot Cruising Cat

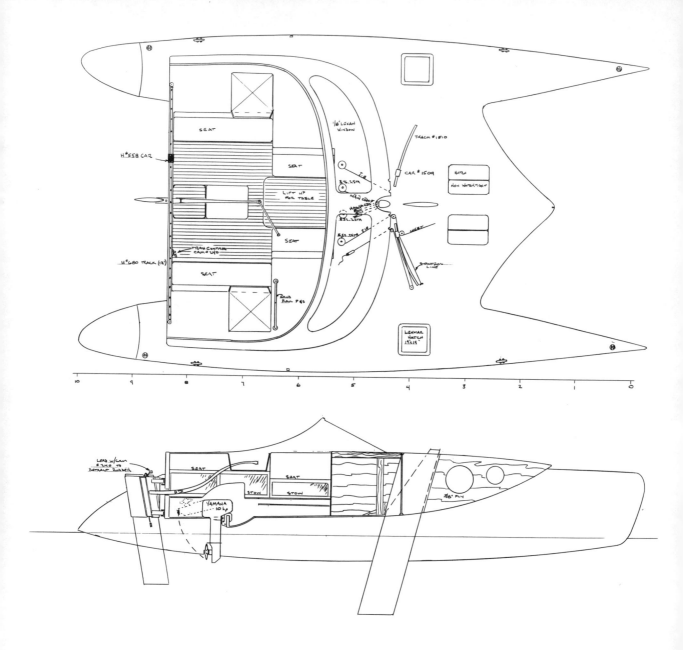

SEAT

SEAT

H.*558 CAR

LIFT UP
FOR TABLE

SEAT

TRAM CONTROL
CAM +240

H.*680 TRACK (12')

SEAT

HAND
RAIL P 45

1/8" LEXAN
WINDOW

TRACK #1510

CAR # 1509

HATCH

NON WATERTIGHT

3/4.25m

MAIN SHEET

MAIN SHEET

6.25m 3/8

6.25m 3/8

WINCH

CONTROL
LINE

LEXMAR
HATCH
19x19"

10   9   8   7   6   5   4   3   2   1   0

LEAD w/CAM
#240 TO
RETRACT RUDDER

SEAT

SEAT

STOW

STOW

YAMAHA
10 h.p.

1/8" PLY

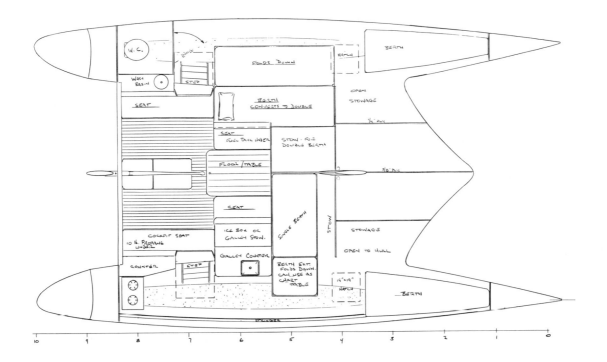

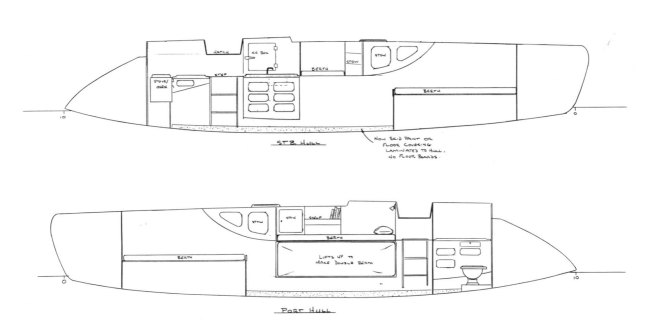

259
29-foot Cruising Cat

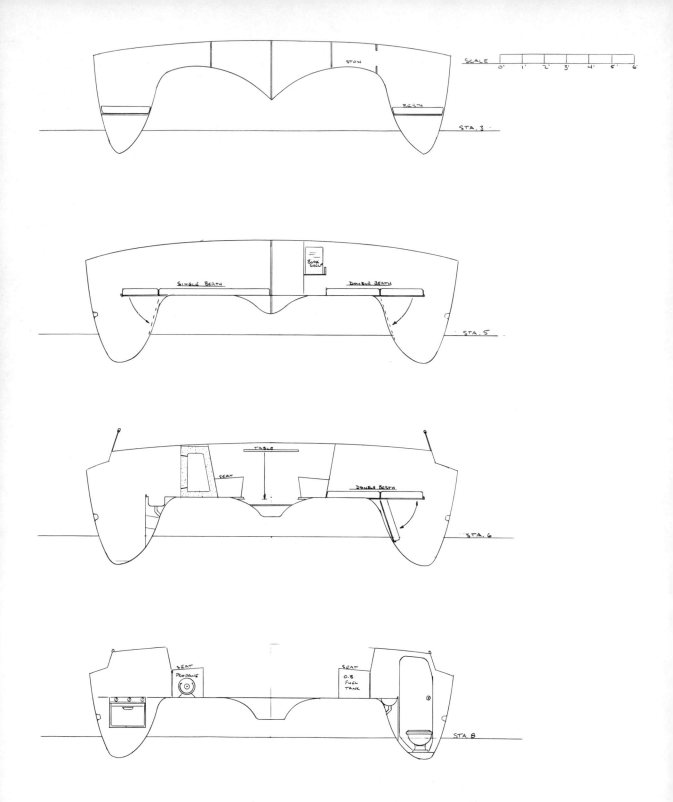

SCALE

0' 1' 2' 3' 4' 5' 6'

STOW

BERTH

STA. 3

SINGLE BERTH

BOOK SHELF

DOUBLE BERTH

STA. 5

TABLE

SEAT

DOUBLE BERTH

STA. 6

SEAT

PROPANE

SEAT

O.B. FUEL TANK

STA. 8

260
29-foot Cruising Cat

JUNIPER II

Length overall: 54'6" (16.6m)

Beam: 31'6" (9.6m)

Draft: 4'6" (1.37m)

Sail area: 1,300 sq. ft. (121m²)

Displacement (fully loaded): 13,500 lbs (6136kg)

Designer: Chris White

An updated version of my own *Juniper,* this design is an extremely comfortable and seakindly boat. Rugged construction, high stability, good payload capacity, and many integral safety features make this an excellent choice for long-distance cruising.

Several rigging options are available, including free-standing, rotating, or fixed aluminum masts. Construction is in wood/epoxy, geared toward simplicity and economy. Auxiliary power is by inboard diesel.

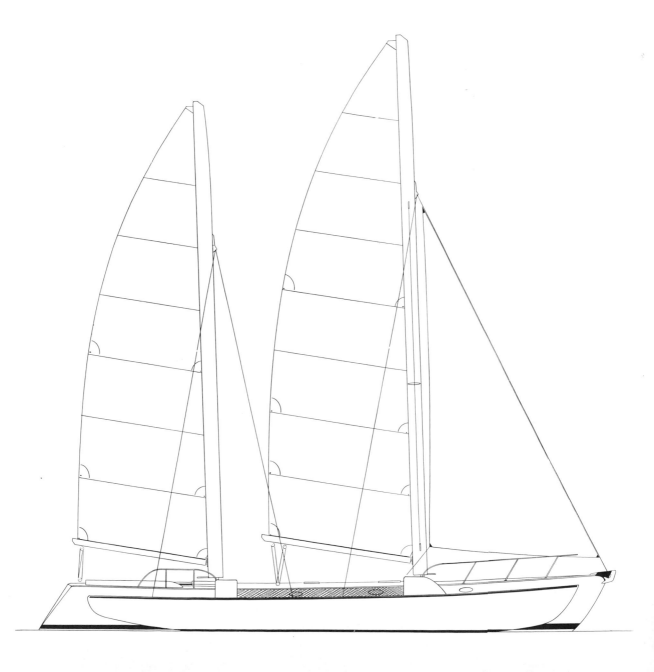

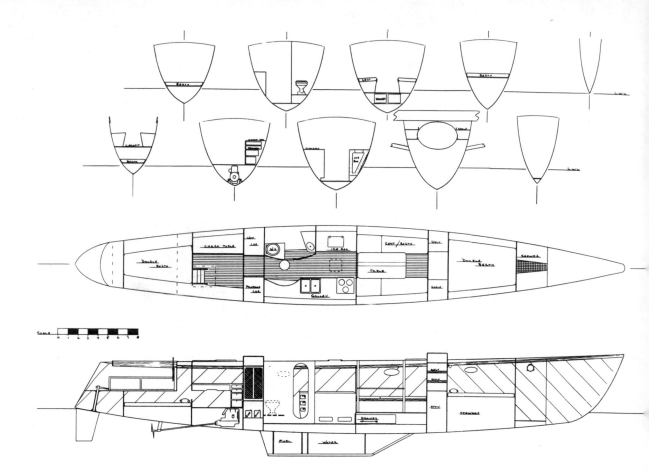

A

accommodations, 10-14, 57-64, 76-78, 105, 129, 143, 150, 160, 185; survival, 187, 216-20
Airex foam, 179-80
Alice Alakwe, 47
aluminum construction, 182-83, 186
Amaryllis, 31
American Bureau of Shipping, 28
anchoring, 18, 232-35
anchors, 232-35; sea, 198, 208-09; parachute type, 210-15, 235
aramid fiber. *See* Kevlar.
asymmetry, 97
Atlantic 46 design, 93
Atlantic 50 design, 83
Atlantic Ocean, 37-40, 196, 205-10, 228
autopilots, 20, 113, 115-17
auxiliary power, 138-48

B

Bacchanal, 36
Bahamas, 15
Balena, 16
ballast keel, 23-25, 27, 29, 194, 196
balsa core, 171-71, 178-80, 186
Baltic 64 design, 17
Banshee, 142
Bartelone, Vince, 254
battens, full-length, 130-34
batteries, 219, 223

beaching, for maintenance/repairs, 18-19, 158
beam, 49-56, 57, 66, 68-69, 97, 117-18, 134-35, 158, 190, 192, 203, 234
Birch, Mike, 207
Blyth, Chay, 200-01
bows, bulbous, 86-89
bridgedeck (catamaran), 90-94, 118, 140, 150, 155, 186-87; full, 78-82; open-wing, 76; partial, 82-86, 147
Bris, 196-97
Brittany Ferries GB, 200-01
broaching, 24, 36, 191-92, 196, 204-05
Brown, "Trimaran" Jim, 5, 37, 114, 124, 140-41, 161, 165, 216, 254
Brown, Woody, 30
Bruce number, 54-56
bulkheads, partitioned (watertight), 42, 184-86, 220
Bullfrog Sunblock, 16
buoyancy, 66-69, 90, 186-88, 216, 218, 220, 225-26

C

C Class, 109-10, 120
cabins. *See* accommodations.
capsize, 24, 26-27, 32-40, 49-50, 52, 55, 120, 184-210; avoiding, 190-215, 235-36; dealing with, 215-28

carbon/graphite fiber, 174
Carlson Marine, 142, 244
carpeting, 6
Casamance 45 design, 247
Cassanova, John and Joan, 210, 212-15
catamarans, 13, 15, 27, 31, 35, 98-99, 127, 130, 139, 140-42, 144-47, 150, 190, 192, 234; design considerations, 45, 53-55, 112, 118, 185-87, 198, 220, 238-42, 244-53, 256-62
centerboards, 100, 104-05, 108
Charis II, 60, 166
Charley, 27
Cheetah, 238-39
chines, 160-61
Choy, Rudy, 30, 86, 97, 254
Clyde Cats, 238-39
coastal cruising, 9-10, 198, 20
cockpit, 76-77, 92-93, 109, 256
cold-molding, 163-68
Coles, Adlard, 214
collisions, 42, 179, 184-86. *See also* bulkheads, partitioned.
comfort underway, 11, 20-23
composite construction. *See* wood/epoxy construction.
compounded plywood construction, 162-63

Constant Camber, 60, 164-68
construction, methods/ standards of, 6-8, 10, 28-30, 42, 44, 94, 121-22, 124, 149-83, 186. *See also* specific types.
cored laminates, 176-80
Corsair Marine, 243
costs, 3-4, 6, 8, 59, 124, 127, 133-34, 138-39, 149-51, 156, 160-61, 173-76, 181-82
Cross Multihull Designs, 5, 254
crossbeams, 69-75, 94, 186-87, 228; demountable, 69-73; folding, 69-70
Crowther, Lock, 80, 86-89, 198, 255
cruising multihulls, classification of, 8-10
currents, 16, 191
custom building. *See* one-off boats.

D

daggerboards, 93, 100-104, 108, 111
Damiana, 7, 60
decks, 187, 228 *See also* bridgedeck, wing deck.
Deguello, 80
design considerations, 45-56, 96-137, 150-51, 184-88, 190-91, 195-99, 228-29; catamarans, 76-95; trimarans,

57-75
diesel fuel, 139, 144, 218
dinghies, 14, 68
dismasting, 194
displacement, cruising, 46-48
displacement-to-length ratio, 53
downwind sails/sailing, 20-22, 134-36, 202. *See also* running off.
drag, 48-49, 53, 65, 67, 86-87, 92, 98, 138, 147, 160, 202, 204-05, 210
drogues, 198, 202-05, 207-10, 214, 235
Drum, 27
DuraKore, 167, 170

E

Edel Cat 35, 250
Edel, Marc, 250
electrolytic corrosion, 182
Elf Aquitaine, 123
engines. See inboard engines, outboard engines.
EPIRB, 221, 223-25
epoxy, 154-56, 159, 168-69, 176-77
Event 34, 5, 248-49
evolution of multihulls, 2-3, 5, 30-32, 57, 97, 149, 151, 160
Explorer 34, 62

F

F-27 Trimaran, 62, 69-70, 243

fairing, 169-71
Farrier, Ian, 62, 69-70, 243
fatalities, multihull-related, 37-41, 187-88, 225, 228
Fay, Michael, 43-44
fiberglass, 159, 164, 171-73
fiberglass construction, methods/standards of, 6, 154-55, 157, 168, 171-81, 186-87
Fidji 39 design, 246-47
fins, fixed, 98-100, 107-08, 113, 184
flares, 220-21
floats (trimaran), 65-69, 185-86
flooding, control of, 184-86
flotation, 39-40, 182, 186-88, 216-17
foam-core, 176-81, 186
fog, 16
Fountaine Pajot, 245-47
Freedom 40 design, 123

G

gasoline, 139, 142, 218
gear. *See* payload capacity, safety/survival equipment, storage.
Gemini, 142
Glennie, John, 218
Gonzo, 205-10, 223-25
Gougeon Brothers, 156, 162
Grainger, Tony, 255
Greene, Walter, 206-10, 223-25
grounding, 100, 102-03, 108, 110,

113, 147, 180
Gulf Stream, 206-10

H

handling, ease of, 11,
  19-21, 124, 139
Harris, Robert, 254
hatches, 186, 222-23
haulout, 158
headroom, 78-80,
  82-86
headstay, 94-95
Heavenly Twins 27,
  242
heaving to, 199-200
heeling, 1, 11-12,
  19-20, 25, 27, 35,
  41, 49, 51, 66-67,
  90, 127, 130-31,
  185, 189, 228
Herreshoff, Nathanael
  G., 30-31
Hobie Cat (Hobie 16),
  76, 97, 108-09
Hopscotch, 12, 62
Horstman, Ed, 212,
  254
Hoyt, Gary, 123
Hughes, Hurt, 254
hull extensions, 59-61
hull shapes, 96-98,
  190; catamaran,
  86-92, 161-62;
  trimaran, 63-65
hurricanes, 205
hydrodynamic lift
  (planing), 67-68

I

inboard engines, diesel,
  143-44; mounting,
  144-48

insulation, 182
interior layout, 10,
  12-14
Intracoastal Waterway,
  8, 19, 56
Iroquois, 142
Iroquois Chieftain 32
  design, 244

J

James, Rob, 41,
  200-01, 231
Jeantot, Philippe. See
  Jeantot Marine.
Jeantot Marine, 182,
  251-53
Jet Services, 77
Johnston, Ian, 16
Joubert-Nivelt, 245-47,
  255
Juniper II , 261-62
Juniper, 12, 17-18, 42,
  61, 63, 75, 113,
  124, 127-29, 145,
  151, 157-59, 167,
  186, 200, 217,
  232-34, 236

K

Kelsall, Derek, 255
Kevlar (aramid fiber),
  174-75
Kinney, Francis, 26, 29
knockdowns, 24, 26-27
Kumalai, Alfred, 30, 97

L

laminated wood
  construction. *See*

cold-molding,
  Constant Camber.
launching, 158
leaks, 29, 185-86
leeway, resisting. *See*
  centerboards,
  daggerboards,
  rudders.
length-to-beam ratio,
  53-54
Lerouge, Eric, 255
life rafts, 14, 216-18
light-air sailing, 19-20,
  97-99, 129, 134,
  161
living aboard, 8, 11,
  14, 57, 64, 80
lofting, 165, 169-70
Lundin, Sven and
  Olga, 196
lying ahull, 199-200

M

maintenance, 146, 151,
  154-55, 157-59
Maldives 32 design,
  245
man overboard, 41,
  228-32, 235
maneuvering (in
  crowded areas), 21
Manureva, 182
Marchaj, C.A., 24, 33
Marples, John, 60,
  161, 166, 254
masts, 117-130,
  194-95;
  free-standing
  (unstayed), 123-30;
  rotating, 118-27,
  129; wing, 120-21,
  123
McAlpine-Downie,
  Rod, 244
merchant vessels,

224-25
Meyers, Hugo, 195
Micronesians, 3, 97
molded-plywood
    construction,
    163-68, 177
molds, 6, 165, 170, 181
monohulls vs.
    multihulls, 1-3;
    accommodation,
    11-14; performance,
    19; rigs/sails, 117,
    119, 124, 127, 130,
    133, 134, 190;
    safety, 26-43, 184,
    235-37; speed,
    15-18; stability,
    22-25, 32-35,
    51-52, 96, 192-99,
    234; steering, 106

N

nacelle, 91-92
Nantucket Splinter, 27
navigation, 15-16
netting, 13, 70-71, 88,
    228-29, 231-32
Newick, Dick, 67-68,
    74, 101-03, 109,
    124, 129, 255
night sailing, 15-16

O

offshore cruising, 3,
    9-10, 26, 28-29,
    36-37, 48, 57, 59,
    69, 76, 80-82, 86,
    129, 136, 187-88,
    195-96, 198-99,
    220, 222
Ohlala Corporation,
    250

one-off boats, 6-8,
    151, 180-81, 187
Oudrup, Lars, 255
outboard engines, gas,
    138-39; mounting,
    139-43
owner building, 4-5,
    121, 150-54, 180

P

Pat's, 129
Patterson, Pat, 242
payload capacity,
    46-48, 54-55, 59,
    86, 94, 161
Peregrine, 12
performance, 10,
    14-20, 43-44, 48,
    53, 65, 82, 89-94,
    97-99, 105, 114-15,
    119, 129-30, 135,
    161, 190
pilothouse, 93
pitchpoling, 36, 52, 212
Piver, Arthur, 5, 32,
    73, 151
planing. *See*
    hydrodynamic lift.
plumbing, 12, 185-86
plywood. *See*
    sheet-plywood,
    molded-plywood
    construction.
polyester resin, 175
ports (windows), 11
pounding, 29, 67, 76,
    86, 90-92
pounds per inch
    immersion, 55
preparation, 37, 188,
    207-08, 218-22, 225
Privilege 39 design,
    182, 251
Privilege 48 design, 81,
    238, 252

Privilege PC 40 Power
    Cat, 253
Proas, 97
production boats, 5-8,
    150, 166, 181-82,
    238-53
propellers, 138, 142,
    144-48, 184
Prout Catamarans, 5,
    146, 238, 248-49
pump, bilge, 185-86
PVC foam, 178-80

Q

Quasar 50 Espace, 79,
    145, 238, 249

R

races (monohull),
    classification of,
    9-10
racing, 2-3, 17, 31-32,
    135, 200-01, 203;
    designs, 76-77,
    100-101, 187-88
radar, 21
radio, VHF, 221,
    223-25
reefing, 19, 56,
    120-21, 123,
    127-29, 131,
    136-37, 189-90,
    199-200, 206
repairs, 18-19, 179
resale value, 151, 161
rescue, 37, 216,
    223-26. *See also*
    man overboard.
resin. *See* polyester,
    vinylester, epoxy.
righting (capsized
    boat), 225-28

rigs/rigging, 17, 19, 24, 54-55, 117-30, 137, 190-91, 194-95, 200
rolling, 20-25, 35, 49, 135, 192-96, 232
rudders, 21, 99, 106-13, 184, 203; fixed, 11-13; kick-up, 107-12; outboard, 106-07, 109, 190
running lights, masthead, 123, 125
running off, 202-10

S

safety (seaworthiness), 2-3, 10, 19, 25-43, 56, 184-237
safety/survival equipment, 10, 187, 202-05, 208-18, 219-22, 229-32
sail area, 19, 54-55, 65, 129, 190
sailboards, 14
sailing, 19-25
sails, 24, 129-37. *See also* reefing.
Sarah Kate, 17
Scrimshaw, 140-41
Seabrake, 204-05
Seaman, Warren, 30, 97
seamanship, 199-215, 229-31
Searunner 31 design, 18, 114, 161
seas, breaking, 138-39, 191-96, 199-201, 204-10, 212-13, 217
seasickness, 11, 22-23
self-righting ability, 32-33, 36, 188, 196-98, 225-28
Shadowfax, 18, 72

Shane, Victor, 213-15
sheet-plywood construction, 160-63, 165
shipwreck, 43
shoal draft, 11, 18-19, 232-33
shop requirements, 153
Shuttleworth, John, 7, 60, 102, 200, 238, 255
SIB, 123, 129, 166
Simpson Design Multihulls, 255
Simpson, Roger, 12
sinking, 26, 32, 36-37, 39, 184, 186-87, 216-18, 235-36
Skyjack, 85, 142
Smeeton, Miles and Beryl, 36-37
Snowgoose 37 Elite, 248-49
Southern Hemisphere, 205, 212
speed, 1, 10, 14-20, 65, 86-87, 144, 161, 190-91, 200-04
spinnakers, 134-35
spreader, 118-20
Spronk, Peter, 85
stability, 1-2, 11, 22-25, 32-37, 42, 48-52, 96-97, 127, 189, 194, 225-26, 235-36; longitudinal, 49-52, 59, 67; transverse, 49-52, 55-56, 66
stability number, 55-56
Stars and Stripes, 120
steering, 20-21, 24, 35, 106-16, 139, 196, 203-04; self-, 113-16
steering station, 92
storage, 13-14, 61, 187, 219, 236
storm conditions/sails,

16, 120-22, 136-37, 198-215, 233
strains on hulls/rigs, 26-29, 117
Street, Don, 30, 32, 34, 42
strip-plank composite construction, 167-171
structural integrity, 6-7, 10-11, 26-29, 42, 44, 69, 72-73, 150-51, 160, 177-79, 183
surfing, 20, 48, 53, 65, 202
survival suits, 221-22, 223, 225
Symons, Bill, 11

T

tacking, 43, 98-99, 135, 190
tank testing, 192-96
tenders. *See* dinghies.
Tennant, Malcolm, 255
Tiki 28, 240-41
tooling. *See* molds.
tools, 220, 223
Tortuga Too, 212
Trailer Tri, 69, 243
trim tabs, 115-16
trimarans, 13, 27, 35-36, 99, 127, 139, 142, 234; design considerations, 45, 52-55, 57-75, 185-86, 198, 220, 243
Tzu Hang, 36-37

U

U.S. Coast Guard, 40

U.S. Navy, 22-23
Underwood, Gary, 47

V

vacuum bagging, 168, 181
vee-section hulls, 161. *See also* nacelle.
ventilation, engine/rudder, 106-07, 109, 138-40
Verbatim, 16
vinylester resin, 175-76

W

Wappl, Wolfgang, 77
water-skiers, 142
waterway cruising, 9-10, 220
waves, 20, 35-36, 41-42, 189, 191-205, 202-03. *See also* breaking seas.
weatherfax, 16
weekending, 16
weight. *See* payload capacity.
West Indies, 15
whales, 42, 184
Wharram, James, 5, 76-77, 161, 240, 255
White, Chris (designs), 12, 47, 62, 64, 83, 93, 255-60
Williams, Nye, 207, 223-24
wind vanes, 113-15
winds, 19, 35, 55, 92, 188-91, 198, 233-34
windward ability/sailing, 20, 43, 92, 189-90, 200-02
wing deck (trimaran), full, 57-59, 70; open (tri), 59, 61-62, 70, 76; partial, 59-60, 70
wood, 154, 156-59
wood/epoxy construction, methods/standards of, 154-71, 180, 186
Woods (Richard and Lilian) Designs, 255

Y

Yanmar Endeavor, 167